Praise for *Wild Mind*

"Once again, Bill Plotkin provides an invaluable field guide to reclaiming and embodying our original wholeness and our inherent kinship with nature, all its species, and all its inhabitants. *Wild Mind* not only ~~~~~~~~~~ us in our endangered world!"

— Angeles Arrien, PhD, cultur

"Bill Plotkin's *Wild Mind* ushers in a new era of depth psychology. For all the penetrating insights flowing from Sigmund Freud and his associates, the field's origin was imprisoned in the worldview that regarded our universe as dead. It was inevitable that psychological work would be confined to conversations between humans, in offices, inside buildings. Plotkin's work shatters that limited conception, for he lives in the creative universe as articulated by quantum physics, indigenous traditions, and evolutionary cosmology. Most helpful of all, Plotkin shares his powerful processes for entering deep conversations with rivers and owls and stone. To study *Wild Mind* is to pass through a magical gateway into one's unique role within the Great Work that Earth is calling us to."

— Brian Thomas Swimme, California Institute of Integral Studies, coauthor with Thomas Berry of *The Universe Story*

"Living as we do in both an external environment and an internal environment, *Wild Mind* is a summons to an evolved eco-consciousness. Both natural settings have been subordinated to narcissistic enlargement by a complex-driven ego, and the price we are paying is personal, cultural, and environmental pathology. *Wild Mind* provides a compelling agenda for the reintegration of these sundered worlds in service to wholeness."

— James Hollis, PhD, author of
What Matters Most: Living a More Considered Life

"*Wild Mind* offers wise and loving medicine for our selves and our world at a time when reinventing how we live on Earth and with each other is more crucial than ever. This brilliant and lyrical book provides an alternative to the outmoded mindset that had us focused on what's wounded or missing in ourselves rather than appreciating our magnificence and the unique gifts we each carry for the world. With this delightful, encouraging, and inspiring read, Bill Plotkin delivers an engaging and tender adventure of reclaiming, healing, and celebrating."

— Nina Simons, co-CEO and cofounder, Bioneers

"Thomas Berry calls us to 'reinvent the human.' Bill Plotkin has been doing his part for decades, principally through leading people into their deeper selves via vision quests in the wilderness. In this book he continues his pioneering efforts in a brave attempt to reinvent psychology with useful practices and a new language that honors the psyche-cosmos relationship."

— Matthew Fox, author of *Original Blessing* and *The Pope's War*

"I have both taught and worked with Bill Plotkin, and I believe that *Wild Mind* is the most mature synthesis of his excellent and much needed vision. Be guided here by a master of listening to both nature and soul!"

— Fr. Richard Rohr, OFM, Center for Action and Contemplation, Albuquerque, New Mexico, and author of *Falling Upward*

Praise for Bill Plotkin's *Nature and the Human Soul*

"Plotkin brings forth a new model for the whole of human life and spirituality in our world.... An essential, weighty book for our perilous times."

— *Publishers Weekly* (starred review)

"With *Nature and the Human Soul*, Bill Plotkin once again works miracles. This vital book provides a road map to help us remember how to be human — which means how to be a human being in relationship to the natural world, to our home. We owe Bill Plotkin a deep debt of gratitude for this important work."

— Derrick Jensen, author of *A Language Older Than Words*

Praise for Bill Plotkin's *Soulcraft*

"As we enter a future where humans and the natural world are more intimate with each other, we will surely be powerfully influenced by this new guide into the mysteries of nature and psyche. In *Soulcraft*, Bill Plotkin gives us an authentic masterwork. In the substance of what he has written, in the clarity of his presentation, and in the historical urgency of the subject, he has guided us far into the new world that is opening up before us. We will not soon again receive a work of this significance."

— Thomas Berry, author of *The Dream of the Earth* and *The Great Work*, from the foreword to *Soulcraft*

WILD
MIND

Also by Bill Plotkin

Nature and the Human Soul:
Cultivating Wholeness and Community in a Fragmented World

Soulcraft: Crossing into the Mysteries of Nature and Psyche

WILD MIND

A Field Guide to the Human Psyche

BILL PLOTKIN

New World Library
Novato, California

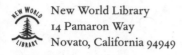 New World Library
14 Pamaron Way
Novato, California 94949

The material in this book is intended for educational purposes only. No expressed or implied guarantee of the effects of the use of the recommendations can be given nor liability taken. The publisher advises that such activities as fasting or wilderness excursions not be attempted or practiced without appropriate guidance and support.

"Soulcraft" is a registered trademark of Bill Plotkin.

Text design by Tona Pearce Myers

Library of Congress Cataloging-in-Publication Data
Plotkin, Bill, date.
Wild mind : a field guide to the human psyche / Bill Plotkin.
 pages cm
Includes bibliographical references and index.
ISBN 978-1-60868-178-5 (pbk. : alk. paper) — ISBN 978-1-60868-179-2 (ebook)
 1. Nature—Psychological aspects. 2. Soul—Psychological aspects. 3. Developmental psychology. I. Title.
BF353.5.N37P56 2013
612.8—dc23   2012050312

First printing, April 2013
ISBN 978-1-60868-178-5
Printed in Canada on 100% postconsumer-waste recycled paper

 New World Library is proud to be a Gold Certified Environmentally Responsible Publisher. Publisher certification awarded by Green Press Initiative.
www.greenpressinitiative.org

10 9

To
the visionary artisans of cultural evolution
and
to the future children of all species.

Nature is an incomparable guide if you know how to follow her.
She is like the needle of the compass pointing to the North,
which is most useful…when you know how to navigate.

— C. G. Jung

…Sometimes…
…I look out at everything
growing so wild
and faithfully beneath
the sky
and wonder
why we are the one
terrible
part of creation
privileged
to refuse our flowering.…

— David Whyte, from "The Sun"

Contents

Introduction

Re-Visioning Our Selves

Let the day grow on you upward
through your feet,
the vegetal knuckles,

to your knees of stone,
until by evening you are a black tree;
feel, with evening,

the swifts thicken your hair,
the new moon rising out of your forehead,
and the moonlit veins of silver

running from your armpits
like rivulets under white leaves.
Sleep, as ants

cross over your eyelids.
You have never possessed anything
as deeply as this.

This is all you have owned
from the first outcry
through forever;

you can never be dispossessed.

— DEREK WALCOTT, "EARTH"

*I*t's time to take another look at ourselves — to re-enliven our sense of what it is to be human, to breathe new life into ancient intuitions of who we are, and to learn again to celebrate, as we once did, our instinctive affinity with the Earth community in which we're rooted. We're called now to rediscover what it means to be human beings in a wildly diverse world of feathered, furred, and scaled fellow creatures; flowers and forests; mountains, rivers, and oceans; wind, rain, and snow; Sun and Moon.

It's time to take an ecological and holistic look at the human psyche, to make a fresh start with Western psychology.[1] In an era when the revealed interdependency of all things is radically reshaping every field of knowledge, what might we discover about the human psyche — the totality of our psychological capacities, both conscious and unconscious — when we consider that we, too, are expressions of nature's qualities, patterns, and motifs?

We're being summoned by the world itself to make many urgent changes to the human project, but most central is a fundamental re-visioning and reshaping of *ourselves*, a shift in consciousness. We must reclaim and embody our original wholeness, our indigenous human nature granted to us by nature itself. And the key to reclaiming our original wholeness is not merely to suppress psychological symptoms, recover from addictions and trauma, manage stress, or refurbish dysfunctional relationships but rather to fully flesh out our multifaceted, wild psyches, committing ourselves to the largest story we're capable of living, serving something bigger than ourselves. We must dare again to dream the impossible and to romance the world, to feel and honor our kinship with all species and habitats, to embrace the troubling wisdom of paradox, and to shape ourselves into visionaries with the artistry to revitalize our enchanted and endangered world.

BECOMING FULLY HUMAN

Emerging in the late nineteenth century, Western psychology was seeded in that era's prevailing practice and philosophy of medicine. Psychology's focus was on diagnosis and treatment of symptoms, diseases, and "mental illness." It was, and in many ways still is, an attempt to identify what could and does go wrong with the human psyche when scrutinized outside its cultural and ecological contexts: neuroses, psychoses, personality and attachment disorders, manias, depressions, obsessions, and addictions. With few exceptions — such as Carl Jung's analytical psychology, James Hillman's archetypal "re-visioning" of psychology,[2] and the new field of positive psychology[3] — there's been too little consideration of what is inherently right and inspiring about human beings. There's been insufficient tending to the process of becoming fully human — an active, deeply imaginative, contributing member of what cultural ecologist David Abram calls the more-than-human world,[4] a world that includes human society as a subset of a much more extensive Earth community.

Western psychology's established ways of understanding ourselves have unintentionally cramped our abilities to grow whole and to fully mature. The agenda of mainstream psychotherapy has been, from its beginnings, remarkably limited and, consequently, limiting. What if, for example, our primary human need and opportunity is not to endlessly attend to our emotional wounds and the eradication of perceived psychological disorders but rather to fathom and flesh out our natural human wholeness and to embody this integral bounty as a gift to others and our world?

Conventional Western psychology has focused on pathology rather than possibility and participation, and this renders it incomplete...and in many ways obsolete.[5]

In Western culture, we've enclosed ourselves within continually mended fences of excessive safety, false security, and shallow notions of "happiness," when all the while the world has been inviting us to stride through the unlocked gate and break free into realms of greater promise and possibilities. Our psychotherapy-fashioned fences have affirmed our flaws and failures and corralled us within psychosocial prisons of our own making. Our mainstream educational and religious institutions likewise have suppressed our human potential and magnificence, or at least failed to evoke and foster our brilliance and virtuosity, our capacity to truly mature and to help make our world a better place.[6]

OUR INNATE HUMAN RESOURCES

Our human psyches possess, as capacities, a variety of astonishing resources about which mainstream Western psychology has little to say. By uncovering and reclaiming these innate resources, shared by all of us by simple virtue of our human nature, we can more easily understand and resolve our intrapsychic and interpersonal difficulties as they arise. We need not be as dependent as we have been on the psychological, social, and professional resources of others — clergy and counselors, family and friends, psychotherapists and psychiatrists — or on the neurological reconfiguration services of psychopharmacological chemicals, whether prescribed or elective.

The alleviation of personal troubles is, of course, important to all of us. But the significance and relevance of our innate psychological resources — largely unrecognized, unvalued, and uninventoried by Western psychology and culture — go well beyond the alleviation of personal troubles. Our untapped inner resources are also essential to the flowering of our greatest potentials, to the actualization of our true selves, and to the embodiment of the life of our very souls. These natural faculties are what we must cultivate in order to actively protect and restore our planet's ecosystems and to spark the urgently needed renaissance of our Western and Westernized cultures. And these innate human resources are precisely those that enable each of us to identify the unique genius and hidden treasure we carry for the world — and, in this way, to participate fully and consciously in the evolution of life on Earth.

These resources — which I call the four facets of the Self, or the four dimensions of our human wholeness — wait within us, but we might not even know they exist until we discover how to access them, cultivate their powers, and integrate them into our everyday lives. Reclaiming these essential human capacities of the Self ought to be the highest priority in psychology, education, religion, medicine, and leadership development. Doing so empowers people to wake up, rise up, and become genuine agents of cultural transformation — and, in the bargain, experience the most profound fulfillment of a lifetime.

The recognition and embrace of these inherent human strengths, capacities, and sensibilities turn much of Western psychology on its head. Our entire approach to understanding and quickening human potential and addressing personal problems shifts radically.

For example, many of the behavioral patterns that mainstream psychology labels as psychopathologies (such as anxiety, depression, manias, phobias, personality disorders, and the tendency to hear or see things other people don't) are not necessarily problems in themselves. How do we know when they are and when they're not? What if most actual pathologies are primarily symptoms of underdeveloped psychological resources — inborn capacities of the Self that await cultivation within everyone? Psychological symptoms may best be relieved not by directly trying to eradicate them, impede them, or mask them but rather by developing our innate resources, the unavailability of which may be the primary reason these symptoms appeared in the first place. Perhaps we exhibit psychological symptoms not so much because we're dis-ordered but because we're deficient in our embodiment of wellness, health, or wholeness.

When we eliminate symptoms without cultivating wholeness, we still have an unwell, unwhole, or fragmented psyche that will soon enough sprout new symptoms that express, in yet another way, the lack of wholeness.

Here's an analogy from ecology: When an ecosystem has been damaged — say, from logging, overgrazing, or chemical-dependent mono-crop agriculture — and then you leave it alone, invasive species typically show up and take over. If you then attempt to simply suppress or eliminate the invasives — whether through pesticide application or heroic weeding — you're not strengthening the ecosystem but rather merely suppressing a symptom called "weeds." In contrast, if you tend the health of the ecosystem — for example, by improving soil quality or planting native species — the invasives find a less suitable landing site and the ecosystem is more quickly restored to its natural and mature wholeness. Likewise, when we tend the well-being of our human psyches — by improving our social and ecological "soil" and cultivating the "native species" of the Self — there is less opportunity for the fragmented or wounded elements of our psyches to take over; the psychological "space" is already occupied by the facets of a more fully flourishing being. We've placed the emphasis on promoting health and wholeness rather than on (merely) suppressing pathology and fragmentedness.

We can douse our psyches with pharmaceutical pesticides and therapeutically weed them, but a much better approach would be to enhance our psychological, cultural, and ecological soil and to cultivate the capacities of our native human wholeness.

A second limiting assumption of conventional Western psychology — in addition to the idea that the symptom is the problem rather than *an indication* of a problem — is that our difficulties are solely or primarily a result of troubles within individual psyches (or, even worse, within individual brains).[7] But in recent decades, we've come to understand that our psychological health relies profoundly on the health of the world in which we are embedded — the psychosocial well-being of our families, the maturity and diversity of our human communities, and the vitality of our natural environments. Indeed, the very meaning of the phrase *psychological health* is interpersonal and ecological and cannot be coherently reduced to something merely subjective, internal, or neurological. Behavioral patterns that some might perceive as psychological disorders are often understandable and natural reactions to a disordered world. Most personal difficulties are symptoms of problems in our relationships, families, societies, and ecosystems.

When a large proportion of people in a given culture have significant psychological troubles, as is demonstrably the case in the Western world today, these people are not to blame. Their culture is. And yet their culture is constituted by the collective actions of its members. It is the responsibility of all capable individuals to help make their culture whole and vital. Those who are most capable in this way are those who are most whole in themselves.

How can we most effectively grow whole and participate in the revitalization of the whole? This book offers an answer.

In these pages, I introduce a map of psychological wholeness, a map that is nonarbitrary and comprehensive precisely because it's rooted in nature's own map of wholeness. The Nature-Based Map of the Psyche serves as a guide to becoming fully human by cultivating the four facets of the Self and discovering both the limitations and the gifts of our wounded, fragmented, and shadowed subpersonalities. This map of the psyche has been in development since the 1980s and has been field-tested and refined by psychologists, counselors, life coaches, educators, clergy, parents, initiation guides, and leaders of wilderness rites in their work with thousands of people of all ages.

For those of you who are psychotherapists, philosophers, professionals in another related field, or simply interested in learning more, I've used this book's endnotes primarily for ideas and references that may be of particular interest to you. Also see the website www.wildmindbook.com, especially the page "For Professionals."

REWILDING PSYCHOLOGY

Beyond its focus on pathology rather than possibility and participation, another feature of conventional Western psychology that renders it incomplete and largely obsolete is that, like mainstream Western culture more generally, it is alienated from the greater Earth community — especially from nature's untamed powers, qualities, species, and habitats. This is a core insight of the developing field of ecopsychology.[8] What makes us human is not merely other humans. We evolved over millennia in response to the challenges and opportunities encountered within a wildly complex web of ecological relationships in a thoroughly animate world. The ways we think, feel, perceive, imagine, and act have arisen in attunement to the rhythms of the day and the turning of the seasons and in intimate relationship with myriad other life-forms and forces. Although in everyday Western life we might feel cut off from our wild Earthly roots and relationships, it nevertheless remains true that the deep structures of our human psyche — the underlying patterns, universal archetypes, innate capacities available to us all, and, yes, even the distinctive ways we are psychologically wounded and fragmented — have emerged from this living web.

What insights, then, about our human psyches appear when we return to Earth, when we remember that we are related to everything that has ever existed, when we reinstall ourselves in a world of spring-summer-fall-winter, volcanoes, storms, surf, bison, mycelium, Moon, falcons, sand dunes, galaxies, and redwood groves? What do we discover about ourselves when we consent again to being human animals — bipedal, omnivorous mammals with distinctive capacities for self-reflexive consciousness, dexterity, imagination, and speech? In what ways will we choose to live when we fully remember the naturalness and ecological necessity of death? Who will we see in the mirror when we face up to the present-day realities of human-caused mass extinction, ecosystem collapse, and climate destabilization? And what mystery journey will unfold when we answer the alluring and dangerous summons now emanating from the human soul, from the dream of the Earth,[9] and from an intelligent, evolving, ensouled Universe?

Beyond insights into the nature of our humanity, what will we discover — or remember — about the most effective methods for cultivating our human wholeness once we liberate psychotherapy, coaching, education, and religion from indoor consulting rooms, classrooms, and churches? What happens when we rewild our techniques and practices for facilitating human development — not by merely getting them out the door and onto the land or waters, but, much more significantly, by fashioning approaches in which our encounters with the other-than-human world are the central feature?

What happens, in other words, when we allow nature itself to be the primary therapist or guide, while the human mentor or adviser becomes more of an assistant to nature, an agent or handmaiden of the wild?

We have a vital opportunity now to shape a new Western psychology that acknowledges humanity as, first and foremost, natural, of nature — not separate from it. It's time to rewild psychology with ideas and methods rooted in the rhythms, patterns, principles, and other-than-human encounters of greater nature. We seek a Western psychology firmly planted in both wild soil and the soul of the world, at once both an ecopsychology and a depth psychology, one that emboldens us to serve the greater Earth community and to enhance the life of all species, and that does not merely tempt us to *use* nature for our own healing, self-centered benefit, or egocentric profit. A mature eco*therapy* does not attempt to decrease our anxiety, outrage, fear, grief, or despair in response to the ongoing industrial destruction of the biosphere; rather, it helps us to more fully experience these feelings so that we can revitalize ourselves emotionally and, in doing so, enable our greatest contributions to a cultural renaissance. This is our current collective human adventure, which theologian and cultural historian Thomas Berry calls the Great Work of our time: "to carry out the transition from a period of human devastation of the Earth to a period when humans would be present to the planet in a mutually beneficial manner."[10] It is what ecophilosopher Joanna Macy refers to as the Great Turning, "the transition from a doomed economy of industrial growth to a life-sustaining society committed to the recovery of our world."[11]

The Great Work of our time calls us to something greater than personal happiness and something more than mere refinements in politics, economy, religion, and education. At its most fundamental level, the Great Work necessitates both a revolution in our understanding of what it is to be human and a revival of our abilities to realize our potential and to transform our contemporary cultures.

It's time, then, to redraw our map of the human psyche, a revision germinated not in notions of symptoms and illness but in our innate wholeness and our foundational and organic embedment in the natural world.

Toward these ends, this book introduces a holistic and integral ecology of the human psyche that encompasses the best insights of existing Western psychologies but also stretches far beyond them, extending our appreciation of the psyche's untapped potentials and its inner diversity, intricacy, and structural elegance.

The Nature-Based Map of the Psyche highlights our positive, life-enhancing resources and perspectives and extols them as foundational to our humanity. The accent is not on our fragmented parts or wound stories, or how our psyches stall out in neurotic patterns, or how we might merely recover from trauma, pathology, or addiction; rather, the accent is on our wholeness and potential magnificence, how we can enhance our personal fulfillment and participation in our more-than-human world, and how we can become fully human and visionary artisans of cultural renaissance.

Chapter 1

The Nature-Based Map
of the Human Psyche

An Overview

> To speak of wilderness is to speak of wholeness. Human beings
> came out of that wholeness.
>
> — GARY SNYDER

W isdom traditions from around the world — including those from
which Western cultures emerged — have looked to nature's seven
directions for a model of wholeness: north, south, east, west, up, down,
and center. These seven directions support us in fathoming the wholeness
of...well, anything that came out of the original wholeness called "nature"
or "wilderness," the wholeness that human beings came out of, as poet
Gary Snyder reminds us. My approach to constructing a comprehensive,
nature-based map of the human psyche begins with the foundational, three-
dimensional pattern of the seven directions.[1] Here's how I've mapped the
psyche onto nature's framework:

The Horizontal Plane

THE SELF. In the four cardinal directions are the four facets of our
innate human potential — the four sets of resources that make up
our horizontal psychological wholeness. Together, these four facets
constitute what I call the Self. As we'll see in later chapters, they
also reflect the qualities of the natural world we observe in the four

directions and, not coincidentally, the characteristics of the four seasons and the four times of day: dawn, noon, dusk, and midnight.

SUBPERSONALITIES. Because each aspect of wholeness also has its immature form, we also find in the cardinal directions the four categories of our fragmented or wounded parts — which I call *subpersonalities*, and sometimes just *subs* for short — again echoing the qualities of the four directions, seasons, and times of day.

The Vertical Axis

SPIRIT. In the upward direction is the dimension of the human psyche that identifies with Spirit (a.k.a. God, Mystery, or the nondual). The upward direction is also known as the upperworld, the heavens, or the vast reaches of the cosmos.

SOUL. Reaching down into depths, we find the human Soul, our unique and deepest individual identity. The downward direction is also known as the underworld, Hades, or the fruitful darkness.

The Center

THE EGO. In the center, at the intersection of the horizontal and the vertical, is the Ego. Its "home" or "natural habitat" is the everyday world or middleworld of family, social, economic, educational, political, and ecological life.

In our three-dimensional wholeness, each one of us is nature in human form, nature in its wholeness of the four cardinal directions, the four seasons, and the four times of day, and also of the upperworld, underworld, and middleworld.

DEFINITIONS

Soul, *Spirit*, *Self*, and *Ego*. "Why all the capitalized words?" you might ask. Simply to remind you, throughout this book, that I'm using these common words to refer to aspects of psyche defined in specific and not necessarily common ways.

Here, then, are my definitions of these and other key components of the Nature-Based Map of the Human Psyche:

SOUL. The *Soul* is a person's unique purpose or identity, a mythopoetic identity, something much deeper than personality or social-vocational role, an identity revealed and expressed through symbol and metaphor, image and dream, archetype and myth. Some other ways to say this: Soul is the particular ecological niche, or place, a person was born to occupy but may or may not ever discover or consciously embody.[2] Or, in a more poetic vein, Soul is "the largest conversation you're capable of having with the world," it's "your own truth / at the center of the image / you were born with," it's the "shape / [that] waits in the seed / of you to grow / and spread / its branches / against a future sky," or it's "your individual puzzle piece in the Great Mystery."[3] For example, the Soul of Irish poet William Butler Yeats can be articulated by way of a poem he wrote (and an experience he had) in his late twenties, as the niche of one who "pluck[s] the silver apples of the moon, the golden apples of the sun."[4] Ecophilosopher, Buddhist, and Earth elder Joanna Macy, at age thirty-seven, experienced a life-transforming inner image of a stone bridge that spanned "between the thought-worlds of East and West, connecting the insights of the *Buddha Dharma* with the modern Western mind." She knew in that moment that her destiny was, in part, to be one of the stones in that bridge — "just one, that was enough."[5] And it might be said that cultural historian Thomas Berry was ensouled as someone who "preserves and enhances [wildness] in the natural cycles of its transformation" and who perceives, articulates, and advocates the "dream of the Earth."[6]

SPIRIT. *Spirit* (or God, Mystery, or the nondual) is the universal consciousness, intelligence, psyche, or vast imagination that animates the cosmos and everything in it — including us — and in which the psyche of each person participates. When consciously attuned to Spirit, we experience a profound connectedness with all things — the "oneness" of Spirit. The manner in which Spirit manifests itself or unfolds has been called, to cite just three examples, evolution's trajectory, the Tao (the way of life), or the Universe story.

SELF. The *Self* is an integral whole, a bundle of innate resources every human has in common, a totality that holds all the original capacities of our core humanness.[7] The Self incorporates the four facets of our horizontal human wholeness, which exist at birth but only as possibilities that, like the Soul, we may or may not learn to access, actualize, and embody. These four facets can be described in terms of archetypes, universal patterns of human behavior and character found in all cultures and in myths, dreams, art, and literature. The Self contains all the resources we need to meaningfully contribute to our more-than-human (which means not-*merely*-human) world in order to live a mature, fulfilling, creative human life, to effectively manifest our Soul's desires, and to align ourselves with Spirit's unfolding. In this book, I use *Self* and *horizontal human wholeness* interchangeably.

SUBPERSONALITIES. The *subpersonalities* are the wounded and sometimes hidden fragments of our human psyches — such as our "inner" Victim, Rebel, Critic, Tyrant, or Addict — each of which attempts to protect us from further injury. These are constellations of feelings, images, and behaviors that operate more or less independently from one another and often independently of our conscious selves (Egos). Subpersonalities form in childhood, with the enduring purpose of protecting us from physical, psychological, and social harm. Often they succeed. Often they also create additional troubles or mischief for us and others. Our subpersonalities are the source or instigators of what Western psychology understands to be our psychological symptoms and illnesses.

I borrowed the term *subpersonalities* from the approach to psychology known as psychosynthesis, developed by Italian psychiatrist Roberto Assagioli in the early 1900s. Other traditions and schools of Western psychology have referred to intrapsychic fragments of this sort as *complexes* (Freudian and Jungian analysis), *parts* (Gestalt psychology), *internal objects* (object relations theory), *ego states* (transactional analysis), or *selves* (Hal and Sidra Stone's Voice Dialogue or Psychology of Selves; and Richard Schwartz's Internal Family Systems Therapy). Each subpersonality functions by way of an interrelated set of ideas, emotions, memories, impulses, and behavioral patterns.

EGO. The *Ego* is the locus, or seat, of conscious self-awareness within the human psyche, the "I." (I also use another term, the *three-dimensional Ego*, or *3-D Ego*, to refer to an Ego blessed with some degree of conscious communion and integration with Self, Soul, and Spirit.) By *personality* I mean the characteristic patterns of behavior the Ego engages in.

How the Ego Operates

When awake, we (our Egos) can, in principle, be conscious through the frame of reference of any of the other four aspects of the psyche — namely, the Self, Soul, Spirit, or subpersonalities. This is to say that we can be conscious as, and act from the perspective of, any one of these four aspects of the psyche. But the subpersonalities are the "default position" for our Egos. Unless and until we cultivate conscious relationships with Self, Soul, and Spirit (and in that way function, at least at times, as 3-D Egos), we experience and behave by way of our psyche's fragmented or wounded parts — from the perspective, for example, of our Conformist, Escapist, or Victim. With a healthy, mature 3-D Ego, we are fully anchored in the fourfold Self, and we more often than not experience ourselves as being in service to Soul and, consequently, to Spirit, too. As 3-D Egos, we can also at times experience ourselves *as* Soul or *as* Spirit.

Self and subpersonalities are not entities or little people inside people. A better way to think of them is as different versions of ourselves that we experience and enact at different times.[8] Here's a slogan to help remember this: "Self and subpersonalities don't do anything; *people* do." People often act by way of or by means of or through their subs, for example, and sometimes they're conscious that they're doing this and sometimes not.[9] But subpersonalities don't act in the world independently of the person of whose psyche they are a component.[10] A given sub is simply one version of the person in action. Same goes for the four facets of the Self.

Our subpersonalities generally function autonomously from other versions of ourselves, which is to say that, when our Ego is identified with a subpersonality, we tend to be undeterred by the perspectives we hold at other times. When identified with a sub, we might be completely unaware of the existence of some or all of our other versions (the four facets of Self as well as our other subpersonalities). In contrast, when our Ego operates by way of the Self, we are aware — or at least potentially aware — of our subs as well as the facets of the Self.

THE MAP AND THE TERRITORY

Something essential to note before continuing: The map is not the territory! In this book I'm offering a way to understand our human psyches, but the reality is always more complex and nuanced than any map can convey. May we always be astounded and humbled by the mystery of our human selves and our animate world.

THE SELF

The Self is what we'll explore in the first half of this book. Even though you may find it less familiar than the subpersonalities (because of what Western psychology and culture emphasize as well as what they neglect), the Self is where we'll begin, because it's the foundation of individual well-being, spiritual development, healthy relationships, and mature cultures. It's also the dimension of our psyches through which we're able to heal the wounds protected by and embodied within our subpersonalities. We must cultivate the resources of the Self before we can truly heal.

Although the Self is a single dimension of the psyche, an integral whole, it has four facets. Here's an initial introduction to these four facets:

NORTH: THE NURTURING GENERATIVE ADULT. This facet is empathic, compassionate, courageous, competent, knowledgeable, productive, and able to provide genuine loving care and service to both ourselves and others. Through the North facet of the Self, we contribute our best and most creative parenting, leading, teaching, directing, producing, and healing. The Nurturing Generative Adult is resonant with archetypes such as Leader, benevolent King or Queen, mature or spiritual Warrior, Mother, and Father.

SOUTH: THE WILD INDIGENOUS ONE. Emotive, erotic-sexual, sensuous, instinctive, and playful, this facet is fully at home in the human body and in the more-than-human world. The South facet of the Self is every bit as wild and natural as any animal, flower, or river and experiences a kinship with all species and habitats. The Wild Indigenous One is resonant with archetypes such as Pan, Artemis/Diana (Lady of the Beasts), and Green Man (Wild Man).

EAST: THE INNOCENT/SAGE. Innocent, wise, clear-minded, light-hearted, wily, and extroverted, the East facet of the Self is fully at home with the big picture, light, enlightenment, laughter, paradox, eternity, and the mysteries of the Divine and the upperworld. The Innocent/Sage wants to lead us up to the realm of pure consciousness beyond distinctions and striving. In addition to the Innocent and the Sage, this facet is resonant with archetypes such as the Fool, Trickster, Priest, Priestess, and Guide to Spirit.

WEST: THE MUSE-BELOVED. Imaginative, erotic-romantic, idealistic, visionary, adventurous, darkness savoring (shadow loving), meaning attuned, and introverted, this facet of the Self revels in night, dreams, destiny, death, and the mysteries and qualities of the underworld. The Muse-Beloved wants to lead us down to Soul and wants us to be continuously dying to our old ways while giving birth to the never-before-seen. In addition to the Muse and the Beloved, this facet is resonant with archetypes such as Anima/Animus, Magician, Wanderer, Hermit, Psychopomp, and Guide to Soul.

As you read about the Self in these pages, you'll likely recognize each of its four facets as existing in (or as) at least one of your friends or family members, in certain public persons or celebrities, and in characters from myths, dreams, art, and literature. You might not at first recognize all four facets in yourself, but they're all there; the "hidden" ones await their discovery by you (the Ego). By locating all four facets of the Self on a single map, we can explore their relationships with one another and with the Ego, subpersonalities, Soul, and Spirit.

In the following chapters, we'll also explore why each facet of the Self is associated with its corresponding cardinal direction or, more precisely, with the qualities of the natural world we experience when we face that direction, and also why it's associated with the related season and time of day. In other words, we'll see how the seasons, the times of day, and the four cardinal directions of the natural world constitute the design pattern enabling us to grasp the nature of the Self.

While the Self exhibits these four facets, it's best understood as a single, integral dimension of the psyche, not merely a collection of four voices. This is why I prefer to say that the Self has *facets* — as opposed to components.

In addition to having the attributes identified above, the Self, as a whole (a "gestalt"), is creative, intelligent, inquisitive, utterly at home on Earth, confident, and joyous. When we (our Egos) function by way of the Self, we instinctively recognize and honor our relationships with other people and all living creatures, things, and habitats — the Self, consequently, is ecocentric.[11] We cooperate with others (including by way of mutually beneficial competition). We protect and enhance all of life.

Whatever we desire to do, we do it most effectively, aesthetically, imaginatively, fairly, and joyfully through the consciousness and resources of the Self.

THE SUBPERSONALITIES

And yet, one inevitable and heartrending feature of being human is that we do not live every moment from or as the Self, no matter how mature, gifted, or lucky we may be. Regrettably, we don't always participate in life grounded in our innate human wholeness. All too often we're in a fragmented or wounded state — physically, psychologically, socially, spiritually. Sometimes we find ourselves feeling unaccountably frightened, for example, or angry with nearly everyone, or unworthy, incapable, on a control trip, confused, subservient, or disconnected. The less healthy our families, communities, societies, and ecosystems, the more wounded and fragmented we tend to be individually. These wounded or fragmented aspects of our psyches are our subpersonalities, the subject of the second half of this book.

In Western and Westernized cultures (now widely understood to be not only adolescent but also pathological and growing increasingly so),[12] most people seem to function more often by way of their subpersonalities than by way of their Selves. Western conversations often sound like two or more subpersonalities comparing notes about life from their wounded or fragmented perspectives. Subpersonality-identified Egos seem to be the most common protagonists in contemporary relationships, politics, news, arts, and entertainment, and the subject matter of most advice columns and pop psychologies. See if you agree as you read the following descriptions.

Subpersonalities might be immature and wounded, but they're doing their best to help us. All four categories of subpersonalities, as we'll see, are attempting to keep us safe (physically, psychologically, socially, and economically) by using the unripe strategies available to them.

Here's an introduction to the four categories of subpersonalities and my names for them:[13]

NORTH: LOYAL SOLDIERS try to keep us safe by inciting us to act small (either beneath our potential or one-dimensionally) in order to secure a place of belonging in the world. They achieve this by avoiding risk, by rendering us nonthreatening, useful, or pleasing to others, or by urging us into positions of immature power over others (dominator power). Versions include Rescuers, Codependents, Enablers, Pleasers, and Giving Trees; Inner Critics and Inner Flatterers (the kind of flattery that motivates us to be useful and nonthreatening to others); Tyrants and Robber Barons; and Critics and Flatterers of others.

SOUTH: WOUNDED CHILDREN try to keep us safe by attempting to get our basic needs met, using the immature, emotion-fueled strategies available to them. They do this by appearing to be in need of rescue (Victims); being harmless and socially acceptable (Conformists); being coercive or aggressive (Rebels); or being arrogant or condescending (Princes or Princesses).

EAST: ESCAPISTS AND ADDICTS try to keep us safe through evasion — rising above traumatic emotions and circumstances and sidestepping distressing challenges and responsibilities. They do this through strategies such as addictions, obsessions, dissociations, vanishing acts, and delinquency. Versions include the *puer aeternus* and *puella aeternus* (Latin for "eternal boy" and "eternal girl"), Blissheads, and Spiritual Materialists.

WEST: THE SHADOW AND SHADOW SELVES try to keep us safe through the repression (making unconscious) of our characteristics and desires that are unacceptable or inconceivable to our Ego. Shadow characteristics can be either "negative" (what the Ego would consider morally "beneath" it) or "positive" (what the Ego would consider "above" it and out of reach). The Shadow is not what we know about ourselves and don't like (or like but keep hidden) but rather what we *don't* know about ourselves and, if accused of it, would adamantly and sincerely deny. Our *Shadow Selves* attempt to maintain psychological stability by briefly acting out Shadow characteristics and doing so flamboyantly or scandalously, but without our being conscious of what we're doing — letting off steam as the only available alternative to complete self-destruction.

———

While the Self, with its four facets, is a single, integral feature of the psyche, the subpersonalities, in contrast, each function as separate and discrete versions of ourselves — as isolated voices. They are multifarious, fragmented elements of the psyche. This seems to be the case even when the subpersonalities join forces for the shared purpose of self-protection. For example, a frightened Wounded Child might plead that you not accept a promotion to the highly visible (socially risky) public role you've aspired to for years; a Loyal Soldier might chime in to say that, if you accept, you'll end up humiliating yourself because you don't have what it takes to succeed ... or even be taken seriously; and an Escapist might suggest that the life of a hermit, ski bum, or drunk would be a much more enjoyable choice, anyway.

In the second half of the book, we'll see that each subpersonality represents a wounded or immature version of the facet of the Self associated with the same cardinal direction.

It seems we never eliminate or finally grow out of our subpersonalities; we can only learn to embrace them from the perspective of the Self and in this way gradually heal our wounds and integrate our subpersonalities into the functioning of our 3-D Ego. Although our subs never disappear, we can mature to the point that we seldom get hijacked by them and instead live most often from our 3-D Ego consciousness as Self, Soul, and Spirit.

On pages 22–23, you can see the horizontal dimension of the Nature-Based Map of the Psyche, which is to say the four facets of the Self and the four categories of subpersonalities. The vertical dimension of the Map — consisting of Spirit and Soul — is not shown here, and you can think of the Ego as being at the center. In order to make it easier to take in, I've divided this horizontal dimension of the map into two parts, which I refer to as map 1 and map 2. Map 1 shows the intrapersonal features of the facets and the subs, indicating how we experience within our psyches our Self and our subs, with the facets of the Self arrayed around the outer circle and the categories of subs around the inner circle. So far in this book, it's this intrapersonal dimension I've introduced you to. Map 2 shows the *inter*personal features of the facets and the subs — the ways others tend to see us when we're embodying these aspects of ourselves. In chapters 2 through 9, we'll explore in some detail both the intrapersonal and interpersonal features of the Self and the subs.

THREE CORE MESSAGES OF THIS BOOK

Now that I've introduced you to the central concepts of the Nature-Based Map of the Psyche, I can state, in one sentence, a core message of this book: The key to healing and to growing whole is not suppressing symptoms, eliminating wounds, or eradicating subpersonalities but, rather, cultivating our wholeness — the horizontal wholeness of the Self as well as the vertical wholeness afforded by our relationships with Soul and Spirit.

The second core message of the book is that there's a vital and synergistic relationship between cultivating personal wholeness and building life-enhancing cultures. Cultivating human wholeness can never be a matter of tending solely or even primarily to the individual human self, as if that self were an isolated entity somehow existing independently of the world of which we are a part. Ultimately, we cannot become fully human without healthy, mature cultures. And such cultures are not possible without healthy, mature humans — and without a healthy Earth community to be part of. Conversely, creating healthy cultures requires more than structural changes in politics, education, economies, religions, food production, energy generation, and environmental protection. It's also essential to tend to human development.

The third core message is this: There are three imperatives of any healthy, mature culture. First is to protect and nurture the vitality and diversity of its environment.[14] Second is to provide adequate numbers of true adults and elders to nurture, educate, and initiate the next generations and to create or revitalize cultural practices for the well-being and fulfillment of its people — economically, socially, aesthetically, and spiritually. And third is to protect and foster the wholeness of the culture's individual members (which is to say the Self of each person and his or her relationships with Soul and Spirit).

MAP 1:

INTRAPERSONAL VIEW OF THE SELF AND SUBPERSONALITIES

(how we relate to ourselves)

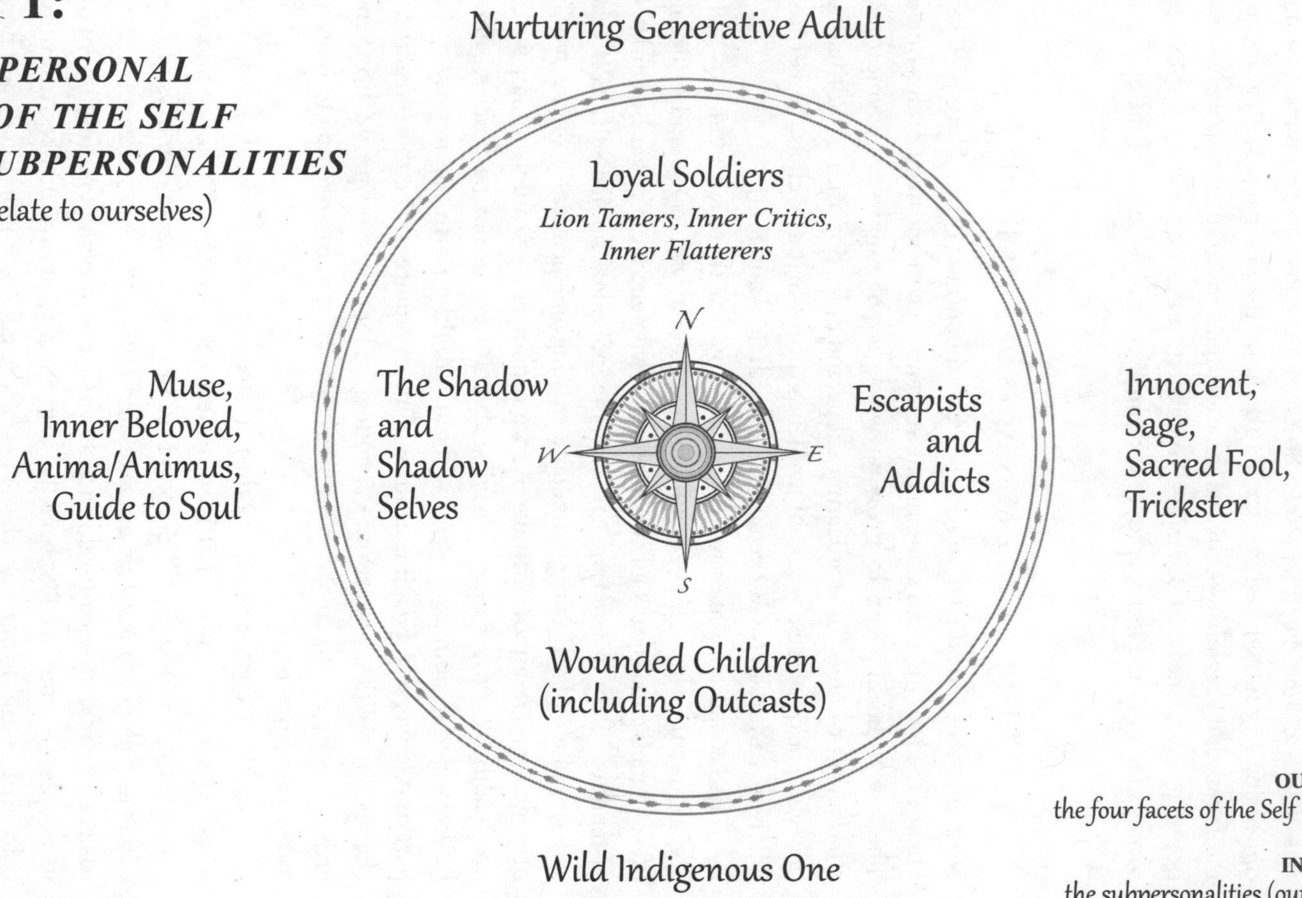

Nurturing Generative Adult

Innocent,
Sage,
Sacred Fool,
Trickster

Loyal Soldiers

_Lion Tamers, Inner Critics,
Inner Flatterers_

Escapists
and
Addicts

The Shadow
and
Shadow
Selves

Wounded Children
(including Outcasts)

Muse,
Inner Beloved,
Anima/Animus,
Guide to Soul

Wild Indigenous One

KEY:

OUTER CIRCLE =
the four facets of the Self (our wholeness)

INNER CIRCLE =
the subpersonalities (our woundedness)

MAP 2:

INTERPERSONAL VIEW OF THE SELF AND SUBPERSONALITIES

(how others see us)

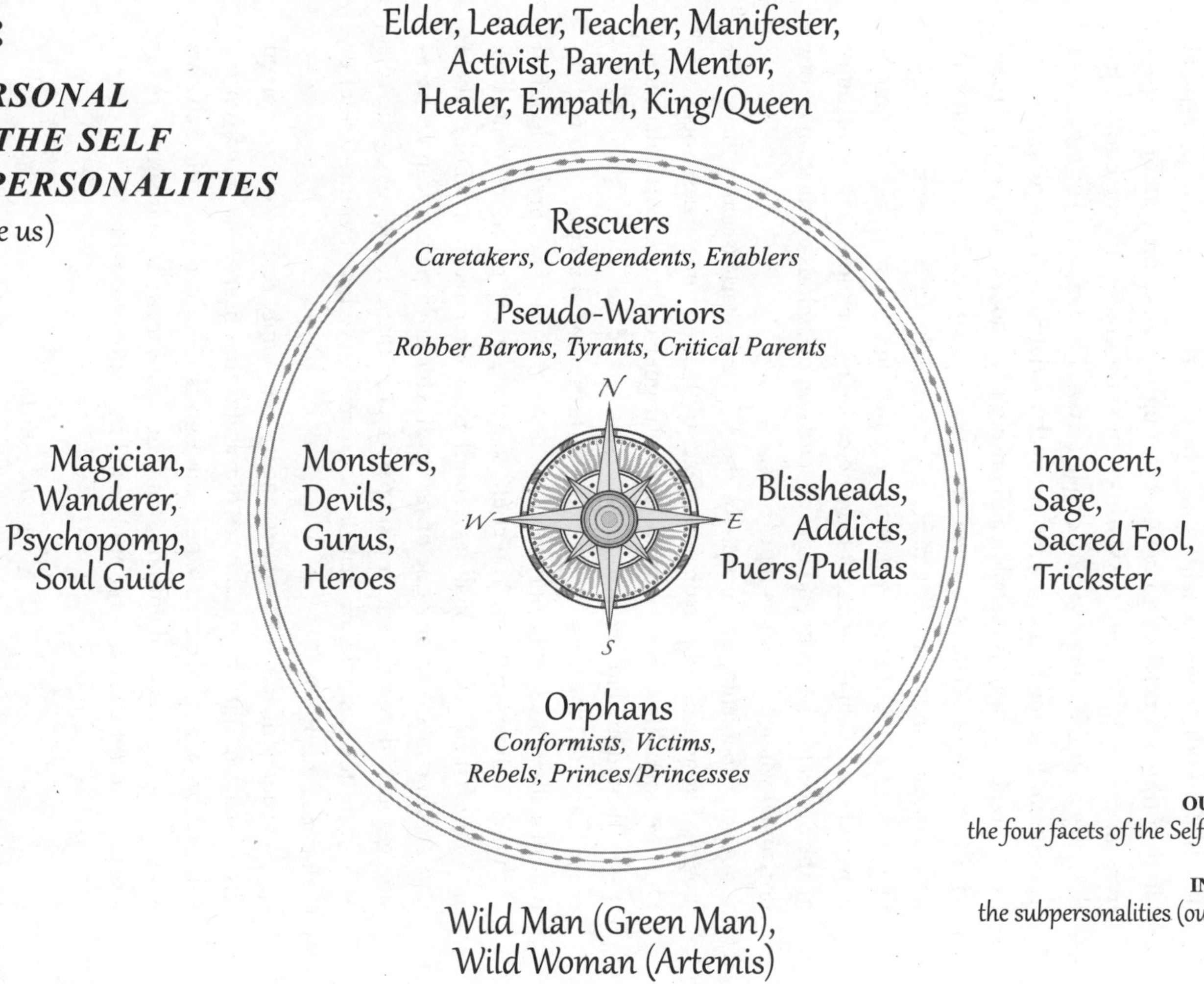

Elder, Leader, Teacher, Manifester,
Activist, Parent, Mentor,
Healer, Empath, King/Queen

Rescuers
Caretakers, Codependents, Enablers

Pseudo-Warriors
Robber Barons, Tyrants, Critical Parents

Innocent,
Sage,
Sacred Fool,
Trickster

Blissheads,
Addicts,
Puers/Puellas

N

E

W

S

Orphans
Conformists, Victims,
Rebels, Princes/Princesses

Monsters,
Devils,
Gurus,
Heroes

Magician,
Wanderer,
Psychopomp,
Soul Guide

Wild Man (Green Man),
Wild Woman (Artemis)

KEY:

OUTER CIRCLE =
the four facets of the Self (our wholeness)

INNER CIRCLE =
the subpersonalities (our woundedness)

HOW THE HUMAN PSYCHE WORKS

The Self and the subpersonalities may be thought of as a set of perceptual filters or frameworks the Ego can look through — an assortment of perspectives on one's self, life, and the world — or as different ways the Ego can tell the story of its life using a variety of narratives. They may also be thought of as different hats the Ego can wear or psychosocial roles it can play. Mature, psychologically healthy people can consciously choose, most of the time, which version or versions of themselves they operate as. But someone with limited psychological development — or a more mature person in temporary, stressful circumstances that trigger the survival strategies of one or more subpersonalities — might have no capacity to choose. The availability of the Self's perspectives and hats depends on conscious cultivation of our horizontal wholeness and its four facets.

A large percentage of people in the Western world seem to be at the mercy of how their subpersonalities react to their circumstances. Social settings, relationships, and traumatic events trigger or evoke particular subs, which then dominate consciousness, choice, and behavior. Many Westerners have no awareness of the Self and no ability to access it, no realization that they have other options; their consciousness is entirely identified with their subpersonalities. You could say that, at any given moment, they *are* one of their subpersonalities...until their circumstances abduct them into another sub. And any one of us, no matter how mature, can on occasion get locked into the rut of a subpersonality that confines us to the role of Victim, for example, or that of Conformist, Addict, Tyrant, Critic, or counterfeit guru.

When identified with a subpersonality, we simply react to our perceived circumstances. But as we cultivate our ability to observe and act from the Self, we become proactive. When our Ego is identified with the Self, we have multiple behavioral options. With the Self's many resources, we're far less likely to get stuck in a rut or hijacked by a subpersonality.

Soul and Spirit

Like the Self and the subpersonalities, Soul and Spirit, too, are filters or frameworks, but they are transpersonal ones, and most people access them far less often than the Self and subs. We might imagine the Soul as the psychospiritual ground into which the 3-D Ego can learn to sink roots. Spirit can be likened to the heavens above, or the air, the wind (the breath of the world),[15] the atmosphere, the entire cosmos, cosmic consciousness, or the great Mystery — the ultimate context within which the 3-D Ego is embedded.

When anchored in our 3-D Egos, we understand ourselves as agents or handmaidens for Soul. The Soul, after all, is the dimension of our human psyche that knows what's really worth doing with our "one wild and precious life," as poet Mary Oliver puts it.[16] Soul holds the knowledge of what we individually were born to do and to be. The Ego, on the other hand, knows how to get things done, to make things happen, but it doesn't know from its own experience what to offer its life to. The genius and beauty of the mature 3-D Ego is that it possesses the ability and creativity to make real the Soul's passions. Indeed, the 3-D Ego is the only means by which the Soul's desires can be consciously manifested in our world. This is why so many mystical traditions speak of a love affair between Ego and Soul, the Lover and the Beloved: Each possesses something the other entirely lacks and longs for. Ego possesses the heart, hands, senses, imagination, and intelligence to manifest, but doesn't know what's worth manifesting; it yearns to know the deeply authentic purpose of the Soul. Soul possesses the song that's worth singing, the dance that wants to be danced, but it has no way to manifest this in the world; the Soul yearns to be made real by the Ego. Ego is long on know-how and short on know-why; the opposite is true of the Soul.

As 3-D Egos, we also understand ourselves as agents or emissaries of Spirit. We experience ourselves as integral participants in the unfolding story of the Universe, as filaments in the vast, singular consciousness that moves through everything. We discover ourselves to be essential extras in a cosmic drama in which Spirit plays hide-and-seek with itself, a pageant in which Spirit occasionally catches a glimpse of its own evolution through the consciousness of self-aware beings. Within this (upperworld) frame of reference, the Ego is entirely at home in the Universe and is cultivating a personal relationship with Spirit, sometimes experiencing itself as a child of Spirit, at other times as Spirit's Beloved or Friend, Partner or Collaborator. A person with a mature Ego understands that by serving as an agent for Soul, she's also serving as an agent for Spirit.

Immature Egos

A person with an immature Ego, in contrast, understands herself as primarily or solely an agent for herself — or at least acts that way, whatever she might believe. Western and Westernized cultures have devolved to the point that many of their members perpetually experience themselves as "looking out for number one." They have little or no direct experience of Self, Soul, or Spirit (or of truly belonging to a human community or to the Earth community or of our interdependence with all things).

Because immature people experience the world, self, and others primarily through their subpersonalities, we can say that their subpersonalities are substitutes (subs) for Self, Soul, and Spirit. (This is another reason for abbreviating *subpersonalities* as *subs*.)

Essential Services Provided by Subpersonalities

As we've seen, the function of the subpersonalities is to protect us, especially psychologically and especially during childhood: they keep us safe by keeping us small. I mean *small* in the psychological and social senses: relatively powerless, nonassertive, harmless, invisible, and unaware; or, conversely, psychologically small by appearing socially, economically, or politically "big" through the wielding of immature, dominator power over others. The four groups of subpersonalities accomplish this in different ways.

The subs protect us by influencing us to act in ways they believe will reduce the chances of our being criticized by others, or humiliated, rejected, ostracized, disempowered, injured, left to die, or killed. Most of them are very good at what they do. Without them, most of us would not have survived as well as we have. We owe them a lot. Probably our lives.[17]

WHOLING, THE FOUNDATION FOR TRUE HEALING

The Nature-Based Map of the Psyche serves as a guide to the healing and wholing practices foundational to becoming fully human.[18] By *wholing*, I mean the cultivation of the Self, including all four of its facets. Wholing — which enables us to understand both the limitations and the gifts of our wounded or fragmented subpersonalities — is a necessary step in optimal human development.

Wholing is the foundation for true healing. Some degree of personal wholing must precede any deep healing, not the other way around. In Western societies, many believe we can't be whole — truly loving, highly creative people contributing to the world — until we have sufficiently healed from our childhood wounds. But I believe the opposite is closer to the truth: Deep psychological healing is the result of learning how to embrace our woundedness and fragmentedness from the cultivated perspective and consciousness of the Self. We must to some degree cultivate our wholeness before we can truly be healed. Wholing comes first and is foundational.

In the predominant paradigm in Western psychotherapy, the therapist acts as the agent of the client's healing. The mature therapist accomplishes this by being present to the client with the resources of the therapist's Self. It's the therapist, in other words, who supplies the wholeness.[19] This Western mode of psychological healing provides a great service, especially when the client has little access to her Self, but this is not the sort of in-depth healing from which we most benefit. It's more of a temporary fix or a relatively shallow healing that might later reveal deeper wounds. The more in-depth healing occurs when we learn to embrace our fragmentedness from our own wholeness. This is self-healing — or, more precisely, Self-healing (healing accomplished by an Ego rooted in the Self).[20]

But once we get started in our wholing, we can begin Self-healing; and Self-healing accelerates our capacity for wholing. Wholing and healing reinforce each other.

Personal wholing and healing, however, require more than simply developing relationships between parts of our own psyches and between our selves and other humans. Psychological wholeness also necessitates a mature and reciprocal relationship with the more-than-human world of which we are members. We are served therapeutically and in so many other ways by nature, yes, but it is also vital that we each step up to our responsibility and opportunity to protect and serve the natural world. We can do this in any number of ways, including planting trees, preserving and restoring habitat, eliminating waste and pollution, protesting ecological crimes, and helping to change the laws, policies, and customs that enable such crimes. Engaging in the good hard work of such service may, in fact, be one of the most effective paths to our individual psychological healing — for many people, ecological service alone (including service to our fellow humans) may be more therapeutic than psychotherapy.[21]

A true adult is in conscious relationship and service to our mysterious and endangered world and, more generally, is a creative, joyful, and contributing member of the Earth community. Our private psyches are meant to be public resources. The personal contributes to the cultural, and vice versa. The personal also contributes to the ecological, and vice versa: as healthy humans, we enhance our more-than-human environment, and we have no life at all, of course, without a thriving environment.

THE PROCESS OF INDIVIDUATION

Individuation is the word Carl Jung used for the cultivation of the psyche into a coherent whole, the process of becoming one's "true self." I think of it as the process of becoming fully human. From the perspective of the Nature-Based Map of the Psyche, the goals of individuation include the following:

- Cultivating our awareness of and our ability to embody the four facets of the Self
- Becoming aware of how our subpersonalities operate and then embracing them from the holistic perspective of the Self, in this way integrating our subpersonalities within the functioning of the 3-D Ego
- When developmentally ready, embarking upon the descent to Soul in order to discover our ecological or mythopoetic place in the world — "the truth at the center of the image we were born with" — and then cultivating our ability to embody or manifest this place or truth
- Developing a personal relationship with Spirit and/or cultivating our capacity to be conscious from the perspective of Spirit
- Applying ourselves to the developmental tasks of the life stage we're in, as well as to the most incomplete tasks of earlier stages (a nature-based perspective on these tasks and stages can be found in what I call the Eco-Soulcentric Developmental Wheel, introduced in my book *Nature and the Human Soul*)

ASSESSING OUR PSYCHOLOGICAL HEALTH

In addition to serving as a guide to the development of wholeness, the Nature-Based Map of the Psyche provides a constructive, person-affirming method of psychological assessment. It's an aid for identifying the innate psychological resources that are most in need of cultivation in an individual, how to go about this cultivation, and what sorts of symptoms are likely to become apparent when these resources are unavailable.[22]

A COMPLETE PORTRAIT OF THE PSYCHE

After considering our humanity from nature's holistic perspective, it seems fair to conclude that previous maps of the psyche offered by Western psychology have been incomplete. The principal intrapsychic elements identified by the major schools of psychology are all represented on the Nature-Based Map of the Psyche (not because I was specifically attempting to include them, but because the seven-directions matrix suggested them), but none of these schools have included all the elements identified by the Nature-Based Map; most incorporate fewer than half, and many essential distinctions are missing.[23] Twentieth-century Western psychology provided many advances in our capacity for self-understanding, but it developed in a time and within a cultural framework that limited its vision, making it difficult for us to see the whole picture.

In contrast to earlier Western models of the human mind, the Nature-Based Map of the Psyche has been constructed using all four of the following design criteria. It is

- nature-based (ecological);
- holistic and integral (comprehensive);
- wholeness oriented (as opposed to pathology oriented); and
- contextual (recognizing that our psychological health depends on the health of our social, cultural, and environmental worlds and our active engagement in these worlds through regular participation, service, and social artistry).

A complete portrait of the psyche, however, makes possible something even more important than advances in psychological theory. It enables us, as individuals, to identify elements of our own psyches whose existence we may never have suspected or that may never have made themselves known to us. The map shows us "where" to look.[24] And psychotherapists, counselors, educators, clergy, life coaches, parents, and other human development facilitators can use this map to help people undertake an inventory of their psyches and further cultivate their relationships with Self, subpersonalities, Soul, and Spirit.

The Nature-Based Map of the Psyche helps us see which of our psychological resources might be underdeveloped or completely cut off from awareness. Without a comprehensive map, we might never know what we've been missing. Hidden and latent facets of our horizontal wholeness (our Selves) often hold the resources we need to solve personal challenges, move through blocks, overcome inner resistance, see our way forward, succeed at careers, develop or improve our relationships, uncover the secrets of our Souls (and live them), and cultivate our personal relationship with Spirit. And hidden and unconscious subpersonalities can control our perceptions and behavior as much as the parts we know consciously, so there's great value in having a map that helps us discover which subs might be operating outside awareness.

The representation of the psyche on the universal nature-template of the seven directions makes it easier to understand psychological complexities, elevates into awareness what has fallen into forgetting, and reestablishes an order that is both comforting and constructively disturbing — comforting because it evokes our original wholeness; disturbing because it summons us to a long and demanding journey.

Part I

THE
SELF

Chapter 2

North

THE NURTURING GENERATIVE ADULT

If we will have the wisdom to survive,
to stand like slow-growing trees
on a ruined place, renewing, enriching it...
then a long time after we are dead
the lives our lives prepare will live
here, their houses strongly placed
upon the valley sides, fields and gardens
rich in the windows. The river will run
clear, as we will never know it,
and over it, birdsong like a canopy....
On the steeps where greed and ignorance cut down
the old forest, an old forest will stand,
its rich leaf-fall drifting on its roots.
The veins of forgotten springs will have opened.
Families will be singing in the fields.
In their voices they will hear a music
risen out of the ground....
Memory,
native to this valley, will spread over it
like a grove, and memory will grow
into legend, legend into song, song
into sacrament. The abundance of this place,
the songs of its people and its birds,
will be health and wisdom and indwelling
light. This is no paradisal dream.
Its hardship is its possibility.

— WENDELL BERRY, "A VISION"

If you've ever felt truly privileged to provide for or care for another being, human or otherwise, even yourself, or if you've ever translated an inspiration or vision into art or song, or into a manuscript, an invention, or a community project, then you've experienced and taken pleasure in the wholehearted and clearheaded qualities of your Nurturing Generative Adult. If you've ever dedicated yourself to the renewing and enriching of a ruined place — a clear-cut forest, a polluted river, or an overgrazed prairie — or rolled up your sleeves and volunteered to serve families or neighborhoods, then you've had a firsthand relationship with the North facet of your Self. If you've ever acted in defense of an oppressed people or an endangered species, spoken truth to power without desire for personal gain, or occupied public space in support of true democracy, then you've known your North Self in masterly action.

To nurture is to care for the well-being of other humans, our fellow creatures, Earthly habitats, and ourselves. To be generative is to design and implement innovative cultural practices that imaginatively and effectively restore, solve, or shelter, that truly serve the whole person and the web of life (endeavors in education, for example, or governance or healing). To be an adult, in this sense, is to enthusiastically and competently embrace opportunities to enhance the vitality of beings, places, and communities, present and future — and, where you don't find such opportunities, to creatively generate them.

Every human is born with the capacity to be abundantly nurturing and generative. Some find it easy and natural to develop and embody this aspect of our humanity. Others experience it as awkward and challenging. But learning to embody the North facet of the Self is always an essential dimension of becoming fully human. We foster wholeness in ourselves when we contribute to the wholeness of something greater than ourselves.

Wendell Berry is a prolific author, an eloquent critic of our culture and economies, and a fifth-generation Kentucky farmer. In his poem that begins this chapter, he offers a vision of the many generations of hard work awaiting us this century and beyond, the labor necessary to restore the land and waters and engender healthy human communities existing in harmony and synergistic partnership with the greater Earth community. The Nurturing Generative Adult is an essential facet of the Self needed to accomplish this demanding and joyous work. Wendell Berry is an inspiring role model of a mature human with a well-developed North.

Thomas Berry — no immediate blood relation to Wendell — was a cultural historian, a Christian monk, and one of our leading twentieth-century environmental thinkers. At age eleven, Thomas ventured out for the first time behind his family's new home in North Carolina. It was late May. He came to a creek, crossed it, and there beheld an astonishing meadow covered with blooming white lilies and filled with song. Writing seventy years later, he reflects,

> A magic moment, this experience gave to my life something that seems to explain my thinking at a more profound level than almost any other experience I can remember. It was not only the lilies. It was the singing of the crickets and the woodlands in the distance and the clouds in a clear sky....
>
> ...Whatever preserves and enhances this meadow in the natural cycles of its transformation is good; whatever opposes this meadow or negates it is not good. My life orientation is that simple. It is also that pervasive. It applies in economics and political orientation a well as in education and religion.[1]

This extraordinary watershed moment during his boyhood informed Thomas's entire life and formed the substance, content, and method of his way of nurturing and providing for his people, who Thomas came to recognize as all the species of our world. His love for creation, for our entire cosmos, stands as a moving example of what it is for a human being to be nurturing and generative.

The North facet of our innate human wholeness is that which enables us to genuinely nurture others, provide for those less able, care for the environment that sustains us all, defend the lives of future generations of all species, carry forward the life-enhancing traditions and wisdom of our ancestors, and contribute to the vitality of our human communities.

NURTURING LOVE

Love. All four facets of the Self begin with love, are anchored in love. Yet each facet features its own favored form of love. The North facet of the Self is rooted in a nourishing and boldly resourceful love, like Thomas Berry's for the Earth, a parent for her child, a devoted teacher for his students, or a true friend for another. This North aspect of love can also be seen in a benevolent leader for her people, a boy for his dog, a mature hunter for each species that feeds her family, and a healthy human community for the particular ecosystem within which it is embedded.

Nurturing love is embodied in a great variety of activities, such as healing, mentoring, parenting, teaching, feeding, protecting, consoling, encouraging, celebrating, and empathically listening and responding.

We are naturally moved and inspired when we meet people who exhibit exemplary development of the Nurturing Adult facet of their Self, or hear stories of their lives, individuals such as Jesus of Nazareth, Francis of Assisi, Mohandas Gandhi, Mother Teresa, and Martin Luther King. But each one of us possesses this capacity for nurturing others in a way that evokes people's courage, magnificence, and ability to self-heal. Each of us can remember times we stretched beyond our usual borders and found ourselves able to support and care for another selflessly and joyously, with love and compassion flowing freely through our hearts and hands. Some of us may have wholly embodied this capacity only a few times in our lives, but the fact that it happened even once confirms that this capacity has always been within us — and that it still is.

One way to evoke your Nurturing Adult is to recall inspiring exemplars you've known — maybe an uncle, your mother, a teacher, or a friend. You might imagine one such person standing behind you with their hands on your shoulders, conveying with a strong, warm touch their love for and faith in you, and imparting with their words their unconditional support and guidance.

I recall a middle-aged woman I met in my twenties, a consummate mentor with an extraordinary capacity to love. Dorothy Wergin had a part-time job as manager of the sleep lab at the university psychology department where I was a graduate student, but she was present on a full-time basis. Few people were aware of what she was actually paid to do. Most of those who visited her office came for the world-class counseling she freely offered. It was her daily pleasure and talent to support people in their confusion, pain, and grief as well as their joy and enthusiasm, all the while assisting them in stepping through the risky but necessary doors into a bigger life and the dangerous opportunities waiting there. In Dorothy's presence the room seemed to fill with more air, more life. Tension eased, previously unnoticed emotions and bodily states arose into awareness, and the way forward became clear.

I find that my own Nurturing Adult is evoked by another person's tender need and simple trust in my capacity to love and support. A friend, child, or someone I'm serving as soul guide might offer this implicit invitation. What a blessing to be invited in this way and be able to respond!

We're also inspired by the nurturing qualities we see in the more-than-human world around us: in mammal mothers and bird parents as they care for, feed, and fiercely protect their young; in the synergy between wildflower and pollinator; even in predator species that evoke the evolutionary development of the species they prey on; and more generally in the way the world provides the resources, habitats, and ecological niches that such an immense diversity of species needs in order to flourish and evolve.

It's obvious that Earth has amply provided for us. Now, in the early twenty-first century, the great question before us is whether each of us can fully access the resources of our Nurturing Adult and learn to sustain and enhance the diversity and vitality of the Earth community, which now wholly depends on our collective awakening to our ecological responsibilities and opportunities.

Embracing Each Other in Our Wholeness

When we're centered in the consciousness of our Nurturing Adult, we're able to accept everything about other people. We understand — or attempt to understand — each characteristic, trait, or state of others as a coherent feature of those individuals, part of what makes them who they are. Naturally, some human traits — such as violence, hatred, or greed — are deeply troubling, but we sense how such characteristics are expressions of others' current conditions. By embracing people in their wholeness, we create the conditions within which they can change or mature. The Nurturing Adult facet of the Self — at any age — enables us to experience others, in their essence, as creative, resourceful, and capable of wholeness. From this perspective, we do not judge, although we are highly, sometimes profoundly, perceptive and discerning. We also act to minimize and heal the damage that people cause through violence as well as through actions that might have been well intentioned but unskillful.

With a well-developed Nurturing Adult, we act from the heart, act out of an uncompromised love for others and for the world. We also act from Soul in the sense that we can see from our own depths into the depths of others and into the depths of the world as a whole. We have the capacity to both discern the truth and respond with love. (Buddhists refer to these naturally paired qualities, those of heart and Soul, as compassion and insight.)

The capacities of our Nurturing Adults also enable us to protect our loved ones and ourselves. When another person is a significant danger to us — despite our attempts to love — our Nurturing Adult will lead us away from the encounter if possible and if doing so is the highest good. With Nurturing Adult awareness, we perceive and feel holistically and ecocentrically, seeking to assist not only individuals but also, even more important, the whole system, community, and ecology to which we belong. On those rare occasions when a choice must be made between the well-being of an individual and that of his environment (the family, community, or ecosystem), our Nurturing Adult chooses to serve the needs of the latter, because without a viable environment all members suffer. But most often our Nurturing Adult sees a way to support both the individual and his ecological or social sphere.

Our North Self enables us to nurture ourselves, too. When we have access to our Nurturing Adult, we can embrace, without judgment, our own woundedness or immaturity, enabling a healing shift when our psyche as a whole is ready for it.

CAREGIVING VERSUS CARETAKING

The actions that characterize the Nurturing Adult can also be enacted by our immature subpersonalities, but the results are utterly different. It's entirely possible, alas, to lead, teach, or encourage others from the woundedness of our North subpersonalities, whose purpose, since early childhood, has been to protect us from harm. What distinguishes one form of caring from the other is our motivation. When centered in our Nurturing Adult, we act with heart (compassion for the other) and with Soul (insight into the real needs of the other). In contrast, our North subpersonalities (our Loyal Soldiers and Rescuers, which we'll explore in chapter 6) prompt us to act on the basis of a persistent and self-diminishing experience of fear and incompleteness. Although these subpersonalities possess a natural human desire to be accepted, this longing is enacted in a manner that is ultimately undermining, family weakening, and self-defeating. When merged with these wounded selves, we might appear to be nurturing — and are, to some degree — but our primary motivation is to avoid abandonment, criticism, or poverty by securing an accepted place in the lives of others. This is a form of "nurturing" that is more properly described as care*taking* than as care*giving*. We appear to be giving, but there's at least as much taking going on. Consider, for example, the socially isolated single parent who does too much for her teenage son because she fears he'll leave home if he's able to care for himself. Or the farmer who grows and provides food but, in order to ensure his profits, knowingly degrades the health of the land, water, and people with chemical fertilizers, pesticides, and genetically modified organisms.

In contrast, caregiving is its own ample reward and source of joy, not a means to garner acceptance or socioeconomic gain. By simply being herself, a person with a strong Nurturing Adult contributes to her family, her community, and the ecology of which she is a member. Cooperating with and supporting others is an authentic and intrinsic expression of her innate human wholeness.

Generative Love

To the same degree that it is nurturing, the North facet of the Self is also generative — supporting us to sustain and enhance life by careful planning; designing and organizing projects; preparing meals; dreaming up stories and telling them; building houses; creating art; taking out the trash (or, better, supporting cultural changes and creating a sustainable lifestyle so that there *is* no trash); governing; and giving birth to children, ideas, or organizations. In short, getting the jobs done — the life-enhancing jobs.

But, again and alas, the Generative Adult is not the only doer in the diverse cast of the human psyche. No doubt our subpersonalities have had a major hand in generating most of the wars, toxic substances, depraved acts, dysfunctional relationships, and life-threatening enterprises of our world.

Here, too, the distinction is a matter of both heart and Soul. A woman with a well-developed Generative Adult does not innovate or fabricate in order to impress others or to secure a place of belonging. Rather, she is simply herself — her Self. If she impresses others, it's because she imagines, designs, and manifests authentically and in a way only she can. She's unique in her way of loving, contributing, and belonging. But she's not inflated about it. Nor is she shy or reserved about what she can do and what she loves. She's both humble and bold.

Although not as common in contemporary Western and Westernized psyches as one would wish, the Generative Adult, by whatever name, is a familiar character found in stories and communities throughout the world, embodied in images such as the good doctor (Jonas Salk, Benjamin Spock), the mature leader (King Arthur, Queen Elizabeth, Abraham Lincoln — even the Lion King), the genius inventor (Leonardo da Vinci, Buckminster Fuller, Martha Graham), or the social activist (Frederick Douglass, Dorothy Day, Nelson Mandela, Wangari Maathai).

In the other-than-human world, we observe life-enhancing generativity everywhere we look. We see that our own lives are made possible by nature's endless giveaways: bacteria, worms, and fungi transforming crumbled rock into fertile soil; herbs and grains providing us with food; ocean-dwelling phytoplankton providing nourishment for other sea creatures and producing oxygen for everyone; mature forests creating wetlands, rain clouds, and habitat for uncountable species; and rock, fossil carbon, and trees providing the materials for our human homes and projects. Everything in nature gives away to others.

Gifting Communities

Those who have cultivated their North facet enjoy nothing so much as offering themselves to the world. They generate opportunities to do so. In the now-rare human communities in which most adults are psychologically mature (which is to say, initiated adults),[2] community life is founded on what Lewis Hyde calls a gifting economy,[3] in which the most important things are not for sale (things like child care, preparing meals, making music, care of the elderly, leadership decisions). Selling and buying tend to distance or impersonalize relationships. Gifting builds, sustains, and grows relationships and real communities. Like nature more generally, everybody in a healthy community freely gives away to others. And there's no waste. Every "by-product" is a resource for somebody or something else.

In Western cultures, people with well-developed Nurturing Generative

Adults operate whenever they can *as if* their community is in fact such a society. Doing so incrementally shifts an adolescent society toward a caring and life-enhancing future.

In this regard, I think of the men and women I've had the honor of guiding on their descent to Soul — the three-phase journey of psychospiritual dying (shedding of one's outgrown social identity), the revelatory vision of a Soul-infused mythopoetic identity, and the embodiment of the new identity in acts of culture-transforming service. Their Nurturing Generative Adult is evident as they go about their world-shifting work. Here are two examples of such individuals, both utilizing the metaphor of song (as well as actual song) as a way to convey the experience of discovering and performing their soulwork.

A Japanese American man, while camped in a wild place, awakened one morning to hear a songbird singing his name: "Awaken to truth and sing its beauty." Having been raised in an American Shin Buddhist tradition, he understood *truth* to be the Buddha Dharma, he told me. But he recognized that "the traditional Shin sound of the Buddha's song was too foreign to be appreciated by the tempo of our times." With this insight in mind, he embarked upon several years of study of Buddhism and transpersonal psychology and was eventually ordained a Shin priest. He has learned to "transpose an ancient truth into a contemporary melody." Although shy by nature, he now teaches the Buddha Dharma with boldness, ingenuity, and modern meaning — and, as he says, "as visibly as a singer on a stage."

A woman on her vision fast was profoundly moved, she told me, by the image of "a deeply rooted tree, a Sitka spruce, a sentient being leaning into the wind to hear the messages of Gaia and to sing and share the beauty, grace, and grief of our world." Living into this image during the ensuing years, this woman has cultivated her voice as a singer and facilitator, creating songs, practices, and workshops that link activism, creativity, and the sacred. She "supports others to grow deep roots of their own, helping people to claim their unique gifts and serve their communities with courage and grace through the gathering storms of our times."

As Wendell Berry declares in his inspiring poem "A Vision," "the songs of [the] people and [the] birds / will be health and wisdom and indwelling / light" — once, that is, we remember as a species how to take our true place in the world, the place ecologist Aldo Leopold called "a plain member of the biotic community."[4]

An initiated adult is motivated, not significantly by wealth, fame, or social acceptance, but rather by the opportunity to offer his hidden, transformative treasure to the world, to deliver, by means of his Nurturing Generative Adult, his most creative, Soul-rooted response to his planetary moment.

But a person need not be an initiated adult to cultivate and embody the North facet of her Self. A psychologically healthy person in any stage of life finds herself naturally drawn to serve and nurture others.

THE NURTURING GENERATIVE ADULT IN CHILDHOOD AND ADOLESCENCE

The North Self is an invaluable psychological resource at all ages and stages, appearing in its incipient form in early childhood. We see it in an infant's empathic emotional response and in a toddler's desire to help. Given a healthy social environment, middle childhood (generally ages four through eleven) gives rise to the North capacity to befriend others, provide care to people and animals, invent games that have rules and structure, and share possessions and knowledge.

A healthy early adolescence promotes additional nurturing and generative behaviors in realms such as courting, environmental stewardship, craftsmanship, and civic responsibility.

Thomas Berry's experience in a springtime meadow at age eleven is an exemplary instance of an experience on the cusp of childhood and adolescence that can inform a long life of mature, ecocentric caregiving and ingenuity.

ARCHETYPES OF THE NORTH

Each of the four facets of the Self is in relationship with each of the other aspects of our psyches as well as with other people. The former relationships constitute the facet's intrapersonal dimension, and the latter the interpersonal.

In its relationships to the other elements of our own psyches, the North facet of the Self is what I think of as our inner Nurturing Parent or Adult, as you can see in map 1. This intrapersonal face of the North Self is our primary resource for healing our fragmented or wounded subpersonalities beset by fear, loss, hurt, addiction, obsession, and other tumults. You might prefer other names for this facet of the Self, such as the inner Comforter, Coach, or Listener.

In its interpersonal face — in its relationships with other beings, human or otherwise — the North facet of the Self is experienced as a variety of cross-cultural archetypes, such as Elder, Leader, Teacher, Parent, Healer, Empath, Mentor, or the (benevolent and compassionate) Queen or King. (See map 2.)

THE NORTH'S PRIMARY WINDOW OF KNOWING: HEART-CENTERED THINKING

Feeling, imagining, sensing, and thinking: together, these four modalities make up what psychologist Eligio Stephen Gallegos calls the "four windows of knowing," the four human faculties through which we learn about self and world.[5] Each of the four is of equal power and importance in living a balanced and creative life. Each is a distinct faculty not reducible to any of the other three.

Let's say, for example, that you want to better understand a woman with whom you have an important personal relationship. You might begin by thinking about her and about interactions you've had with her, and this will lead to some valuable insights and conclusions, or at least hypotheses, about her. If you then let yourself feel the full range of emotions evoked by her and by the qualities of your relationship, you'll learn additional things you wouldn't have otherwise appreciated — often surprising and as valuable and relevant as what you learned through thinking alone, possibly more so. You might then use your imagination to empathize with what it's like to be her, to have that particular life with those gifts, difficulties, and opportunities. Doing so will result in additional discoveries you'd never have made by thinking or feeling alone. And the next time you two are together, you might carefully observe the way she walks and gestures and laughs, or you might listen mindfully to changes in the texture of her voice as she discusses different topics. What do you learn about her through your senses?[6]

As we'll see, each of the four windows of knowing has a special resonance with one of the four facets of the Self. The four natural pairings are North and thinking, South and feeling, East and sensing, and West and imagining. By cultivating our relationship with all four facets of the Self, we are in this way also cultivating our capacity to use all four windows of knowing, which in turn enhances our ability to fully know the world in all *its* facets. The most accomplished scientists, artists, musicians, and journalists, for example, are those who are adept at feeling and imagining as well as thinking and sensing.

Of the four windows of knowing, it is thinking that's most closely partnered with the North facet of the Self, because the Nurturing Generative Adult depends on keen insight and clear planning in order to provide effective care and leadership. However, the specific mode of thinking that characterizes the North facet of the Self is *heart-centered* thinking, not the merely logical, analytical, deductive mode of thinking more common in the contemporary Western world. Heart-centered thinking is independent, creative, moral, and compassionate. It is "critical" in the sense that it reflectively questions assumptions, discerns hidden values, and considers the larger social and ecological context. Entirely distinct from the rote memorization commonly stressed in mainstream Western schools, heart-centered thinking is distinguished by an animated curiosity that leads to a constantly adjusting, in-depth knowledge of the environment, the human culture, and its individual members. The Nurturing Generative Adult is a compassionate systems thinker, understanding the patterns and dynamics that connect the interdependent members of the more-than-human community. The Self, by way of its North facet, possesses an avant-garde insight into how our current actions ripple across space and time to other places and future generations.[7]

THE NURTURING GENERATIVE ADULT'S PLACE ON THE MAP OF THE PSYCHE

Why have I placed the Nurturing Generative Adult in the north of the Nature-Based Map of the Psyche? What, exactly, is it about the north that suggests nurturance and generativity?

The north is, implicitly, where the Sun goes after it sets in the west and disappears for the night before rising again in the east — a place of coldness, darkness, and stillness.[8] Even during daylight hours, the north-facing sides of things are the darker, colder sides. At most times of year, the winds from the north are the colder and mightier ones. The north is also associatively partnered with the middle of the night, the time of least light and least plant growth, the winter solstice, and, consequently, the ripening depth of winter.

As with winter, the north direction is a place of hardship, but hardship that has become familiar and accustomed (in contrast with the sudden changes associated with the west, which represents the sunset and the mere start of the long night). By the middle of the night or the winter, with its dangers and challenges, we've adapted to darkness and devised means to survive and do well. It takes knowledge, skill, and fortitude to thrive in the cold and dark, and so the north is linked with the generative qualities of intelligence, foresight, competence, endurance, and strength. And it is these very qualities that we most need during the dark times, the qualities that enable us to care for and nurture ourselves and others.

The north, then, is said to be the place of healing, service, caring, and creative thought — in short, nurturance and generativity.

PRACTICES FOR CULTIVATING THE NORTH SELF

Because the four facets of the Self are innate resources existing in latent form within each of us, cultivating them can proceed by our simply choosing to embody or enact them the best we can in any moment. To evoke our wholeness or any one of its four facets, the single most important step is just to remember to do it!

Yes, sometimes this is easier said than done. As we begin our conscious cultivation of the Self, we may discover that our subpersonalities are in charge most of the time. But by regularly reminding ourselves and each other to practice the conscious shift to wholeness, we develop the habit and it becomes more natural and instinctual.

What part of the psyche calls on the Self when it is not already the perspective from which we're functioning? The 3-D Ego: that neutral pivot of consciousness cognizant of its rainbow range of possible manifestations, like a craftsman with an array of tools or an artist with a palette of colors. The 3-D Ego has access to all the capacities of the Self, as well as to the contributions and vulnerabilities of the subpersonalities.

The primary practice, then, for cultivating the North Self is to simply turn inward and call upon this facet to make itself present to you, or to feel yourself stepping into the North's perspective, experiencing the world from the North's wholehearted and clearheaded point of view. As often as you can remember to do so, pause for a moment and ask your Nurturing Generative Adult to step forward into consciousness, into your embodied experience of being present to your world as you find it right then. You might remind yourself of other times when you fully experienced yourself inhabiting this generous and effective North perspective — perhaps when you were compassionately caring for another or in a leadership or teaching position or when engaged in a challenging project that demanded great skill or courage. Or you might call to mind one or two inspiring role models. As you move into this North consciousness, notice how your experience of being in your body shifts. Now, from this North perspective, what feels like the best and most important thing to do in this moment? Or what seems like the best way to proceed with what you're already in the midst of? What opportunities for nurturing and generative loving offer themselves to you right now?

You can also cultivate your North Self by enrolling in courses and programs that focus on Northerly realms, such as leadership development, nonviolent communication, negotiation skills, sensitivity training, parenting, conscious loving and intimacy, sustainability, permaculture, creative expression, social artistry, and cultivating genuine participatory democracy.

Next are four of the best general self-development practices I know, followed by some additional activities specifically designed for accessing and cultivating the North facet of the Self.

Voice Dialogue, Four-Directions Circles, Dreamwork, and Deep Imagery with the Nurturing Generative Adult

These four self-development practices work equally well for cultivating all four facets of the Self and also for healing the four groupings of subpersonalities. Because these four practices apply to all aspects of healing and wholing, I've placed them together in the appendix, rather than dividing them up among eight chapters. I recommend you consult the appendix and use these practices regularly.

North Walks

Go for a walk in a neighborhood, city park, state or national park, or wilderness area. Lead with your Nurturing Generative Adult. Be aware of how you walk, sit, look, listen, think, imagine, and feel from this North perspective.

Be in relationship to the things, creatures, and other humans you encounter. What opportunities for service, compassion, or caring arise? What insights emerge about the authentic way you belong in the more-than-human community of life? What emotions or longings surface? Record your discoveries in your journal.

Another walk: Wander in a wild or semiwild place where there are few other humans, asking the world or Mystery for help in finding — or being found by — a nurturing, other-than-human thing or place. Take your time with this; don't settle for something that doesn't truly feel nurturing to you. If you find such a thing or place, sit or lie down there and let yourself fully feel, viscerally and emotionally, the nurturing love present in this place. If you can't feel this everywhere in your body, notice if even one part of your body can receive it. If so, allow the experience of that love to spread throughout your body. Then, in your imagination, let yourself merge with this thing or place, experiencing the world from its nurturing perspective. Allow this to feed your remembering of your Nurturing Generative Adult. Perhaps you'll write one of the following letters while in this place.

Love Letter from the Nurturing Adult

Write yourself a letter of fiercely loving support from the perspective of a mature and unconditionally accepting parent. Embrace all your current emotions and life challenges and help yourself appreciate what each tells you about your relationships to yourself, to others, and to the world. Offer advice about what you could courageously do to further grow or develop those relationships. While in this consciousness, embrace your strengths and your weaknesses. Remind yourself, as you write your letter, that the goal of individuation is wholeness, not perfection.

Write a series of these letters and notice how they change over time. If you'd like, make a copy of one, place it in a sealed envelope, give it to a trusted friend who knows you well, and ask him to mail it to you when he intuits you could use some support from your North Self.

Love Letter to Another

The love letter from the Nurturing Adult to yourself aims at cultivating the intrapersonal dimension of the North facet of the Self. The interpersonal dimension can be cultivated by writing a love letter from the North Self to

another being, usually another human, or possibly a member of another species or a whole species.

This love letter, and the ones that follow, can also take the form of a song
or a poem, a dance or performance art, or a painting, sculpture, or weaving.

Love Letter to a Mountain, River, or Watershed or to the Earth, Sun, Milky Way, or Universe

In order to access and cultivate the ecological or cosmic dimension of your
Nurturing Generative Adult, write a love letter to an ecological feature of
your world — a particular mountain, river, desert, forest, marsh, or glacier.
Or write a letter to the Earth. Or to our local star. Or to our galaxy or the
entire Universe.

Love Letter to the Mystery

Write a love letter to the vast Mystery that informs and expresses itself as
every thing in the Universe. For example, Rainer Maria Rilke, the great German poet, wrote more than 150 such letters, in verse, when he was in his
midtwenties. These letters Rilke bound together in his *Book of Hours: Love
Poems to God*, in which he acknowledges that he has a personal relationship
with Mystery, has personal obligations *to* Mystery, and has opportunities for
passionate and wild celebration of this relationship. You, too, may want to
acknowledge your relationship with Mystery — from the consciousness and
perspective of your Nurturing Generative Adult. Rilke recognized that Mystery appears as universally as "the Limitless Now," on the one hand, and as
uniquely and specifically as mountain, fire, or "a wind howling from the desert's vastness,"[9] on the other. The Self of every person knows this to be true.

A Vow to Your Soul

If you have come to understand your Soul's desires mythopoetically (namely,
in the Soul's own language of metaphor, symbol, archetype, and image),
write a vow of commitment to enacting or deepening your soulwork, your
own unique life mission, personal mythology, or sacred story. Express your
vow in writing, or sing it or dance it on a hilltop, and be sure to do so from
the embodied perspective of your Generative Adult. Don't hold back! Let

Mystery know you say yes boldly, despite your appreciation that being so bold will occasionally lead to humiliations — mortifications (ego deaths) necessary for transmuting you into ever more effective shapes and semblances for embodying Soul.

And this probably goes without saying, but I'm going to say it nonetheless: as helpful and facilitative as vows are, much more important is the follow-through — the actual performance of your Soul-infused vision as a gift to others.

THE NORTH FACET OF THE SELF
AND THE DESCENT TO SOUL

So far we've mostly been exploring how the Nurturing Generative Adult functions in the middleworld — our everyday reality of family, friends, school, work, and community. But the North facet of the Self is also an essential resource in the transpersonal journey to the underworld of Soul.

The descent to Soul offers some of the most harrowing challenges of a lifetime. There we encounter dangerous opportunities that range from the physical to the psychological to the spiritual. On the way to Soul, we might be compelled by our initiation guide or by our own psyche to wander into wilderness (remote mountain ranges, claustrophobic caves, or searing deserts) or into our own psychospiritual wilds (core emotional wounds, Shadow realms, nightmares, memories of personal or collective trauma, or confrontations with our own mortality) that demand a well-honed capacity for self-care, self-reliance, and creative response if we are to benefit from these experiences — or even survive them.

In *Soulcraft* I explore the many capacities that must be honed for a fruitful descent, or that are at least invaluably facilitative. The self-nurturing subgroup of these skills includes the abilities to relinquish attachment to our former identity, quit addictions (explored in chapter 8 of this book), welcome home our Loyal Soldiers (chapter 6), explore our core wounds (chapter 7), choose authenticity over social acceptance, and make peace with our past. The complementary set of generative skills for Soul encounter include those of soulcentric dreamwork, deep-imagery journeying, talking across the species boundaries, self-designed ceremony, symbolic artwork, journaling, and the arts of wandering, Shadow work (chapter 9), soulful romance, and mindfulness. Cultivating and deploying these two sets of underworld-relevant skills require a well-developed Nurturing Generative Adult.

And after underworld encounters, the work of embodying Soul likewise necessitates a well-honed North Self. Living our mythopoetic identity for the benefit of the more-than-human community requires determination and perseverance, as well as the skills and knowledge that constitute a delivery system (a Soul-resonant craft, career, profession, art, or discipline). As initiated adults, we also need to hone the strengths of character and the skills required to face active resistance or censure from those threatened by our culture-reshaping contributions, or to respond effectively to the often de-stabilizing projections of others — the positive ones as well as the negative.

THE NORTH FACET OF THE SELF
AND THE ASCENT TO SPIRIT

The North facet of the Self is also an essential resource in the transpersonal ascent to Spirit, in which the Ego aims to merge with Mystery. On the path to cultivating spiritual equanimity, universal compassion, self-transcendence, and nondual awareness, there are a great variety of challenges, distractions, and pitfalls. In order to stay on the path, we need a well-developed capacity to nurture ourselves in the face of sometimes overwhelming emotions and memories, interpersonal antagonism and discord, the boredom that can accompany contemplative practices, or our own wounded subpersonalities screaming for their needs to be met or their addictions to be fed. And in the course of sustaining a contemplative, meditative, or yogic discipline, we require the mature generative capacities to care for ourselves, our families, and our environment — to sustain health and well-being.

WHAT WE NEED IN ORDER TO GROW WHOLE

If each one of us is born with the breathtaking bundle of latent human capacities I call the Nurturing Generative Adult, then perhaps you wonder if this set of potentials might be all anyone needs for living a fully human life. It isn't. There are three additional treasure troves of psychological resources we must cultivate in order to grow whole — three additional and essential facets of the gemstone that is the human Self. Let's turn now to the first of these three.

Chapter 3

South

THE WILD INDIGENOUS ONE

Owning up to being animal, a creature of the earth. Tuning our
animal senses to the sensible terrain: blending our skin with the
rain-rippled surface of rivers, mingling our ears with the thunder and the thrumming of frogs, and our eyes with the molten
gray sky. Feeling the polyrhythmic pulse of this place — this huge
windswept body of water and stone. This vexed being in whose
flesh we're entangled.

Becoming earth. Becoming animal. Becoming, in this manner, fully human.

— DAVID ABRAM

The South facet of the Self — what I call the Wild Indigenous One — is
fully and passionately at home in the human body and in the natural
world. The South Self has a sensuous, erotic, emotional, and enchanted relationship with what David Abram calls "this huge windswept body of water
and stone" and with each living thing in it — and, from the perspective of
the South, everything in our world is alive, each rock and river as much as
every herb and animal. The Wild Indigenous One is our most instinctual
dimension, every bit as natural and at home on Earth as any elk, elm, or alp.

Like a youth in midsummer (someone, that is, in the south season of life
during the south season of the year), the Wild Indigenous One is that dimension of our innate wholeness deliriously in love with our enthralling, sacred,
animate world. The South facet of the Self would have us dancing through
sun-drenched meadows, paddling down wildly leaping rivers, rowdily

celebrating the full rainbow range of emotions rollicking through the embodied psyche, and recklessly declaring devotion to lovers in the form of blossom, bison, canyon, woman, or man. When in the consciousness of our Wild Self, we're sometimes so at home in our world, so in love with Earthly creation, so fully present to our moment and place that, in an ecstatic rapture, we lose awareness of all obligations. Canadian mountain poet Robert MacLean celebrates a liberation of this sort:

> Tent tethered among jackpine and blue-
> bells. Lacewings rise from rock
> incubators. Wild geese flying north.
> And I can't remember who I'm supposed
> to be....[1]

Thanks to our Wild Indigenous One, we possess an uncanny ability to emotionally empathize and somatically identify with other life-forms, and are sometimes even able to shape-shift *into* them. The capacity to merge our consciousness with that of other species and terrestrial forms is something we used to enjoy as a matter of course when we lived in nature-based clans. And even our own children still do this — without our ever suggesting it or showing them how. Probably even we did this in early childhood. We can remember to do so again, as did Hermann Hesse:

> Sometimes, when a bird cries out,
> Or the wind sweeps through a tree,
> Or a dog howls in a far-off farm,
> I hold still and listen a long time.
>
> My soul turns and goes back to the place
> Where, a thousand forgotten years ago,
> The bird and the blowing wind
> Were like me, and were my brothers.
>
> My soul turns into a tree,
> and an animal, and a cloud bank.
> Then changed and odd it comes home.
> And asks me questions. What should I reply?[2]

Is everyone capable of such communions and ecstasies? You *know* your own psyche includes a wild, indigenous dimension if you've ever felt privileged to be embodied as a sensuous human animal; or if you've ever looked into the eyes of a wild mammal, or a companion dog, cat, or horse, and experienced an irrefutable kinship with a fellow Earthling. Without doubt, you've had direct, unmediated experiences of your Wild Indigenous One if you've ever enjoyed the thoroughly somatic experience of a powerful emotion — not just the visceral participation in fabulous feelings like joy, but also in grief, fear, and anger, too — or if you've ever made love with abandon, howled into a starlit night, or skied powder snow as instinctively as a dolphin dances in the ocean or a hawk rides the wind. Indeed, your Wild Indigenous One was in full play the last time you were in ecstasy as you simply chopped wood, carried water, prepared a sumptuous meal, or savored a long yoga posture.

The capabilities and sensibilities of the Wild One are especially vital for those of us born into Euro-American cultures, because our South facet has been a primary target of Western cultural suppression. It is our South that enables us to most fully experience our unconditional belonging in this world, our native kinship and interdependence with every other thing and place on Earth. And it is precisely this sense of belonging and kinship, if widely experienced, that would render impossible the Western and Westernized cultures we now live in, which, despite our aspirations to the contrary, are largely ecocidal, genocidal, dog-eat-dog, materialistic, unjust, defensive, imperialistic — in short, isolated and isolating, the obverse of affiliated and collaborative. By cultivating the Wild Indigenous One in ourselves and in our children, we'll go a long way toward forging new cultures that are not only life sustaining but also life enhancing.

David Abram reminds us that to be fully human we must fully inhabit our sensuous animal bodies, our enfleshed forms inextricably embedded in an animate world. By rewilding ourselves in this way, we moderns will rewild our world as well. This reenchantment is nature's windfall awaiting us once we learn again to access, embrace, and cultivate the South facet of our Selves. And although this might not be easy, it's simple. As poet Mary Oliver advises, "You only have to let the soft animal of your body love what it loves."[3]

SOUTH LOVE: EMBODIED, PASSIONATE ATTRACTION

In the previous chapter, I suggested that while all four facets of the Self are anchored in love, each facet features its own *way* of loving. While the North is rooted in a nurturing and generative love, the South mode of love is sensuous, sexual, emotional, and playful, like that between uninhibited lovers.

The modern Greeks use the words *philia* and *storge* for the North variety of love, both words connoting affection between friends and family members, or the love of parents for their children. *Eros*, in contrast, is the Greek word for passionate love, which can be understood as a combination of romance and sexual attraction. Romance is the West facet's mode of love (which we'll explore in chapter 5), while the South mode of love is a carnal attraction, a form of allurement we usually think of as existing exclusively between human lovers, but which also occurs between nonhuman beings and between humans and other members of the Earth community. It helps to remember that healthy sexual attraction is a much more extensive realm than the mainstream Western fixation on genitals. Sexual-erotic allurement is full-bodied and multisensory; it engages the intellect, emotions, and imagination as much as the flesh. Healthy humans naturally experience this kind of somatic rapture with sunshine, flowers, ocean, trees, fragrance, breeze, and land shapes. More on this later.

NATIVE TO EARTH

From the perspective of the Wild Indigenous One, we are wild not in the sense of being out of control, deranged, or barbaric but in the sense that we are terrestrially natural, as a wildflower is wild — native to its particular place, surviving and thriving in its ecosystem without deliberate introduction or manipulation by others. When animated by the South facet of our Self, we know in our bones and bellies that we emerged from this world and were shaped in body and mind through interaction with the other creatures. From the vantage point of the Wild Indigenous One, we know that each thing on this planet has become what it is by virtue of its ever-evolving relationships with all other things; instinctively we know we're not an exception.

There are at least three ways in which someone can be indigenous: culturally (of a particular people or tribe), ecologically (of a particular ecosystem or geographical place), and terrestrially (of Earth), each kind having an essential relationship with the other two.

Most Americans — in fact, the majority of contemporary humans worldwide — have lost touch with the cultural traditions, wisdom, and mode of consciousness of their ancestors, those who were psychospiritually rooted in the place they lived: their particular river valley, mountain range, desert canyon, seacoast, forest, island, or savanna. In this sense, most people today are neither culturally nor ecologically indigenous.

. But the Wild One within us preserves and sustains our more general terrestrial indigenity, a resource of the greatest significance and potency, especially now in the twenty-first century. Our being native to Earth is, after all, foundational to our ever having been culturally or ecologically native. What enabled our indigenous ancestors to truly and fully belong to their geographic place and to generate life-enhancing cultures there was the fact that their physical and psychological capacities were shaped by the terrestrial world that we have in common with them. They emerged from this world in a specific place *and lived accordingly*. And by living accordingly, they engendered particular cultures — ways of living — that were inherent elements of their more-than-human community. Their cultures were organic fruitions of their place: indigenous. Human culture and environment were interdependent: mutually shaping and mutually enhancing.

By learning to access and cultivate our Wild Selves, we can once again become indigenous to the place we live — our valley, watershed, or bioregion — and collectively engender ways of life fully resonant with and integral to our local ecosystem, cultures that harmonize with the songline of our place. This will take a good deal of time — likely several generations. All the more reason to celebrate the small but growing number of communities throughout the Western world that are now two or three generations into this process of relocalization, of returning home to place.

CAPTURED BY THE MAGIC AND UTTER MYSTERY OF EACH THING

From the perspective and experience of the Wild Indigenous One, we are enchanted, and in two ways. First, the South Self is utterly moved by, deeply touched by, the things of this world — its creatures, greenery, landforms, weather, and celestial bodies — and recognizes that each thing has its own voice and presence. It's as if we're under a spell — enchanted — captured by the magic and utter mystery of each thing. And when we're alive in our South facet, all that we do, even "work," becomes play. The world fills us with wonder and awe. Sometimes we're terrified by the deadly potential of terrestrial forms and forces such as tornadoes, grizzlies, and hornets, sometimes simply exhilarated, sometimes both at once.

We're also enchanted in a second, reciprocal sense: The things of the world are allured *by us* and *to us*! We ourselves, individually and as a species, are a magical power or presence in this world. The other-than-humans recognize in us a form of mystery no less stunning than their own. We, too, place other beings under a spell (including each other).

Enchantment, most fundamentally, is about how a thing belongs to its world. To thoroughly belong to a place is to experience both it and ourselves as enchanted. Through the consciousness of our Wild One, we're allured by our terrestrial place and, through that allurement, come to experience how we were *made* for that particular place. We cannot experience our own magic without experiencing the world's. Each requires the other. Conversely, the world becomes disenchanted when we no longer feel and act on our deep and innate belonging to it. To reenchant the world requires us to rediscover, reclaim, and embody our sacred and interdependent relationships with all things. We must learn again to experience and treat each thing and the world itself as alive and ensouled, each being as having its own interior life. As Thomas Berry regularly reminded us, the world is not, in fact, a collection of objects but a communion of subjects.

Enchanted derives from the French *enchanter*, which means "to be sung." The Wild One is enchanted because it has been sung into the world *by* the world *and knows this*. And the Wild One's song harmonizes fully with the grand song of the world itself.[4] Indeed, the world's symphony cannot realize its fullness without each thing — including each human — joining in with its own life melody, each of which is one note in the composite song of the world. Industrial dominator societies have been damaging and destroying Earthly biomes, but domination is not our natural or instinctive tune. The Earth needs humans to be healthy and mature if it is to be fully itself and if it is to evolve and fulfill its destiny. David Whyte writes,

> ...As if your place in the world mattered
> and the world could
> neither speak nor hear the fullness of
>
> its own bitter and beautiful cry
> without the deep well
> of your body resonating in the echo....[5]

In Sensuous Communion with the World

The Wild Indigenous One is sensuous and body centered. We are embodied in flesh and are in communion with the world through our eyes, ears, nose, tongue, and skin, as well as through our indigenous heart and wild mind. When animated with the Wild One's sensibilities, we live this corporeal reality in every moment. We delight in playful contact with the flesh and fur of fellow living animals, with bark and seed, husk and fruit, wind and water. We're thrilled by the scent of jasmine, the taste of honey, the spectacle of elk or eagle, the roar of thunder or the buzz of bees, or by full-bodied immersions in ocean, storm, or the final dazzling rays of sunset.

Our sensuous communion with the world sends shivers of seductive appreciation through our limbs — the visceral, blossoming experience of the Southerly Indigenous One aroused within us.

Emotionally Holy

In addition to being enchanted and sensuous, the Wild Indigenous One is wholly emotive and emotionally holy. Within our embodied wild consciousness, we live and breathe the sacredness and pleasure of all the emotions. *All* of them. To the Wild One, there are no toxic emotions, not even shame.[6] Each emotion is an experience alive in our bodies. The Wild One is exhilarated by each tremor, moan, or howl of feeling. Every emotion is a valued experience of assimilating the vicissitudes of life, of social, corporeal, and spiritual existence.

Through our South *subpersonalities*, however, we experience our emotions quite differently. As we'll see in chapter 7, when we react to events through the filter of our woundedness, our emotions often seem unpleasant, and we may then end up *acting* on our emotions in ways that harm ourselves or others.

It bears emphasizing that the mature human — the human Self — is not a dispassionate, merely logical functionary. We do not do well in any domain of life — even (or especially) in government, business, religion, or education — without the free flow of our feelings. "Emotional intelligence" is as essential to our humanity as any other mode of intelligence, including intellectual, imaginative, sensory, ecological, and musical, to name just a few. Individual humans burn out and human organizations self-destruct without emotional aliveness.

Some people believe we'd be better off without emotions because "emotions are irrational." But, in fact, our emotions always make sense when we're able to fully understand ourselves, and there's a treasure in each emotion. Without emotions, we're not human.

Each emotion, if we know how to embrace it, provides guidance in modifying or celebrating our relationships to others, to life, to our world. Positive or negative, emotions are not experiences we choose. They occur without deliberation in response to our ever-changing relationships to self and others, relationships that manage to regularly get out of balance. The information contained in our emotions, however, can help us recover that balance, repair or refashion our world, and enable us to participate in communities in more fulfilling ways.

A short list of emotions: mad, sad, bad, glad, scared. Every emotion contains a message. Each type of emotion (for example, mad versus sad) offers a particular kind of revelation about self or about the relationship of self to others or the world. What we call negative emotions tell us that something seems off to us and that attempts at improvement are called for. What we experience as positive emotions embody our appreciation or celebration of a good thing. Every emotion suggests particular kinds of actions that can bring the world back into balance or, in the case of positive emotions, can maintain, enhance, or celebrate balance that already exists.

For example, what makes us mad or feel hurt? Every instance of anger or hurt evokes questions such as: How do I believe I deserve to be treated? How should another person or a community of people be treated, or a particular place, or, more generally, the planet? What seems to be wrong with the world? In what way might I be part of the problem?

What we believe we or others deserve is, of course, not necessarily an accurate assessment. The value of the questioning is to help us understand ourselves — our beliefs and attitudes — as well as the moral and social conventions of our people. Sometimes we discover our beliefs are mistaken. At other times our investigation yields confirmation. In both cases, we can learn how to act on our anger and hurt. In particular, we can learn how to respond to others in a way that fosters healthy relationships.

When we're sad, a different set of questions arises: What do I love, admire, or desire that I've lost or fear I'm about to lose? What can I do to keep the loss from happening or getting worse? If it's too late, how can I mourn what's been lost? What does my love or desire say about who I am? How might I praise the things of this world?

When we feel bad (guilty or ashamed): What is expected of me? What do I expect of myself? What are the right ways for me to be and to act? What are my genuine values, and which ones have I violated, knowingly or unknowingly? How do I make things right again with others and with myself?

When we're glad: What makes my world better, more complete? What, in general, do I rejoice in? What does this say about who I am, what I value? How might I praise or celebrate what is good?

When we're afraid: What is dangerous and therefore to be escaped, avoided, or approached cautiously? What do I need to do to protect myself or others? What degree of risk is tolerable in pursuit of which goals? Given that zero risk can be deadening, what degree of risk is optimal? What is true security? Given life's inherent risks and dangers, what skills or resources do I need in order to take care of myself and others?

The Four Steps of Emotional Assimilation

In healthy cultures and families, we learn in childhood how to embrace our emotions in ways that serve ourselves and others. In contemporary Western cultures, most people must learn this later in life. Many never do.

Embracing our emotions can be understood as a journey through the four cardinal directions. Ideally, each of the four steps is thoroughly completed before we move on to the next. The first step — a talent of the South facet of the Self — is to thoroughly experience the raw emotion itself, beginning with how it feels in our body, allowing the emotion to express and embody itself through us, using sound, movement, gesture, or posture. In this step, there's no interpretation, censoring, or sanitizing of the emotion, only the full visceral experience of it. Second, from the mature perspective of the West Self, we explore what the occurrence of that emotion in that particular situation tells us about ourselves (not about others), about our expectations, values, needs, desires, attitudes, and so on. This is intended not as harsh self-criticism but rather as compassionate self-examination. Third, we express our emotions to others, in word and action, in a nonviolent, kindhearted way that makes our social world right again, or that celebrates what's already right (nurturing action is a North skill). And fourth, we review the entire cycle of the emotional process now being completed, seeing how it fits within the big picture of our individual life's story, and, hopefully, have a wholehearted laugh with ourselves and perhaps others about this adventure of being human (an East gift). Through this sunwise (clockwise) cycle — from south to east — our emotions support us in bringing our outer world of relationships into alignment with our inner world of experience, and vice versa.

A Full Emotional Response to Our World

When it comes to our emotions, it's the Wild One — the South facet of our Self — that feels, embraces, and expresses the full range of our responses to our world: from our ebullient joy over the astonishing spontaneities of Earthly life, to our anguish, outrage, and grief over the devastations and deprivations of its creatures, soils, waters, and air. Wendell Berry has expressed *his* anguish and grief in this way:

> It is the destruction of the world
> in our own lives that drives us
> half insane, and more than half.
> To destroy that which we were given
> in trust: how will we bear it?
> It is our own bodies that we give
> to be broken, our bodies
> existing before and after us
> in clod and cloud, worm and tree,
> that we, driving or driven, despise
> in our greed to live, our haste
> to die. To have lost, wantonly,
> the ancient forests, the vast grasslands
> is our madness, the presence
> in our very bodies of our grief.[7]

As ecophilosopher Joanna Macy reminds us, we humans are full-fledged ecological members of our world, a world suffering unspeakable losses every day.[8] Given our interdependence with the biosphere, it's simply normal and healthy to respond with a great wailing grief-cry over the loss of species, habitats, clean air and water, of a safe enough world for our children and ourselves. It's normal and healthy to feel vulnerable, or overwhelmed at times, to experience a shuddering fear for our world, anger and shame over our collective human carelessness, or outright despair over the survival prospects of our biologically diverse planetary ecosystems. Profound feeling is a natural consequence of our deep belonging and participation in our world, our utter dependence on the vitality of the greater Earth community. These emotions inspire and empower us to act in defense of life.

The South Self's emotionality is mature compared to that of the South subpersonalities — our Wounded Children, which we'll explore in chapter 7. The emotions of our Wounded Children tend to be reactive (triggered by conflict and frustration), egocentric (self-centered), self-protective, and self-justifying, while the Wild One's emotionality is more often proactively ecocentric (supporting our life-enhancing contributions to the more-than-human world) and worldcentric (supportive of all humans, regardless of race, gender, sexual orientation, capacity, or age).

When our Egos are dominated by our Wounded Children, our consciousness is anchored in childhood, especially its traumas. But when our Egos are functioning from the perspective of our Wild Indigenous One, our consciousness is rooted in a web of life as extensive and diverse as the entire Earth community, a web very, very old indeed.

THE TWO-MILLION-YEAR-OLD MAN

Much has been written about human instincts, innate behavioral patterns ascribed to primitive and enigmatic elements of our psyches that remain fully connected to nature and our origins as a species. Reflecting on this primal dimension of humanity, Carl Jung spoke of an "archaic man" or the "two-million-year-old man," an unconscious layer of our psyche that still enjoys a full communion with all the forms and forces of the Earth community. At our depths, in other words, there remains an indigenous man or woman within each of us. Jung personally experienced this as the "primitive" within himself.

The "archaic man" within us takes nature as his guide. For him, wisdom derives primarily from daily natural occurrences, from signs and omens experienced through his senses, emotions, dreams, and visions. Jung believed that "most of [modern people's] difficulties come from losing contact with our instincts, the age-old forgotten wisdom stored in us."[9] Likewise, the cultural ecologist Paul Shepard suggests that if we are to live again in fulfillment and in balance with the rest of nature, we must reclaim our Pleistocene psyches.[10] The Wild Indigenous One encompasses much of what I believe Jung meant by the "archaic man" or Shepard by our Pleistocene psyches. But a caveat is necessary: In contemporary people, much of the instinctive self is not only unaccessed, uncultivated, and unembodied but also actively repressed, both collectively as a result of Western cultural biases and individually as a result of the pathological and egocentric nature of childhood development in modern societies. Consequently, much of our South wholeness is now submerged and buried in what Jung called the Shadow (constituting the West subpersonalities, which we'll explore in chapter 9).[11]

But our natural instincts need not be nearly so repressed as they are in contemporary Western peoples. Healthy, mature parents know how to preserve and safeguard something essential: their child's original, natural wildness — her instinctive, sensuous, emotional, and imaginative qualities, those that exist before any cultural shaping. This aspect of the psyche is what Freud called the id. However, Freud's soul-suppressing agenda was to tame and supplant that wildness, not nurture it. "Where id was, there shall ego be," he advised.[12] In contrast, one of the goals of mature parents is for this dimension of their child's psyche — the Wild Indigenous One — to be encouraged, celebrated, and incorporated into the emerging personality.[13]

We need to preserve and embrace this priceless resource, our individual wildness — "our treasury of ecological intelligence"[14] — in order to become fully human. And, as a species, we need the preserved wildness and diversity of the land, air, and waters in order to *remain* fully human.

POLYMORPHOUS EROTICISM

In addition to being indigenous, enchanted, sensuous, emotive, and instinctive, the Wild One is also the primary feature of our psyches that enables and ignites our sexuality and our polymorphous eroticism.

People with a well-cultivated South Self enjoy a sexuality that is untamed, sensual, wholehearted, playful, and intoxicating. And because the Wild One is only one of four facets of our horizontal wholeness, the sexuality of the Self is also nurturing and tender (North), magical and romantic (West), and innocent and lighthearted (East).

But what about "polymorphous eroticism"? Here we must first distinguish between the sexual and the erotic — the erotic being a far wider range of experience. Eros is the life force that allures, that draws one thing toward another, the way gravity "takes hold of even the smallest thing / and pulls it toward the heart of the world."[15] Eros, which, as noted earlier, has both West and South qualities, evokes in us a passionate curiosity, a wonderment that impels us to explore relationship and communion. Sexuality is a particular (and special!) variety of eroticism, a South variety. Sexual arousal spurs us to surrender to and avidly explore the allurement between our enfleshed self and that of another.

And here's where "polymorphous" comes in. When embodying our Wild One, we are allured not merely by other humans but also by landscapes and seascapes, trees and forests, by ideas and poetry, art and music (rhythm as well as melody), and by eloquent spoken language and the fragrance and flavor of succulent cuisine. We find ourselves somatically aroused by the world, seduced and captivated by the everyday wonders of Earth. In the Western world, we've made erotic love too small; we've isolated it and ourselves from the animate planet within which we are immersed. As D. H. Lawrence famously lamented,

> Oh what a catastrophe, what a maiming of love when it was made a personal, merely personal feeling, taken away from the rising and the setting of the sun, and cut off from the magic connection of the solstice and equinox! This is what is the matter with us. We are bleeding at the roots, because we are cut off from the earth and sun and stars, and love is a grinning mockery, because, poor blossom, we plucked it from its stem on the tree of Life, and expected it to keep on blooming in our civilised vase on the table.[16]

The Wild Indigenous One is sensuously, emotionally, instinctively, and viscerally crazy about creation, enchanted by all things and possibilities.

ARCHETYPES AND EXEMPLARS OF THE SOUTH

As with the other three facets of the Self, the South has an interpersonal guise as well as an intrapersonal one, the latter — the Wild Indigenous One — having been the focus in this chapter so far. The interpersonal guise of the South is how we appear to others when we are fully embodying our Wild One. At such times, we incarnate the archetype of the Wild Man or Wild Woman — the Green Man, for example, or Artemis. (See maps 1 and 2.)

Green Man refers to nature spirits or flora deities found in a great variety of cultures and traditions throughout the world, including our own Western traditions and religions. Often depicted in carved wood or stone as a face with branches or vines sprouting from nose or mouth, the Green Man is a symbol of rebirth, fertility, or the cycle of plant growth initiated each spring. Some say the Green Man possesses the ability to work with tireless enthusiasm beyond normal capacities.

When a man has a particularly well cultivated Wild One, he might appear to others as a Green Man, an Earth-infused creature of sky and ground, tree and birdcall, fruit and herbs, effortlessly and endlessly bearing the natural abundance of the land.

Artemis is an ancient Greek goddess variously known as Lady of the Beasts, Goddess of the Wildlands, and Mistress of the Animals. She is the Hellenic goddess of the hunt, the wilderness, and both virginity and childbirth, and she brings as well as relieves disease in women. Artemis is often depicted as a huntress carrying a bow and arrows.

These Southerly archetypes are found in Western culture in many forms and guises, as, for example, satyrs and wood nymphs, Puck (the mischievous nature sprite, who also appears in Shakespeare's *A Midsummer Night's Dream*), Robin Hood, Peter Pan, Diana (the Roman goddess of the hunt, Moon, and birthing), a variety of fertility gods and goddesses, and innumerable other characters from literature, art, and mythology. Examples of Southerly individuals in Western culture — people who seem to be fully at home in their bodies, in the more-than-human world, and among the other creatures, and who seem to be instinctive and/or sexually vibrant — include authors Jean Giono, Henry Miller, Anaïs Nin, D. H. Lawrence, Linda Hogan, Alice Walker, and Jim Harrison; poets Pattiann Rogers, Walt Whitman, and Gary Snyder; dancers Mata Hari, Vaslav Nijinsky, Martha Graham, and Gabrielle Roth; feminists Eve Ensler and Naomi Wolf; and environmentalists John Muir, Aldo Leopold, Jane Goodall, and Julia Butterfly Hill.

Without a well-developed Wild Indigenous One, we cannot be at home on Earth or in communion with the others, nor can we experience full emotional health and vivacity, sexual fire, or erotic vibrancy. Like the other three facets of the Self, the South grants an indispensable key to being or becoming fully human.

The Wild Indigenous One
in Childhood and Adolescence

The Wild Indigenous One in healthy children is fully embodied and easily observed. Human infants and children are by nature emotional, enchanted, sensuous, and erotic. In early childhood, we respond to our world instinctively and emotionally, as seen, for example, in our joyous wonder and delight during first meetings (with cat, puddle, raspberry, friend, song); our happy pleasure evoked by another's smile, hug, or laugh; the emotional wounding of a critical word; the bodily hurt of a thunderclap or a hot stove; the sudden fright of a snarling dog or family uproar.

We are, of course, born wild, in the sense of undomesticated — naturally, perhaps blissfully, ignorant of cultural conventions and niceties. We begin life with an innate human enjoyment of an intuited kinship with all beings and things. We're as happy to trade speech with a bird or a brook as with a fellow human. And not merely speech: we naturally desire touch and taste, too. As children, we recognize ourselves as sensuous, breathing, animate creatures in communion with — erotically captivated by — other such beings.[17]

Later, in a healthy middle childhood, the Wild One is expressed and experienced in the sensuous, instinctive, earthiness of free play in wild or semiwild environs — building castles on the beach and forts in the forest, gorging on wild berries, and making golden dresses out of Scotch broom blossoms. The South Self is also seen in a child's instinctive practice of imitating the gestures and calls of birds and animals, in her endless curiosity about bugs and trees, caves and stars, in her wonderment about her own and other human bodies; in his instinctive, enchanted, audacious response to song and games and dance, and in his readiness to surrender his body to the pulse and timbre of the assorted emotions that flow through him unbidden.

And in the teen years of a healthy adolescence, the Wild One manifests in sexual aliveness and a hormone-enhanced psychosocial curiosity and exploration of the infinite possibilities of social presence, personal style, and relationships. The healthy teenager also discovers her innate yearning to explore self and world from nonordinary states of consciousness — in part achieved through Southerly pursuits such as music, rhythm, extreme sports, entheogens (psychoactive substances), and yoga — because the Wild One has always known the world is far more enchanted than has yet been discovered.

THE SOUTH'S PRIMARY WINDOW OF KNOWING: FULL-BODIED FEELING

Feeling, of course, is the window of knowing that is native to the South facet of the Self, the window most resonant with the Wild One. I'm referring not only to the kind of feeling we call emotions but also to our bodily feeling, including our awareness of our internal organs (interoception) and the positioning of our limbs (proprioception and kinesthesia, or "muscle sense"), as well as to the "feeling in our bones" (premonitions, hunches) we get about particular social gatherings, city neighborhoods, or natural habitats, not to mention interpersonal vibes, sexual passion, and our general sense of corporeal well-being, malaise, or dis-ease.

To have heartfelt and gratifying relationships with our fellow humans, as well as with the other creatures and places of our world, we must proceed, first and foremost, by way of full-bodied feeling. True communion is impossible without feeling. The other beings indigenous to our world do not speak our human languages, but we can nevertheless come to know them deeply and intimately — through feeling, through a kind of nonphysical touching.[18] Our Wild Indigenous One instinctively translates *by way of feeling* what's being "said" by the nonhuman flora and fauna (and stones, rivers, and forests). This ability to know-by-feeling is the most natural thing in the world for nature-based peoples. And when it comes to communion with others of our own species, we must remember that we are at least as much feeling infused as we are linguistically inclined. What on Earth would our relationships be like if we couldn't sense social vibes, read the emotional field, or discern the bodily states of our friends and family? (Well, actually and sadly, the worst of contemporary mainstream Western culture is an all too apt answer.) And certainly our sexuality is founded on our capacity to feel, in all senses of the word. To be fully human we must fully feel.

THE WILD INDIGENOUS ONE'S PLACE
ON THE MAP OF THE PSYCHE

What is it about the cardinal direction of south that resonates so surely with the Wild One? The south (for people in the Northern Hemisphere, that is; for those in the Southern Hemisphere, this is the north) is the place of greatest warmth and light, the south being where the Sun is at its midday zenith. The south-facing sides of hills, groves, canyon walls, and dwellings are the warmest and brightest. At all times of year, the winds from the south are generally the most temperate and often, but not always, the mildest.

South, then, is naturally mated with the flowering and growth of plants, the early development of young animals, and the child's emotions and vulnerabilities, as well as with his playfulness, delight, and sense of wonder. Because of its direct connection with the warmth and comfort of the Sun, the south is also affiliated with the warmth of the human heart and emotional connectedness. And in the warmth of the southerly season of summer, people are outside for longer hours and have greater opportunities to explore the other-than-human world.

Consonant with these qualities of the south, the Wild Indigenous One is emotionally alive and expansively at play and at home amid the fecund wonders of our more-than-human world. The Wild One celebrates its embodiment and its communion with all living things, just as nature does more generally in the warmer parts of the day and year. Both the Wild One and our experiences in the cardinal direction of south are lush, sensuous, abundant, energetic, and animated.[19]

PRACTICES FOR CULTIVATING
THE SOUTH FACET OF THE SELF

Not everyone has well-honed access to their Wild Indigenous One. This is especially true of contemporary Western men who've been taught from the get-go that feeling is unmanly. Feeling is in fact a foreign faculty in immature men mired in macho and military misconceptions of manhood. The fully embodied man, in contrast, is in a sensuous and emotionally vibrant relationship with the diverse beings and things of his world, which enables him to be most empathically responsive to, appreciative of, and supportive of his fellow humans, the other creatures, and the shared environment in which they are all participatory members. This is, of course, equally true of the fully embodied woman.

Actually, it's rare for the South facet of the Self to be well developed in *anyone* in the contemporary West, because of the culture's pervasive alienation from the other-than-human world. Few Westerners experience kinship with undomesticated fauna. Few are deeply moved or inspired by rivers and mountains or by any flora beyond the garden. This is primarily due to a lack of exposure or interest. Too few families, schools, and religious organizations introduce children to their greater world in any meaningful or comprehensive way.[20] As noted earlier, the Wild Indigenous One is actually a direct threat to industrial dominator societies. If a majority of Westerners were to viscerally experience the sacred kinship they naturally have with all life, we'd see an abrupt collapse of the extractive, synthetic economy and imperial politics on which contemporary Western culture is built. Egocentric, patho-adolescent culture has a major stake in suppressing the South of our Selves.

The good news, however, is that cultivating the Wild Indigenous One is not difficult. As with the North facet, the primary and most portable means of accessing the South is to simply call on it, because it is, after all, waiting within our psyches.

For example, sit outside, or even by an open window in your city apartment, and feel the wind or sun move across your skin. Let the distinctive mood of that place on Earth and its weather penetrate you like the sound track of a rousing drama. What feelings are stirred in you? Or, at any time and any place, very carefully observe your emotions and bodily sensations, even the subtlest ones, as you encounter another person — a stranger sitting across from you in a train, or your own beloved, or anyone else. What do you feel between you? What vibes do you detect? Or walk through undomesticated country and offer your full-bodied attention to each unexpected thing you encounter — a flower, frog, rivulet, bone, stone. What is the particular feeling of that thing, your embodied knowing of it? While there, very consciously take in all the fragrances and whatever they evoke in you — images, memories, or bodily sensations. Do the same at home as you roam through your spice rack. Again, what feelings (bodily and emotional) are evoked? Or, if your circumstances permit, take off your clothes and let your whole body fully feel your world — perhaps in a meadow, your backyard, or your living room. What feels good against your skin? Not so good? What emotions or longings are evoked? Or offer your full attention to the sounds of the world, preferably while outside in a wild place, discovering the auditory nuances, distinguishing different pitches, melodies, and rhythms. Make a song of them. What feelings are stirred?

At any moment of the day, whether you're at work in the shop or office or garden, at play on the field or court, at home with your family, or en route between one and the other, remind yourself of your wild, sensuous, emotive, and erotic indigenity. As you re-member yourself in this way, what do you notice about the way you physically move through your activities? What shifts do you notice in your relationships? What now feels most alluring or compelling? How's it feel to be in your body? In your animate surroundings? What emotions are viscerally present? How's it feel to be immersed in the land? Are you fully at home? How could you be more so?

Your Wild One Awaits Deployment

Consider enrolling in a wilderness program that gets you traveling by foot or boat or skis in unpredictable weather through untamed lands or seas. Or simply wander off on your own, if you have the skills and knowledge to do so. Take experiential courses in animal tracking, birding, gardening, or permaculture. Study massage (and get some) or other somatic practices such as Feldenkrais. Sign up for courses in sensory awakening, Gestalt awareness, sacred sexuality, yoga, drumming, singing, or dance.

And here's one of my favorite South practices: skipping! Yep: Bouncing from one foot to the other while maintaining dynamic forward momentum. Just do it, for at least five minutes. You can skip in the hallway or on the sidewalk or field, but if you really want to supercharge your skipping practice, try it on earthen trails with a downward slope of, say, ten to thirty degrees. Then you can *really* catch some air between hops. Sure, be careful. Take it slow at first. But if you do this for five minutes, you'll be surprised at how alive you become, how your blood surges, your emotions stir, your senses become vibrant — your eyes feasting on colors and textures you had previously missed, your ears now awakened to the songs of birds and the calls of animals and the murmur of wind in the pines, your nostrils flaring to take in the fragrance of roses. Your body feels, well, a bit more wild, yes?

Voice Dialogue, Four-Directions Circles, Dreamwork, and Deep Imagery with the Wild Indigenous One

Turn to the appendix to get a better feeling for these four core methods of cultivating wholeness, including your Wild Indigenous One.

South Walks

Wander into a place with no or relatively little human impact. Let your Wild Indigenous One feel your way in. From your South perspective, be in embodied relationship with the things and creatures you encounter. How does each thing feel? How does it provoke or inspire you? Take in both the minute details and the big picture. Let yourself be moved by the way light plays upon a rose or the way a cloud's shadow races across a hillside and what these experiences stir in you. Touch things you've never touched before, or as if you haven't. Sing the songs you feel emanating from things. Drum their rhythms. Dance for or with them. Echo birdcalls, or offer your own language in response. Play with your capacity to be immersed in all your sensory fields simultaneously. What do you hear? (The wind? Surf? Crickets? Trees creaking? Water flowing?) What are the fields of fragrance, sometimes subtle, that you move in and out of as you stroll? Can you feel the changes in air temperature or humidity as you approach or leave a watercourse? Are there berries to taste? Salt in the ocean air? What does all this arouse in you?

As you walk in full embodiment of your Wild Indigenous One, what opportunities for communion or celebration arise? What insights emerge about your authentic place in the world or about the integral way you belong as a member of the more-than-human community of life? What emotions surface? Record impressions in your journal.

Wild Conversations

Here's one approach, in five steps, that will catalyze conversations with other-than-human beings, or what Gary Snyder calls "talking across the species boundaries."²¹ Feel free to add or subtract steps or do them in a different order.

1. Go wandering outside. Bring your journal. Be prepared to offer a gift — a poem, tears of grief, an expression of yearning or joy, a song, a dance, a lock of hair, tobacco, cornmeal, water, a handful of your breath. Early on, cross over a physical threshold (a stream, a stick, a passageway between two trees) to mark your transition from ordinary consciousness to that of the sacred. Beyond the threshold, observe three cross-cultural taboos: do not eat, do not speak with other humans, and do not enter human-made shelters.

2. With the perspective of, and through the embodiment of, your Wild Indigenous One, wander randomly until you feel called by something that strongly draws your attention because it attracts, intrigues, allures, repels, or scares you. This might take some time. Don't simply choose something with your strategic thinking mind; wait until you're called. It might be a bush, boulder, anthill, waterfall, or snake, or maybe a rotting animal carcass. Sit and observe it closely for a good length of time, offering your full sensory and emotional attention. Record in your journal what you observe. Perhaps offer a gift at this time.

3. Then introduce yourself, out loud. Being audible is important. Tell the Other about yourself, who you *really* are, but from the perspective of your Wild Indigenous One. Be prepared to go on for fifteen minutes or more. Perhaps tell it why you have been wandering around waiting to be called — not merely because someone recommended it, but because of the ways the idea resonated with you. Then tell your deepest, most intimate truths or stories that arise in the moment, or your greatest doubts or most burning questions or yearnings, or all of these. In addition to ordinary human language, you might "speak" with song, poetry, nonverbal sound, images (feel yourself sending these images to the Other), emotion, or body language (movement, gesture, dance). Then, using the same speech options, tell the Other everything about *it* that you've noticed. Describe its features (out loud, if using words, song, or sound), and respectfully tell it what interests you about its features, and what the

fact that you find them interesting tells you about *you*. Keep communicating...until it interrupts you (if it does).

4. Then stop and be receptive — with your senses, intuition, feeling, and imagination. "Listening" to the Other (direct, prereflective perception) is different from fabricating metaphors (such as a tree "telling" you to stand tall). With true listening, you're simply being receptive to the Other through your feeling and imagination without striving for a response. Fabricating metaphors, on the other hand, consciously enlists the strategic thinking mind, which asks "What is this like?" and reaches for an answer by means of reasoning. To really listen, it helps if you expect to be surprised. If you "hear" something predictable, you're probably not really listening.

5. Keep the conversation going for several rounds. Don't end the interaction prematurely. In your journal, record or draw what happens. Offer the Other your gratitude and a gift, if you haven't already. When you're ready, return to the place of your original threshold and cross back over, ending your observance of the three taboos.

In this practice, the Other might reflect something back to you about you, but, more generally, the goal is to learn something about the Other. Or about both you and the Other. Or about the web that contains you both. It's best to enter wild conversations with the central intent to become better acquainted with a nonhuman being, rather than, say, to receive some oracular information about yourself.

THE SOUTH FACET OF THE SELF
AND THE DESCENT TO SOUL

The underworld of Soul is a wilderness — an outback defined not by a particular geographical location but by a state of consciousness, a frame of mind, a realm of the psyche in which meaning, metaphor, and symbol percolate from their generally invisible depths and flow through our moment-to-moment experience like creatures from another world. Sometimes it seems to be a circus world, but more generally it's a sacred one, a heaven or a hell exuding eloquent signs of portent or promise. Here, denizens of our personal unconscious mingle, strangely, with archetypes of the collective human unconscious and creatures of the terrestrial wild, and it is often difficult to discern which are which. To our astonishment or bafflement, our own individual Souls might appear in a great variety of shapes and guises. Characters from dreams and nightmares materialize out of nowhere. We find ourselves faced with unavoidable and seemingly fated tasks and trials — supremely challenging adventures, perhaps impossible but nonetheless necessary ones — and we recognize that how well we engage with these quandaries will determine whether or how fully we'll realize our destiny in this lifetime. Every move we make seems critical and fraught with significance.

In order to thrive in such circumstances — and certainly to benefit psychospiritually — we require an instinctive aliveness, an ability to respond without thinking, or prior to thinking, like an animal with corporeal faith in its natural embeddedness in the world, an animal equipped with instincts not merely for survival or defense but for imaginative response and enchanted play. What is needed is an experience of belonging to one's place so profound that it seems as if the place itself thinks and feels for you, that it opens the way for you to proceed simply by virtue of the fact that it knows you and recognizes how you are meant to be there.

In other words, in the underworld, you need to be rooted in your human wildness and your indigenous belonging.

And you need to be emotionally alive, too, because your emotions provide you with invaluable clues to how well you're currently adjusted or acclimatized to the underworld and to the others you encounter while in that state of mind, and clues to what to do if you're not. You want to be able to trust your embodied feelings.

You want to be able to trust your *body*, more generally. You want to be confident that your body will react and move you toward your true place in the world. You want, that is, to know what to move toward without having to first (or ever) rationally analyze your situation. You want to have faith in your faculty of allurement, your gift of feeling the more-than-human relational possibilities in the shimmering, interactive field within which you find yourself at any moment while in the depths.

An excursion into the underworld is one hell of an adventure, and your Wild Indigenous One knows and loves sacred adventures of all kinds. You wouldn't want to embark on the descent to Soul without some prior cultivation of this South facet of your innate human wholeness.

THE SOUTH FACET OF THE SELF
AND THE ASCENT TO SPIRIT

The ascent to Spirit is the merging of our individual consciousness with the one consciousness that pervades and animates the Universe. Why is this considered an ascent? Partly because the Universe is a totality (it includes and enfolds everything), the Earth is just one infinitesimal element of it, and we instinctively point upward to indicate what is beyond Earth. However, since we know that Earth is a planetary sphere, it would be more accurate to say that the bulk of the Universe is not up but out (out beyond the Earth). From this perspective, we don't so much ascend to Spirit as we expand out to Spirit (out from our everyday consciousness, which is anchored in our individual Egos).[22]

In the process of ascending to the upperworld of Spirit, our everyday consciousness expands out and ultimately merges with the one consciousness that fills (and forms) the cosmos. One path to this experience is the cultivation of our capacity to feel fully at home in this world, to recognize ourselves as belonging unequivocally to the Universe. We embrace and merge with the whole by deeply experiencing our kinship with each thing.

Being fully at home in the world is the genius of the South facet of the Self. The South facet, then, is key to the ascent to Spirit when approaching Spirit by way of our embodied experience. Spiritual paths that are grounded in, or that at least honor, our fleshly embodiment and erotic powers include Hatha, Kundalini, and Tantric yoga; Buddhist Tantra; Hindu Tantra; and some of the mystical branches of Christianity, Judaism, and Islam.

One of the doorways, then, to experiencing our oneness with all things begins with cultivating consciousness of our interrelationship with *each* thing by way of an embodied, sensory communion. We progress from reverent observation to empathy to identification; this final step is the experience of merging with another being or thing or place. Like the descent, this journey of ascent is a great adventure, one that can be thoroughly embraced by the Wild Indigenous One.

There are, of course, other paths to enlightenment, ascetic paths that proceed by denying the needs and desires of the self and the body. These function not by expanding the Ego to encompass the All (the One) but by annihilating the Ego that experiences itself as separate. Ascetic paths might evoke transcendent experiences, but they do so at the expense of the South facet of our human wholeness and, consequently, compromise both our middleworld and underworld lives and identities.

NORTH AND SOUTH AS PAIRED OPPOSITES

You may have noticed a dichotomy, perhaps a familiar one, between the North and South facets of the Self, a contrast that shows up in philosophy, mythology, psychology, and literature. In Western culture, perhaps the most common means of symbolizing this distinction is by way of the Greek gods Apollo and Dionysus and the differences between them. Apollo is said to be rational, ordered, serene, calm, poised, and self-disciplined. Dionysus, in contrast, is sensuous, spontaneous, emotional, uninhibited, undisciplined, and even orgiastic or chaotic. Apollo is the god of the Sun, music, and poetry (in other words, he's generative), while Dionysus is the god of wine, wild nature, and ecstasy (a rather feral fellow).

You can see that the Apollo-Dionysus opposition parallels that between the Nurturing Generative Adult and the Wild Indigenous One. But not precisely. Perhaps all such dualities are merely approximations of archetypal distinctions impossible to express precisely, definitively, or once and for all.

Like all paired opposites, Apollo and Dionysus are not at all incompatible. Nor are the North and South facets of the Self. Rather, they represent two dimensions of a dialectical unity. Perhaps the most important thing to remember about the Self, in this regard, is that it is *both* Apollonian and Dionysian.

Although the North and South facets of the Self enjoy between them some dynamic tension, they are also, curiously, favored with a commonality that distinguishes both of them from the East and West facets. The horizontal plane of the Map of the Psyche is composed of two axes: the north-south and the east-west. And these axes are orthogonal — at right angles to each other — and consequently address different dimensions of the human psyche. The north-south axis incorporates the intrapersonal and interpersonal — our everyday, social, and psychological experience, whether generative and disciplined or emotional and spontaneous. And the east-west axis encompasses the *trans*personal — our spiritual or mystical experiences of both the dark (West) and the light (East) that lie hidden beneath or beyond the everyday. Let's turn now to the transpersonal axis, beginning with the East.

Chapter 4

East

The Innocent/Sage

Every day
  I see or I hear
  something
    that more or less

kills me
  with delight,
  that leaves me
  like a needle

in the haystack
  of light.
  It is what I was born for —
    to look, to listen,

to lose myself
  inside this soft world —
  to instruct myself
  over and over

in joy,
  and acclamation.
  Nor am I talking
  about the exceptional,

the fearful, the dreadful,
  the very extravagant —
  but of the ordinary,
    the common, the very drab,

the daily presentations.
  Oh, good scholar,
    I say to myself,
      how can you help

but grow wise
  with such teachings
    as these —
      the untrimmable light

of the world,
  the ocean's shine,
    the prayers that are made
      out of grass?

      — MARY OLIVER, "MINDFUL"

"Well, which is it, then," you might ask, "Innocent or Sage? How could someone be both innocent and wise?"

"Well, why not?!" giggles the Innocent.

"How could one *not*?" queries the Sage enigmatically.

This is the way it is with the East facet of the Self, and we just have to learn to live with it. Paradox is its friend and ally; "both/and" is its stock in trade, its modus operandi. This is why I've placed a slash rather than a hyphen between the two parts of its name. The Innocent/Sage sometimes appears naive and uncomplicated, and sometimes seasoned and sagacious, but it's really unfailingly both. The Innocent/Sage is always having a good time, and that twinkle in its eye — is this naïveté or wisdom? Ingenuousness or ingeniousness?

When you sit long enough with the paradox, you discover that innocence and sagacity actually have quite a bit in common: purity, virtue, and incorruptibility, for example.

To further complicate the matter and spice up the prospects, there seem to be not just two but actually four archetypes that resonate equally well with the East facet of the Self: not only the Innocent and the Sage, but also the Sacred Fool and the Trickster.

Consider Mary Oliver's "Mindful," an extraordinary exemplification of the East, in which we find echoes of all four archetypes. We sense the Innocent in her declaration of a life purpose so wondrously simple: "what I

was born for — / to look, to listen, / to lose myself / inside this soft world."
But this is followed up with: "to instruct myself / over and over / in
joy / and acclamation," which delightfully resonates with the Sacred Fool (I
imagine the poet standing in front of herself, whimsically instructing). And
then we find both the Fool and the Sage in: "Oh, good scholar, / I say to
myself, / how can you help / but grow wise / with such teachings / as these
— / the untrimmable light / of the world, / the ocean's shine." You can
feel how she's having a good time, maybe making fun of herself, and yet in
the end evoking, with great wisdom, the miracles revealed through her full
presence in every moment. And then she concludes with a return to pure,
poetic innocence: "the prayers that are made / out of grass."

The world itself is the Trickster in this poem, a Trickster who evokes
in the poet (and in us, her readers) the experience and outlook of the Innocent and the Fool, for the world, like every genuine Trickster, staggers us,
boggles our minds with its constant outlandishness: "Every day / I see or I
hear / something / that more or less / kills me / with delight."

Do we all have a facet of our psyches that is both innocent and wise,
both joyous and serene, both goofy and insightful, that can help us lighten
up and live beyond conventional rules and norms, and that can trick us and
others out of everyday routines? Well, have you ever been dazzled mute by
the miracle of a sunrise or the night sky, or found yourself perfectly still and
at peace while in a temple or cathedral or an old-growth forest? Have you
ever had a good laugh with (and maybe even at) yourself about how you
tend to take certain things oh so very seriously, as if those things — getting through traffic, winning a game, writing a decent sentence — are, in
the moment, the only important considerations in life? You *know* you've accessed your Innocent/Sage whenever it feels to you as if a veil has lifted and
you're able to see a situation, a person, or a place in utter clarity, and you
wonder how you could have been so blind for so long. For sure, the East
facet of your Self was in full play the last time you felt and acted a little imp-
ishly or behaved a bit impulsively, and on the occasion when you were able
to instinctually lighten up a tense social situation with just the right quip, or
if you ever took a social, professional, or artistic risk even though you knew
you'd look foolish — or perhaps even because you would.

The Innocent/Sage is that aspect of the Self that grants us access to the
purity and grandness of life lived simply, spontaneously, gratefully, and

joyously. When we haven't cultivated this East facet, our lives are liable to turn humorless, stress filled, heavy, and dull, perhaps even gloomy.

The Innocent, Sage, Fool, and Trickster — these four archetypes (and their cousins) are alive and well in all of us, even if, in some of us, they haven't gotten much airtime for a while...if ever.

EAST LOVE: TRANSPERSONAL COMPASSION

The love emanated by the East facet of the Self is a spiritual love that instantly dissolves our defenses, sees us to our core, and embraces our deepest human nature. East love nudges us out of our relatively small, everyday story and helps us grasp and celebrate a bigger, transpersonal narrative, a story whose sweep gathers up all historical epochs, all species, the great array of cultures, the pathos and rapture of being human — indeed, the very space-time continuum and vast imagination of the cosmos.

Sometimes the East confers a Trickster's love, the love we feel in the whack on our shoulders from a Zen master's stick, or the version of God's love that the fourteenth-century Sufi mystic Hafiz evoked with great, Trickster-ish humor:

> Love wants to reach out and manhandle us,
> Break all our teacup talk of God.
>
> If you had the courage and
> Could give the Beloved His choice, some nights,
> He would just drag you around the room
> By your hair,
> Ripping from your grip all those toys in the world
> That bring you no joy....[1]

Agape is the Greek word for transpersonal compassion, whether fierce or farcical or both. Christian theology borrowed the word from the Greeks to mean God's or Christ's love of humans or the human reciprocal love for God. But the meaning of *agape* also encompasses spiritual love between people, often said to be unconditional and self-sacrificing.

THE INNOCENT

A dimension of every human psyche is born innocent — simple, naive, free from moral wrong — and remains so throughout life, regardless of the traumas, wounds, or ordeals the Ego may suffer along the way. The East facet of the Self is uncorrupted, even in the midst of calamity and tragedy, shows up fully but is not attached to outcome, and is always innocently present to the wonders of our world, unhampered by our socially learned filters and blinders.

Innocence implies and requires present-centeredness and receptivity — being here now, fully and simply, in relationship to each thing wholly in the way it is sensed and felt in the moment. The Innocent facet of our psyche is permeable, completely open to the world as it is — not ruminating on past hurts or successes or future consequences or aspirations — and living as if the world will take care of us.

Our capacity for present-centeredness is essential to our psychological health throughout life. Innocence is akin to what Buddhists call "beginner's mind," allowing us to see with fresh eyes, respond with a young heart, act without guile or deception, love like we've never been hurt, and dance like nobody's watching.

With our innocence intact, we plunge ourselves into the now — in a spring meadow, during an embrace with a lover, or while absorbed in a work of art. We offer ourselves fully to the world.

We tend to think of innocence as being opposed to experience, as if through living we inevitably lose our innocence. We do indeed grow beyond our original ignorance of how the world works, but in all other senses we can keep alive our innocence by cultivating the East facet of our Self. And we must. Innocence is the foundation of our ability to be in relationship and to cooperate, and cooperation is essential to life-enhancing societies.[2]

THE SAGE

The Sage aspect of the East Self possesses an innate sort of wisdom, a mountaintop perspective. It's essential here to distinguish wisdom from knowledge, the latter being an accumulation of facts, the former pertaining to superior discernment and understanding. Like an oracle or prophet, the Sage (within us or in others) inspires us to let go of the lesser things in our lives and to ask ourselves to consider more deeply what is of true and lasting value.

The Sage's awareness, like the Innocent's, need not reach beyond her current moment. In making choices, she doesn't have to begin with a review of the larger context of her actions — the more-than-human community, the Earth, the Universe. This is because she is, in a sense, already merged with the Universe. Her way of being is intuitively in tune with the cosmos.

The Sage dimension of our psyche experiences all of creation as "ours" in the sense that the Universe is our primary felt membership. This mystical realization is difficult to articulate in everyday language. As the poet Robinson Jeffers writes,

> ...they have not made words
> for it, to go behind things, beyond hours and ages,
> And be all things in all time, in their returns and passages, in the
>   motionless and timeless centre....[3]

Being merged with the whole, the Sage within us understands that the vitality and ongoing evolution of the whole — of Earth as a living being, for example — has a distinctly higher value than the survival of any of its components, including any of its particular peoples, institutions, or nations. This perspective might seem to lack compassion, but the Sage is exquisitely aware that all things suffer or perish if the whole is harmed.

My favorite exemplar of the Sage archetype is the Taoist master Lao-tzu, whose philosophy has been described as "common-sense mysticism" and "creative quietism" and, by Lao-tzu himself, as the way of the "simpleton" or the "do-nothing," designations that suggest the Sage's kinship with the Innocent and the Sacred Fool. The wisdom of Lao-tzu, a legendary Chinese mystic from the sixth century BCE, is preserved in eighty-one sayings that evoke core East-Self qualities such as humility, graciousness, and transcendence of the separate finite self.[4] Lao-tzu's best-known adage, "the way to do is to be" — action rooted in essence or being — is a root paradox of the East Self.

The blending of wisdom and innocence is a quality of many spiritual masters. The current (fourteenth) Dalai Lama, for example, Tenzin Gyatso, is well known for his delightful innocence as well as for his sagacity and insight. Although the spiritual leader of Tibetan Buddhism, he describes himself as "a simple Buddhist monk."

Although wise, the Sage does not personally experience himself this way. Merged as he is with the Universe, the Sage believes it's the Universe that's wise. The Sage feels that he himself does nothing. The Sage in each one of us simply admires nature's way.

Some say that wisdom is simply innocence seasoned by experience.

THE SACRED FOOL AND THE TRICKSTER

The Sacred Fool doesn't play by the rules or standards of everyday society. Not caring what others think of him, he's neither for nor against social niceties, conventional morality, or even sanity. He's not interested in progress or getting somewhere other than where he already is. He's beyond or prior to custom, etiquette, propriety, and protocol — and sometimes even personal safety. In card zero of the Tarot, we see him strolling blithely ahead, seemingly unaware that he's about to walk off a cliff.

The thirteenth-century Persian mystic Jelaluddin Rumi audaciously expresses the archetype of the Sacred Fool in this way:

> Conventional knowledge is death
> to our souls, and it is not really *ours*.
>
> We must become ignorant
> of what we've been taught,
> and be, instead, bewildered....
>
> Forget safety.
> Live where you fear to live.
> Destroy your reputation.
> Be notorious.
>
> I have tried prudent planning
> long enough. From now
> on, I'll be mad.[5]

In common parlance, "fool" and "sage" appear to be opposites, one connoting ignorance and the other wisdom. At their depths, however, both exhibit a nonattachment to form or outcome. The Sacred Fool acts from what often seems to be innocence, insanity, or lampoonery but is no less wise for it. We think of a Sage, in contrast, as strictly sober; but because she doesn't strive and doesn't seek positions of elected or hired leadership, the true Sage has neither investment in sobriety nor compulsion to comply with rules.

The Sacred Fool dimension of our own psyches merges the innocence of the child and the wisdom of the elder. Both draw on the capacity to perceive simply and purely, to be fully present to the moment and to all things existing and happening within it.

The Sacred Fool — in others or in ourselves — helps us grasp the big picture by poking fun at himself (and, in so doing, at all of us) or by making fun of us directly. He also might respond to our solemn questions and conceptions with perspectives that reject or reframe our most cherished assumptions.

Psychologically mature comedy and clowning have their roots in the East facet of the Self. Some spiritual approaches seamlessly combine wisdom and comedy, as seen, for example, with Roshi Bernie Glassman, the Zen master and clown. Wise comedy is never only about laughs. Roshi Glassman, for example, is internationally recognized as a pioneer and role model of socially engaged Buddhism. By embodying the jester or clown as Sacred Fool or Trickster, he can fly beneath our everyday-identity-defending radar, nudging us to see the larger picture that galvanizes our social, environmental, political, or cross-cultural activism.

Possessing countless cross-cultural forms, the Sacred Fool or Trickster shows up in myth and ritual in guises such as Nasruddin from the mystical Sufi tradition of Islam, the familiar Native American Tricksters Coyote and Raven, the Heyoka clowns of the Lakota or the Mudheads of the Hopi, American rodeo clowns, European court jesters, and the clownlike figures in Japanese Kabuki theater.

The Sacred Fool is at once an artless and innocent clown, sly Trickster, and sage teacher. She helps us break out of the common trap of taking ourselves too seriously, a hazard as common in our spirituality as it is in our work, play, and love lives. Sacred Fools and Tricksters help us see the psychospiritual armor we might be inadvertently sealing ourselves within. They also have the job of keeping our leaders honest — to increase the chance that the priests, kings, queens, CEOs, and politicians act with integrity. Perhaps more important (and more achievable), their task is to raise our consciousness about what our leaders are actually up to. In early-twenty-first-century America, we see this role brilliantly embodied by comics such as Jon Stewart and Stephen Colbert.

The Sacred Fool shows up in your own human psyche, too. He can appear anytime in your life when, against all odds, you suddenly lighten up about matters you had been treating so solemnly. When the perspective of the Fool breaks through, you're able to laugh at yourself, appreciating your immediate circumstances from a larger perspective.

The Trickster, too, exists within you. He exposes your illusions and evokes in you a larger understanding of events and of yourself by devising pranks and creating mischief, confronting you with paradox, and helping you lighten up in the midst of the oh-so-serious business of work, love, and spiritual development.

At Home with the Mysteries of the Divine

The East is the facet of the Self most at home with the mysteries of the Divine, with the upperworld, light, enlightenment, eternity, and the non-dual. The Innocent/Sage wants to lead us up to the realm of pure conscious-ness, beyond distinctions and striving.

And yet it's important to remember that our East Self, whose place is on the psyche's horizontal plane, is not the same as Spirit (nor is the East the same as the upperworld) — any more than our West Self is identical with Soul (or the West with the underworld).

The East Facet and the Ego

Is the goal of the East to get rid of the Ego (as I define it in this book — as that element of the human psyche that is conscious of itself)? Not at all. The Ego, after all, is what renders us human. The contemporary problem with being human is not that we have Egos but that too many people have *immature* Egos, many of them patho-adolescent Egos. As an Ego heals and matures, it journeys through a series of Ego-deaths and Ego-rebirths, but it never disappears — until, perhaps, death.

Ego*centrism* is the problem, then, not Egos. Egocentric people are agents for themselves only (and perhaps also for their immediate families), without awareness of or tending of the social and natural environments that sustain their lives. Their consciousness is Ego-*centered*. A person with a healthy, ma-ture Ego, in contrast, is *eco*centric; she understands herself as, first and fore-most, an agent for (the health of) her ecosystem (and second, as an agent for the health of her human community, which dwells within that ecosystem;

and third, as an agent for her immediate family and self). Spiritual practice helps mature our Egos.

Faced with the assertion that the goal of spiritual practice is to eliminate the Ego, the East facet of the Self might respond with a hearty laugh and the blended perspectives of the Trickster, Fool, and Sage, as, for example, expressed by Jay Leeming:

> Trying to get rid of your ego
> Is like trying to get rid of your garbage can.
> No one believes you are serious.
> The more you shout at the garbage man
> The more your neighbors remember your name.[6]

Rather than attempting to jettison the Ego, a sensible person draws on the resources of her East Self to cultivate her relationship to innocence, wisdom, humor, and the great, transpersonal, and universal mysteries of life.

INTERPERSONAL AND INTRAPERSONAL FACES OF THE INNOCENT/SAGE

One of the curious aspects of the East facet of the Self — as you can see reflected in maps 1 and 2 — is that, unlike with the other three facets, its interpersonal and intrapersonal faces are identical: Innocent, Sage, Sacred Fool, and Trickster. These are the ways the East facet appears both to us (our Ego) and to others. The Innocent/Sage, in its simplicity and purity, doesn't make a black-and-white distinction between subject and object, between you and me, between acceptable and unacceptable. When anchored in our East Self, we aren't trying to manage our social impression in order to attract or repel others. We are what we are, to others and to ourselves.

THE TRANSPERSONAL AXIS OF THE MAP

The Innocent/Sage represents one of the two poles of the transpersonal, or spiritual, axis on the horizontal plane of the Nature-Based Map of the Psyche. The other is the West facet of the Self, which we'll explore in the next chapter. While the East resonates with the transpersonal mysteries of light and the universal, the West embodies the spiritual mysteries of darkness and the unique.

The East-West axis can also be thought of as the continuum between extroversion (East) and introversion (West). The East facet moves us beyond our everyday self-focus to a greater awareness of the whole within which we are embedded. The West facet, in contrast, ushers us deeper inside, inviting an understanding of ourselves more profound and meaningful than our everyday social identity. East is wide-angle big picture; West zooms in to the particular.

The Innocent/Sage in Childhood and Adolescence

Like the other three facets of the Self, the Innocent/Sage is present in our human psyches at birth and fully embodied during early childhood. But our conscious access to the Self tends to fade later in childhood, especially in egocentric society. This is why the Self must be consciously cultivated as we grow into adolescence and adulthood. Ecocentric families and societies support personal wholeness in every dimension of social, educational, recreational, religious, and work life.

Young children, of course, embody innocence more fully and naturally than humans at any other stage of development. But children, as we all know, possess their own variety of wisdom, too ("out of the mouth of babes"), as well as Sacred Fool zaniness and Trickster impishness.

Teenagers, even in Western mass culture, sometimes exhibit a type of wisdom less prevalent in older members of society. In the handful of years after puberty, the rare Western teens who are psychologically healthy reel with epiphanies about the stifling social realities of mainstream mass culture, on the one hand, and the alluring psychospiritual potentials of human life, on the other. Their fresh perspectives enable them to ask questions and seek possibilities that their older, more established family and community members have forsaken or forgotten. A healthy teenager's discerning questions and social observations are often a great embarrassment to her parents and teachers, both secular and religious. In egocentric societies, countercultural teenage fashion, language, and exploits — embodying a blatant antithesis or critique of the conventional — often have a Trickster-ish effect on society, exposing the illusions and hypocrisies of the so-called adults.

The East's Primary Window of Knowing: Full-Presence Sensing

In keeping with the simplicity, purity, and openness of the East, clear and keen sensing is the Innocent/Sage's native window of knowing — in particular, the five senses of vision, hearing, taste, smell, and touch. The East facet of the Self has an uncomplicated way of knowing the world, in which cognition (North), imagining (West), and feeling (South) are secondary to the straightforwardness and immediacy of perception.

The sharp and nuanced sensing we're capable of with a well-developed East Self contrasts with the diminished perception typical of people in egocentric cultures. In the mainstream Western world, the senses are dulled by disinterest, disuse, and stultifying cultural activities that take place indoors and in denatured outdoor environments with a woeful constriction in the diversity of things that can be seen, heard, touched, smelled, and tasted. Too few contemporary people are intoxicated by the songs of birds and bowled over by their colored plumage. Can we feel the delicacy of a cool breeze jostling the hair on our sun-baked arms? Do we linger with the perfume of peonies?[7]

Keen sensing is a talent, one that must be cultivated and practiced in order to be maintained and honed. The Self, by way of its East facet, does not merely favor sensing among the four windows of knowing. The Innocent/Sage, to be more precise, is a connoisseur of the senses, a practitioner of full-presence sensing. More generally, the Self (as a whole, as a gestalt) is a devotee of the rainbow spectrum, a maven of music (the songs of creatures, wind, and waters, as well as of humans), an epicure of food and drink (from fine cuisine and wines to a draft of spring water or a single grape simply but thoroughly enjoyed), an aesthete with an exquisite appreciation of texture and textiles, and, quite frankly, a full-on freak of floral fragrances.

The Innocent/Sage's Place on the Map of the Psyche

What exactly, you might ask, do the archetypes of Innocent, Sage, Fool, and Trickster have to do with the cardinal direction of east?

The east, of course, is where the Sun rises, granting us light after the long night. The east, then, is commonly affiliated with beginnings, origins, and birth, and also with illumination and enlightenment and, as a consequence, with Spirit, too. Beginnings and enlightenment suggest innocence and wisdom.

With the return of the light each morning, we can more readily appreciate the big picture, our world expanding beyond the immediate fears and concerns of our contracted night-selves. The east, then, is also allied with qualities that widen or sharpen our perception or understanding, qualities such as the simplicity of the Innocent, the wisdom of the Sage, the humor ("lightening up") and transcendent brilliance of the Fool, and the Trickster's gift of paradox.

With the light of the new day, we walk out into the world — into public places and into our more communal roles. This is why the east is coupled with extroversion — the directing of our attention and intention beyond ourselves.

The east is associated with the end of the twenty-four-hour day as well as its beginning. The end flows seamlessly into the beginning. In this way, the east is yoked with our final and physical death, as well as with our birth. It paradoxically bonds the newborn and the elder, our innocence and wisdom.

PRACTICES FOR CULTIVATING
THE EAST FACET OF THE SELF

In the mainstream world of Western and Westernized cultures — an aggressively competitive world in which the Ego exists as an agent primarily for itself and its small-story desires and needs — the Self is not only abandoned early in life but also actively suppressed by family, schools, and religious practices. This suppression is essential to the existence of egocentric culture; a human being in vibrant contact with her wholeness would be a poor candidate for the social roles of consumer, worker bee, or soldier — the pawns and minions, the cogs and cannon fodder that enable military-industrial society to function. The roles of tyrant, tycoon, and taskmaster would be equally unattractive to a fully human being. Bred for such roles at any rung of the dominator hierarchy, most members of egocentric society have completely lost touch with their wholeness by their midteens.

In contrast, in ecocentric families and communities, all four facets of the Self are supported and encouraged from birth onward. The Innocent/Sage dimension of the Self, for example, is routinely recognized and nourished in children and adolescents, so there's rarely a need for remedial cultivation of innocence, wisdom, spontaneity, transcultural humor, or transpersonal awareness.

As with the other three facets, the handiest method for cultivating the qualities of the East Self is to innocently call on its many resources, which, after all, have always been waiting within. The most essential step is to simply remember to open the way. At every opportunity, when your awareness may otherwise be idling — while waiting for a pot to boil or a friend to arrive — remind yourself of your inborn capacity to dwell in the calm center of the frequent storms of your life, or your ability to smile at the comedy or absurdity of being human, including your frequent insistence that life unfold one way rather than another. Or, in your imagination, you might transport yourself to a mountaintop from which you can sense a larger story unfolding, or you might imagine yourself decked out in your favorite clown suit in the midst of the somber business and busyness of life. As you are gently lifted onto this Eastern platform, what do you now feel about yourself and others? What are the most important lessons or principles to remember going forward? Can you find the place where you can open to whatever pain is present without having to experience it as suffering? Where in your life do you find joy? Can you have a good laugh with yourself?

As for more traditional and systematized approaches, the Innocent/ Sage can be awakened and ripened through the study and practice of meditation, contemplative prayer, and mystical-spiritual disciplines such as yoga, Taoism, Buddhism, Kabbalah, or Sufism. The study and practice of stand-up comedy or clowning are excellent options, too, because they support us in accessing the Sacred Fool, Trickster, Innocent, or Sage.

The practice of mime is another path to East cultivation. An accomplished mime — especially a white-faced guerrilla mime playing with receptive people on city streets and in public shops — attends to everything with exquisite care, has a finely honed sense of humor; appreciates, from a particularly broad perspective, the human condition; operates within both the guise and archetype of the Sacred Fool; and tricks others out of their too-serious identification with the small self.

Movement-based meditations such as tai chi and qigong support the cultivation of the East facet's simplicity and present-centeredness, as can the practice of trance drumming or dance. Meticulous and devoted nature observation will also evoke these qualities.

Then, of course, there is the pancultural opportunity of apprenticing to natural, bona fide Innocents and Fools — namely, infants, toddlers, and young children. Spend an hour or a day hanging out with one or more little ones. Abandon your "grown-up" agenda and follow the lead of your companion: how does he play, attend, emote, desire, laugh, cry, sing, dance? Give it a whirl.

Voice Dialogue, Four-Directions Circles, Dreamwork, and Deep Imagery with the Innocent/Sage

Consult the appendix now for sensible guidance in using these four key practices for cultivating the Innocent/Sage.

Praise Walks

First thing in the morning, before breakfast (in other words, close to sunrise, the east time of day), go outside and, as an Innocent and/or Fool, praise each thing in nature that moves you in any way. Speak directly to the things (not about them) and praise them out loud in your most eloquent or brazen speech. You might also praise with dance, verse, song, or chant. Feel free to clown it up with exaggerated gestures if you'd like, but be entirely genuine in your praise. Or praise in a very quiet, reverential self-effacing way, if you prefer. The important things are to praise and to do so in a way more embodied than still and silent appreciation. Don't look for meaning or try to determine what anything might tell you about yourself. Praise the "others" for the simple magnificence and miracle of their autonomous existence.

In your praising, perhaps adopt Mary Oliver's attitude expressed in the opening poem of this chapter: "Every day / I see or hear / something / that more or less / kills me / with delight."

Sunrise Practice

Arise early, when it's still dark. Whether you must drive partway or not (ideally, not), walk to a place with a low eastern horizon, a place from which you can watch the Sun rise — perhaps you'll be on a hilltop, at the edge of the ocean or a large lake, or on a great prairie or desert. Stand or sit in silence and stillness while you wait for dawn. Let all your senses take in the unfolding miracle: the very gradual return of light, from gray to first colors, the birds beginning to sing, the subtle changes in the movement of air, the first color appearing on the eastern horizon (perhaps the yellow-orange of pollen), the very first rays of sunlight sneaking over the rim of the Earth and lighting up your face, the first sensation of the Sun's warmth on your skin, the colors on the clouds and clear sky. Greet the Sun with whatever simple movement, gesture, or dance occurs to you in the moment. Let any emotions, memories, or symbols emerge in your awareness. If you'd like, remind yourself that the Sun's apparent movement actually reveals the revolution of the planet you're standing on, as you and Earth slowly tilt forward toward the Sun. Experience fully, purely, and simply the sunrise. Allow it to reverberate through you.

Meditation Practice

A pancultural means of cultivating the East facet of the Self is, of course, meditation practice or contemplation. There are many traditions and approaches. If you don't already have a meditation practice, find an instructor or consult a text by a meditation teacher. Meditation cultivates the resources of the Innocent/Sage through the regular practice of stillness, silence, and simple but steady attention.

A very effective and nature-based form of meditation, rarely taught, is to simply walk on the land, very slowly, just wandering, especially in a wild or semiwild place or in a city park, with all your senses fully open to everything, neither clinging to nor avoiding any experience or encounter. Walk with an attitude of loving-kindness toward all beings, human or otherwise. Whenever you notice that your attention has wandered away from where you are and from the other beings you are walking among, simply and gently bring your attention back to the here and now.

THE EAST FACET OF THE SELF
AND THE DESCENT TO SOUL

The state of consciousness or dimension of the psyche known as the underworld can get pretty wild. To the Ego, it often seems like a madhouse of maelstroms or a precarious precinct of pandemonium. If there were ever moments in life that could sweep you from your feet so surely you might never again right yourself, your underworld hours are the ones. And yet these are the times when keeping your wits about you means everything. Your potential for creating meaning in your life, for discerning your way toward your destiny, depends utterly on your capacity to be fully present with the chaos of your underworld encounters.

You want to be sure not to close down at such times. While in the domain of Soul, you must be as open and receptive as you've ever been — an Innocent. You don't want to be analyzing underworld events while they're happening — that can wait for another time. You want to be absorbing everything that's unfolding. To enter underworld consciousness and fully benefit from your encounters there, you need the East's capacities for presence and equanimity.

And you don't want to be defensive, trying to save your life at all costs, when, after all, the underworld is the "place" into which you've descended in order to transform that very life. And surely you understand transformation as a death-rebirth experience and know you can't skip over the first half, as much as you might wish to.

While in the underworld, you need a cultivated capacity for present-centeredness and receptiveness, as well as a certain nonattachment to your own life, at least as it has been — the sort of transpersonal perspective embodied by the Fool.

Equally essential during underworld journeys is the wisdom of the Sage, enabling the big-picture perspective that allows you to remember what's most important and to choose well.

And when faced with choices during underworld encounters with personal demons, Shadow figures, or traumatic memories, we often need the perspective-shifting tactics of the Trickster. We'll never deeply understand our demons, Shadow elements, and traumas as long as we approach them from the restricted perspective we retreated to long ago in order to keep ourselves safe from them. At some point, before true healing is possible, we must be able to see how our demons are actually our partners in the individuation process, how they hold the missing segments of our path to wholeness. This psychoperceptual shift is precisely the domain of the Trickster, who knows how to lure us out of our defensive positions (our caves and fortresses) to glimpse at last, from a vast perspective, the terrific and terrifying terrain of our unfolding personal mythos.

Upon our return from underworld sojourns, when it comes time to embody the Soul's desires, we find ourselves struck by the seemingly impossible demands and dimensions of the task. Without a sense of humor at such crossroads, without an appreciation of the big picture of living a human existence, we're surely sunk. The Innocent's perspective is also necessary at such times, because unless we approach the dangerous opportunity of Soul embodiment with freshness and conscious presence to each moment, we'll never succeed. The task of living as an initiated adult is always a unique undertaking. We can't manage it by following another's path or by trying to figure it out. We must rely, in part, on simplicity, humor, wisdom, and, at times, trickery.

Even though it sits opposite the West (the direction most resonant with the underworld), the East facet of the Self is essential on the descent to Soul.

THE EAST FACET OF THE SELF
AND THE ASCENT TO SPIRIT

It's not surprising that the East facet of the Self is essential on the ascent. In order to lift the veil that obscures our Ego's oneness with the Great Imagination that animates the cosmos (the universal psyche), we surely require the intrapsychic support of the Innocent/Sage.

Consider the everyday preposterousness of the upperworld project: "You mean that I — little me — am the One Who created the world and sustains it? Are you *nuts*?" You can see that it takes a certain innocence — naïveté, even — to embark on the ascent, because there's no way your Ego is going to understand at first what the endeavor really entails, or what the experience of the destination might actually be like. Someone might explain, "No, it's not your *Ego* that created the world; rather, there's a vast consciousness or imagination that weaves the evolving story of the cosmos, and your Ego partakes in — is an element of — that consciousness. Your individual consciousness is a drop in the ocean of that greater consciousness and is, in this sense, no different from it. There's no boundary between you and it." But, let's face it: you're still going to need a good deal of innocence to embark on the journey.

And the journey is going to entail maintaining a sustained and careful attention to what *is* — through practices such as meditation, contemplation, and compassion (for self and other). The Innocent/Sage, as we've seen, is your foremost resource for present-centeredness.

Spiritual teachers say the one who embarks on the path of enlightenment will not be the one who survives it. A necessary event along the way is the death of the Ego that aspires to know the truth.[8] Indeed. Given this state of affairs, who would choose to begin... or persist? Only a Fool.

It's possible to realize your original Oneness with everything only because this is who you already are and always have been. And, within you, one of the representatives of this truth is your Trickster, ever ready to do its best to pull the rug of egocentric identity out from beneath you. You were born with this intrapsychic capacity to get over yourself.

Your Sage, too, is necessary for the ascent. There are many moments on the upperworld journey in which we need wise and sane counsel, and it won't always be available from sources beyond our own (alleged) individual psyches. And our Trickster and Fool do not, quite frankly, come across as particularly sane. Our Innocent, perhaps yes, but he does not possess the kind of wisdom you need at the times when you would be best served by clear advice, guidance, encouragement, humor, and compassion. When the outer Sage is not available, the inner one might be.

Chapter 5

West

THE MUSE-BELOVED

I glanced at her and took my glasses
off — they were still singing. They buzzed
like a locust on the coffee table and then
ceased. Her voice belled forth, and the
sunlight bent. I felt the ceiling arch, and
knew that nails up there took a new grip
on whatever they touched. "I am your own
way of looking at things," she said. "When
you allow me to live with you, every
glance at the world around you will be
a sort of salvation." And I took her hand.

— WILLIAM STAFFORD, "WHEN I MET MY MUSE"

Romance is how love is experienced by the West facet of the Self —
romance, that is, in its grand and all-embracing sense of seeking and
surrendering to those mysterious and enigmatic fascinations that promise/
threaten to devastate us in all the right ways, turn our lives upside down and
inside out, plunge us into magic and rapture, and, in the bargain, liberate us
from whatever doldrums our everyday lives may have marooned us in.

A love affair with another human is surely a treasured instance of romance, but the West facet of the Self is not a specialist in human liaisons
alone. The West facet is equally a devotee of sunsets and sunrises, storms
and waterfalls, armadillos and rattlesnakes, watercolor and cosmology, jazz
and poetry. The West revels in the great romance with our wildly diverse

world, is a connoisseur of the multifarious adoration, is profoundly moved by the mystique of the manifold.

By imaginatively romancing the world and its endless unique wonders — both human and other — we keep our lives new, forever evolving, and, in so doing, we participate in the ongoing evolution of the world itself. But personal evolution — individuation — necessitates a periodic reshaping of our lives that is often deeply challenging. By opening our hearts and imaginations to the daily mysteries, a romance with the world upsets our routines, making us vulnerable to the great changes destined in our Souls and in the Soul of the world, the *anima mundi*.

The West, then, is not only the place of romance but also the change place, the dimension of our human psyches that seeks and savors ecstatic and troubling transformations.

How does the West facet of the Self embrace change — real change, deep change? By falling in love with things — with an idea, a meadow, a melody, a woman or man, an endangered planet — and striving to understand what each beloved thing is at its core, intuiting what it is destined to be, and then assisting it (or him or her or ourselves) to unfold uniquely. The West is a genius at wholeheartedly grasping the meaning of things, in part by enabling us to fathom how one thing, symbolically or metaphorically, is often like another that at first appears quite different.

In this chapter, we'll explore the West facet's transformative Muse-methods of romance, imagination, and metaphor.

LOVE AND DEATH

The romantic love particular to the West is not necessarily sexual in the way South love is. But when we think of fully fleshed-out human love affairs, we recognize that they exhibit the love of all four facets of the Self: the sexual love of the South and the dark romanticism of the West, but also the nurturing care of the North and the simple-wise-lighthearted-spiritual love of the East.

But an allurement can be and often is exclusively West, utterly romantic and enigmatic without the love qualities of the other three directions: for example, an intense but platonic friendship that exudes themes of fate or karmic bonding; or perhaps an inscrutable attraction to a mountaintop, desert canyon, swamp, or seashore, a locale where a terrifying and liberating revelation awaits; or a bewitchment by a musical instrument, such as a lyre or bassoon, or a pull to poetry, painting, or a performance art that somehow, as you engage in it, reminds you of your true name; or a fascination with an esoteric spiritual path — Sufism, Kabbalah, or Tantra — that seems to vow/warn that it will alter your world conclusively and irreversibly.

When we enjoy a vibrant relationship with the West facet of our Self, our world and everything in it comes fully and staggeringly alive, each thing shimmering in its unspeakably unique mystery, meaning, and momentum. And in its transience or mortality, too.

Because the West facet, after all, is as much at home with death and decomposition as it is with romance. From the West's perspective, to love something is to assist it to unfold and evolve, and this requires a recurrent dying to what it has been. The West, then, is an apprentice to death as well as to dreams, destiny, night, the unknown, and the underworld of Soul. It wants to draw us down — and can — and wants us to continuously surrender and sacrifice our old ways while giving birth to the never-before-seen.

The West knows that by embracing death — the ending and recycling of things — we serve life. And by serving life, we foster love.

THE DARK MUSE-BELOVED

Seen from one angle, the West facet of the Self is our Muse, our intrapsychic source of inspiration, creativity, and deep imagination. The Muse allows us to experience the world in a way that only we can and to dream the future from our unique perspective and with our distinctive resources. As the Muse of poet William Stafford said, "I am your own / way of looking at things." And when we look through her eyes, we see the world in its great depth, diversity, eloquence, and potential: "When / you allow me to live with you, every / glance at the world around you will be / a sort of salvation." *Will* we allow her (or him) to live with us? And, if we do, will we be prepared to find, astonished, the restoration of our vision — our ability to look deep into the heart of things? We might be so moved by the wonder and terror we behold that the world itself changes: the sunlight bends and the ceiling arches.

But the Muse is not the only archetype that resonates roundly with the West facet of the Self. We experience the West in a variety of ways, all of them related by the West's three constant themes of romantic allurement, hidden or veiled meanings and depths, and the undoing, dying, and reshaping of things.

For example, sometimes we experience the West dimension of our own psyche — this is the intrapsychic view (see map 1) — as the Anima or Animus, or the Inner Beloved, or the inner Guide to Soul (all of which I'll say more about shortly). And when we're strongly manifesting our West qualities for other people, they'll tend to see us (the interpersonal view; see map 2) as Magician, Wanderer, Psychopomp, or Guide to Soul.

With all these seductive Westerly archetypes to choose from, it's been challenging for me to settle on just one or two as this book's "official" designation for the West facet of the Self. But this can be no surprise or misfortune: The West — the sunset place — is inherently mysterious, cryptic, or shrouded. It does not wish to be pinned down or defined too precisely. Whatever we think it is, after all, is only partially correct. Its meanings tend to shift, like tectonic plates on molten rock.

Well, then, using the West's own preferred method, let's muse as we peruse the possibilities…

Guide to Soul is a tempting choice because it plainly names one of the West's most celebrated roles; but alas, the descent to the underworld is only one of the West's proclivities, only one of its enticements. The West finds more than enough enchantment and seduction, darkness and decomposition, in the breathtakingly strange middleworld of everyday life.

Anima/Animus would be an accurate portrayal, but readers not familiar with Jungian psychology may find these Latin terms odd and may not even know they refer to the (often hidden) feminine nature of a masculine person (the "inner woman," or Anima) and the (often hidden) masculine nature of a feminine person (the "inner man," or Animus).

Inner Beloved correctly implicates the West as the hidden and largely unconscious other half of our psyches that both allures and terrifies us. And this is also, after all, close enough to what Jungians mean by *Anima* and *Animus*.

Wanderer is a fitting icon for the West because it implies exploration of the unknown. But by itself it doesn't connote enough mystery and darkness, both of which are at the core of the meaning of the West.

You may have noticed, by the way, as I just did, that I've written this chapter, so far, in a rather Westerly way. I'm musing on meanings, pondering appellations, trying to get inside or beneath things, letting myself be allured by the enigmatic and furtive, sometimes wandering in circles or getting lost, dawdling dreamily, seeking the evasive truth and surreptitious treasure, flirting with literary transgression and scientific blasphemy, risking immobility in the muddy meanders of meaning. Come to think of it, my writing in this chapter could turn out to be sufficiently abstruse or cryptic that you may find yourself wondering if I'm a Jungian.

Now, from where did I wander off? Oh, yes: potential names for the West facet.

I'm personally partial to *Magician* because, of the four directions, the West best resonates with real magic and chthonic mysteries. But there's a connotation problem with *Magician* that could lead many modern readers to imagine party entertainers or jesters, and that would be much too East and frivolous for the West.

Psychopomp! Oh yes, that's very good...except for the inconvenient detail that it's a truly weird word and practically no one knows it derives from a Greek phrase and from Grecian myth, or that it refers to one who guides (*pompos* means "conductor") souls (*psyches*) to the place of the dead. And the everyday Ego — I can just hear it now — is going to grouse that this is too morbid.

So, I'm sticking with *the Muse*, for now — the Muse, who imagines deeply, wildly, and from beneath things, and who inspires us to all sorts of revolutions and psychospiritual deaths and rebirths. And with *the Beloved*, that mysterious other-gendered half of our psyches that calls us to foreign, risky, and yet alluring perspectives and so has much in common with the Muse. Merging these two archetypal terms, my "official" reference to the West facet of the Self is the Muse-Beloved. But I'll confide in you: because this hyphenated hybrid handle overlooks the cryptic, shrouded, and death-captivated aspect of the West, and because I'm personally drawn to such realms myself, I actually prefer: the *Dark* Muse-Beloved. You can use this, too, if you'd like.

THE MUSE

We've already seen that the Muse is our own unique and wildly creative way of looking at things — the wellspring of our deep imagination. By *deep*, I mean its symbols and metaphors arise unbidden from the nether lands of our psyches, in contrast to the relatively shallow ideas and fantasies mustered by the everyday Ego.

In Western and Westernized societies, many people have no or little or only sporadic access to their Muse, because of educational, social, religious, and recreational suppression of our fierce and feral creativity. The atrophy of the deep imagination in the Western world (ironically, the loss of the West in the West) has resulted in too many pedestrian, utilitarian, unimaginative projects that are disconnected from nature's ways and that undermine the health and survival of humanity, other species, and Earthly habitats.

The reason we can trust the Muse's proposals to be nature compatible is that they emerge from nature itself — namely, from our deep imagination, one of the ways nature expresses itself through the human.

In the mainstream Western world, we've forgotten the ancient understanding that the strategic mind (the everyday Ego) does not, by itself, possess the ability to determine what's worth doing in life. This ability belongs to a partnership between the Soul and the Muse. The Soul, if and when we're developmentally ready, reveals to us our individual destiny on the metaphorical, mythopoetic level — the truth at the center of the image we were born with, how we uniquely fit in the more-than-human world, the nature of the mysterious and singular gift we were born to contribute. But it is the Muse who inspires the choice of *delivery system* for the Soul's desires. The Muse holds the key to selecting a particular career, craft, or project that is meaningful, fulfilling, and life enhancing. It is the Muse who imagines the underlying form of each original and distinctive thing we create.

In contrast to the Muse and the Soul, the mature Ego has the task of implementation — of manifesting the desires of the Soul and doing so by drawing on the deep imagination of the Muse; the skill, knowledge, and strategic thinking of the Generative Adult; the wisdom of the Innocent/ Sage; and the emotional passion and terrestrial-rootedness of the Wild Indigenous One.

The Muse would much rather explore a mystery than solve it, would much prefer to describe an enigma than explain it. Author Ken Kesey puts it this way: "The answer is never the answer. What's really interesting is the mystery. If you seek the mystery instead of the answer, you'll always be seeking. I've never seen anybody really find the answer — they think they have, so they stop thinking. But the job is to seek mystery, evoke mystery, plant a garden in which strange plants grow and mysteries bloom. The need for mystery is greater than the need for an answer."[1] And novelist John Fowles writes, "Mystery has energy. It pours energy into whoever seeks an answer to it. If you disclose the solution to the mystery you are simply depriving the other seekers...of an important source of energy.... [Humankind] needs the existence of mysteries. Not their solution."[2]

We live in a culture that understands too many things too precisely and in too small a way, rendering our lives and our world too predicable and controllable, too sterile. We would be much healthier if we could regularly imagine the impossible, be open to surprise and unexpected discovery, and change course, turning on a dime, especially when something alluring crosses our path. We tend to dwell too much in "farmer consciousness": focused and intent on getting a predetermined thing to grow in a specific place with a particular expected result. We haven't sufficiently honed our native human "hunter consciousness": diffuse, open, always scanning, and attuned to the arrival of subtle clues, the unexpected, novel associations, and the idiosyncratic, quirky, and outlandish.

The Muse is an inventive and visionary hunter: a lover of diversity, wildness, revolution, evolution, and transformation.

Everything we do is more fulfilling when done with a wild imagination. Indeed, most things worth doing — raising children, teaching, creating art, doing science, making love, cooking, praising the Divine, or romancing the world — cannot genuinely be done at all without the dynamic imagination of the West facet of the Self.

The Nine Daughters of Memory (or Earth)

The Muse appears in many realms and guises. In my own life, the Muse often shows up as an intrapsychic presence overflowing with surprising and innovative ideas, images, and associations. I become aware of her in a variety of circumstances, but most commonly first thing in the morning upon awakening, or soon after, perhaps during a yoga pose or later in the day while wandering in a wild place.

The Muse also appears in our dreams, perhaps as an Anima or Animus figure, and in our waking lives in the form of a woman or a man (or sometimes an animal) who inspires our creative endeavors. Some would say that the Muse not only appears in our dreams but also may in fact be our Dream Maker or Dreamer.

The archetype of the Muse appears prominently in ancient Greek mythology, in which there are, most commonly, nine Muses: wildly imaginative goddesses who inspire the creation of literature and art and are considered the source of all knowledge.[3]

The Greek poet Hesiod, from the seventh century BCE, tells us that the nine Muses were the daughters of Mnemosyne, goddess of memory. This makes sense if we bear in mind that imagination is often the remembrance of things long forgotten or once experienced but never consciously registered. And conversely, memory utilizes the imagination in order to recall the past. (Imagination is also used to discern the future and to experience the present moment more fully.)

It's no coincidence that in English the Muse is implicit in words such as *music*, *musing*, *amuse*, and *museum* (the latter originally meaning a place where the Muses were worshipped, now a place for the public display of art and knowledge).

Do *you* have a Muse dimension to your psyche? It's hard to imagine otherwise! (I didn't consciously intend this double entendre, but apparently my Muse did, or perhaps it was "only" a coincidence — an amusing one.) Have you ever slept and dreamed? From where in your psyche, pray tell, do you imagine these other worlds spring? Have you ever had an inner lightbulb go on, or fathomed a solution to a dilemma before you could even put words to it? Ever compose a song that seemed to have a life of its own? Do helpful or intriguing images appear in your mind's eye? Have you ever been enthralled by a mystery? Ravaged by a romantic obsession? Dismembered by beauty? Smote by magic?

In addition to being sparked and animated by those Muses who exist in our own psyches, or appear as occasional flesh-and-blood humans who enigmatically enliven us, or take the form of electrifying characters from myth and literature, we're also inspired by the astounding imagination of Earth itself and of the cosmos more generally. Anyone who has contemplated the extraordinary diversity of terrestrial life-forms and the fecundity of the land, air, and waters has simply been brought to their knees in wonder and praise. Who other than a god or goddess could have imagined geysers, rainbows, snowstorms, orchids, humpback whales, peregrine falcons, or, for that matter, humans? Or how about butterflies, hummingbirds, mushrooms, or the miracle of slime mold? Or galaxies, nebulae, or — get *this* — the curvature of space-time? As the eighteenth-century English poet-artist William Blake remarked, "To the Eyes of the Man of Imagination, Nature is Imagination itself."[4] In one Greek myth, the nine Muses are the offspring, not of Mnemosyne, but of the Earth goddess, Gaia, who mated with her son and husband, the sky god Uranus.

We humans are among the countless offspring and beneficiaries of Earth's profound imagination. As Geneen Marie Haugen — an inspiring Muse, for me — muses, our grandest potential as humans might be to serve as the forward-seeing imagination of the Earth.[5] Earth imagines us into being and, by doing so, enables us to imagine Earth's future — and to make it manifest. Our destiny is to creatively and responsibly partner with Earth in her evolution. Our capacity to support Earth's unfolding derives in part from our own deep imagination, our Muses — the West facet of our Selves.

What will we end up manifesting for Earth and ourselves? Resorting to the tormented, shallow imagination, will we bring about a postapocalyptic, nuclear-winter nightmare? Perhaps instead we'll learn to collaborate with the deep imaginations of the Muse, of Soul, and of Gaia and engender a new era in which Earth and humanity become mutually enhancing, an era in which we allow Earth to heal herself and in which we create postdemocracy biocracies, a possible future that Thomas Berry has called the emerging Ecozoic era.[6]

THE INNER BELOVED

From the perspective of the West facet of the Self, romance between humans marries attraction and danger, enticement and peril. When we fall in love in a West way, we feel an overwhelming yearning to merge with another, but also a trepidation that in surrendering to the magnetic draw we might be radically reorganized. Our hard-earned identity and social adaptation could be shattered on the rocks of the other's shore. We might never be able to go "home" again. Just for saying yes to love!

Here, Rumi says yes to the change incurred by loving:

I would love to kiss you.
The price of kissing is your life.
Now my loving is running toward my life shouting,
What a bargain! Let's buy it.[7]

Metamorphoses, disintegrations, and obliterations by way of romance: the West facet of the Self wants to take things apart so they can be reassembled in new, startling, and life-enhancing ways.

True romance with another person, whether spiritual or carnal, always entails both an attraction (a falling) and a devastation (a falling apart) — and with good fortune, a rebirth, too. But this is equally true for the *inner* romance.

For it is said that there is an Inner Beloved, and that this archetypal partner is in fact the existential prototype that we project onto outer lovers. Despite ourselves, we fall in love with the people who have something essential in common with our Inner Beloved. We can't help it. Apparently we're made this way.

In contemporary Western cultures, people often refer to their life partner as their "other half" or even their "better half." But this is, at best, a metaphor. In actuality, it's the Inner Beloved who truly is our other half — the other half of our psyche.

And yet the Inner Beloved, like the Muse, is at least as dangerous and attractive as any flesh-and-blood person could be. The Inner Beloved is irresistible because she possesses precisely what our everyday Ego doesn't but most needs for the experience of full aliveness. And yet the Inner Beloved is also a grave threat because he wants us to abandon the story we've been living. The Inner Beloved has glimpsed a deeper, truer, and more fulfilling story. This sounds and feels good to us (the Ego) in theory — and this, in fact, accounts for what we find so attractive about the West. But the price often seems too high. (In egocentric culture, the price almost *always* seems too high.)

The Inner Beloved is both opposite and complementary to the Ego, to the ways we understand and experience our Self. It's common to imagine this relationship in terms of gender: to the extent that our Ego is masculine, our West is feminine, and vice versa. This is independent of whether we're anatomically male or female. If we are feminine at the core of our psyche, our Inner Beloved is said to be masculine, whether we are a man or a woman. And, we'll be strongly and naturally attracted to people who are masculine at their core. And vice versa.

The Anima (inner woman) holds much of a masculine person's intuition, faith, and psychic sensitivity to himself and others. The central theme or resource here is creativity or the deep imagination: the ability to recognize and appreciate that which cannot be proven, deduced, observed with the senses, or figured out with the strategic mind. The Anima, in this sense, is the feminine dimension of a masculine person's imagination.

The Animus (inner man) holds much of a feminine person's mature initiative, capacity for innovative action, and philosophical insight. These qualities are, as with the Anima, expressions of deep imagination, but in this case the masculine dimension of it. These qualities enable a feminine person to imaginatively act on and express what might otherwise only be felt or intuited.

You can see that to be whole, to participate fully in the world, a masculine person needs to access his Anima, and a feminine person her Animus. Otherwise, the masculine ends up insensitive, literal, overly logical, and overly analytical, and the feminine helpless, conventional, and mute or empty-headed.[8]

The Inner Beloved appears to us in a variety of ways. We recognize his or her presence in our own Anima or Animus capacities and impulses or as qualities we catch ourselves actually embodying, often to our own and others' amazement. We can also recognize the Inner Beloved when she or he appears in our dreams and visions — for example, as exceptionally feminine or masculine characters that we feel both attracted to and wary of. And we can detect the Inner Beloved in the way we project his or her attractive qualities onto other people, especially when we fall in love with a stranger, or when we're offended or repulsed by someone on whom we've projected the more frightening qualities of the Inner Beloved. In the latter case, the Inner Beloved might appear as a demon, witch, or assassin.[9]

The existence of the Inner Beloved does not imply that outer romance is second best or a mere substitute! Human romance provides an opportunity that complements but is distinct from the relationship we cultivate with the Inner Beloved: In outer romance, we learn to love — and be loved by — not our other half but someone who is truly other. And in such a relationship, we also discover where we are wounded, where we are not yet whole, and where we have unfinished emotional business to attend to. When we get stuck in our attempts to love another, this often exposes our failure to have fully embraced and integrated our true other half, our Inner Beloved. We need the resources of the Inner Beloved in order to be more whole in our outer romance. This is the way in which romantic relationships provide the opportunity to find our true (inner) other halves.[10]

LOVER OF FRUITFUL DARKNESS

For the Muse-Beloved, the dark is not a bad, dangerous, fearful, or sinister place. Rather, it's the treasured Unknown, the not-yet-known, which is to say it's filled with mystery, possibility, unremembered resources, and not-yet-embraced powers. To the everyday Ego, much of what lurks in the dark is indeed dangerous or even abhorrent, but this is because all Egos — even healthy, mature ones — have some natural and understandable fear of change. To the Muse-Beloved, in contrast, the dark is a storehouse of boundless potential. It's filled to the brim with dreams, visions, images, and stories that have not yet become conscious, have not yet informed and blessed our sunlit world. For the West facet, the fruitful darkness is a place to revel in and wander through. The nightworld is something to cherish; it overflows with treasures the daylight and firelight don't have — and couldn't.

You, too, harbor within you a faithful lover of fruitful darkness. What are the dark and unexplored realms in your life, the enticing ones you've timidly steered clear of? Perhaps these include certain kinds of fascinating but offbeat people (gypsies? shamans?), unusual social or recreational pursuits (trance dancing? skydiving?), unconventional vocational angles (priestess? sexton?), nonordinary states (elicited by Afro-Cuban drumming, Dervish whirling, or entheogenic plants?), unfamiliar arts or music (mime? jazz?), exotic city districts (ghettos? bohemia?), wild terrain (deserts? swamps?).

The Muse-Beloved is a lover of the world — of *everything* about the world and particularly its transformative mysteries. Although the West facet of the Self is seduced by the green sprouts of new life, the perfumed radiant blossoms, and the succulent fruit, this facet is also and especially mesmerized by decay, decomposition, rot, by worms and maggots — the composting of dead things that prepares the ground for new life. The Muse-Beloved is entranced by the supernovae blasting away entire worlds and not just by the dazzling, multicolored spinning galaxies and nebulae; by the sun-drenched meadow, yes, but also by the forest-shredding cyclone; by predator mountain lion no less than prey fawn; by torturous nightmares every bit as much as sweet dreams.

EAST AND WEST AS COMPLEMENTS: THE TRANSPERSONAL AXIS REVISITED

Although the East and West together compose the transpersonal axis of the Self, their partnership is the two-opposed-poles-of-one-thing type. Where the East gets high with the universal, the West gravitates toward the unique. The East wants to ascend to the heights and shine its dazzling light on the big picture, while the West longs to get down in the shadowy sewers of life with a magnifying glass, up close and personal, wandering in the fruitful darkness. East is extroverted, West introverted; East lighthearted, West happily wallowing in gravitas. East and West are each portals for — or mediators of — our spiritual lives, but East specializes in the vast universal transpersonal (Spirit, Tao, God) and the West in the unique unusual transpersonal (Soul, daemon, mythopoetic identity).

Together, Spirit and Soul (the upperworld and underworld of the vertical axis) represent the two complementary halves of our human spirituality. Either alone is incomplete. Without Spirit, Soul becomes too heavy and self-centered. Without Soul, Spirit becomes ungrounded and too otherworldly.

But it bears repeating that the East facet (Innocent/Sage) is much more than a portal to the upperworld (and is itself decidedly not Spirit), just as the West facet (Muse-Beloved) is a whole lot more than a portal to the underworld (and distinct from Soul).[11]

THE MUSE-BELOVED IN CHILDHOOD AND ADOLESCENCE

Young children are notorious for their exuberant Muse-Beloveds. Healthy four- and five-year-olds are constantly enchanted by and musing about the meanings of almost everything they encounter: blossoms, worms, the color of the sky, the changing shape of the Moon, grandpa's beard, Aunt Sophia's scent. And their Muses love to fabricate all manner of stories about why these and other things are the way they are. As healthy children in healthy settings, we are deeply imaginative wonder wizards. This is how we discover the enchantment of our world, its creatures and possibilities. This is how we learn to become fully human. The surprising thing is not that we're born with such a strong and vibrant Muse-Beloved but that egocentric culture can so effectively quash a child's imagination.

In a healthy, *eco*centric family and culture, children deepen their romance with the world as they get older (starting around age seven) and begin to roam farther from home — geographically, socially, and psychologically. They even begin to wonder about Westerly things like death, dreams, basements, extraterrestrials, the conundrums of mathematics, ghosts, buried treasure, and circus life. And, as they approach puberty, they naturally find themselves deeply imagining what their lives might be like when they get older, in this way preparing the soil of their young psyches to later receive the seed of destiny from Soul.

In a healthy early adolescence, the Muse-Beloved becomes increasingly evident in teenage crushes, in musings about the mysteries of sex, in ruminations on being the other gender, and in daydreams of falling under the spell of another and submitting to rapture.[12]

THE WEST'S PRIMARY WINDOW OF KNOWING: DEEP IMAGINATION

Like the other three facets of the Self, the Muse-Beloved employs all four windows of knowing: thinking, feeling, sensing, and imagining. But as you've seen in this chapter, it's the latter window in which the Muse specializes — in particular, the *deep* imagination, experiences we cannot command or control but that arise unbidden in the form of images, symbols, dreams, visions, and revelations that surprise us and yet possess the immediate ring of truth.

In Western, egocentric cultures, the imagination has been contrasted with and pitted against truth and reality: "It was just my imagination." "Leave the dull, everyday world behind, and escape to the Land of Imagination." But in fact the deep imagination is an indispensable faculty for discovering the truth about everyday life, no less essential than observing, thinking, and feeling. The deep imagination not only shows us what might be but also illuminates what already is. It reveals things we may never have detected with our senses or emotions or by deduction. The nineteenth-century German chemist August Kekulé discovered the ring shape of the benzene molecule after having a reverie of a snake seizing its own tail. By way of an image that suddenly appears to her inner eye, a psychotherapist might grasp — accurately — her client's long-standing conundrum.

The deep imagination is also our primary resource for recognizing the emerging future, for "seeing" the visionary possibilities of what we can create right now — individually and collectively — and consequently for creating a better world. It is our essential resource for all genuine human creativity.

Sadly, through unimaginative education, entertainment, and religion, egocentric culture has suppressed and deflected the deep imagination. And yet the Muse or Dreamer waits within everyone to be reclaimed as an indispensable resource for liberating ourselves from the flatlands and wastelands of the mainstream and for designing and building new life-enhancing societies.

WESTERLY PERSONS

People naturally strong in the West facet of the Self tend to gravitate toward social and vocational roles that feature the hidden, esoteric, magical, romantic, or dark; or that delve into the unknown, occult, sinister, cryptic, sacred, or holy; or that revel in symbols, mythology, transformation, or the search for meaning. These people commonly end up as depth psychologists, mythologists, bards, poets, underworld guides, wilderness explorers, astrologers, undertakers, shamans, clergy (priests and priestesses), and magicians.

Examples of well-known people who exhibit exceptionally potent West facets include the psychologists Carl Jung, James Hillman, and Jean Houston; novelists J. R. R. Tolkien, Hermann Hesse, Doris Lessing, Cormac McCarthy, and J. K. Rowling; poets Rainer Maria Rilke, Adrienne Rich, William Stafford, and David Whyte; consciousness explorers G. I. Gurdjieff and Aldous Huxley; philosopher-theologian-mystics Rudolf Steiner, Pierre Teilhard de Chardin, John of the Cross, and Hildegard von Bingen; artists Salvador Dalí, René Magritte, Maxfield Parrish; and filmmakers Federico Fellini and Martin Scorsese.

The Muse-Beloved's Place
on the Map of the Psyche

Why locate the Muse-Beloved in the west?

The west is where the Sun sets, descending toward the horizon and seeming to sink beneath the ocean or prairie or beyond the forest or mountain. The west delivers the conclusion of day, escorting us into the night, corresponding psychologically to our being ushered into the darkness of the psyche, turning inward and wondering about the meaning of things.

As day ends, shadows lengthen, reaching their greatest extension at sunset. The west, then, is often paired with the domain of mystery and shadow — the occult, esoteric, and secret, the ambiguity of the hidden and the danger of specters. The west evokes the hidden dimensions of the psyche, too — the repressed, censored, forbidden, or unconscious. Carl Jung employed the term *Shadow* to identify those aspects of the psyche that the Ego insists are not-self, our rejected and denied traits and experiences. (We'll discuss the Shadow in depth in chapter 9.)

At sunset, we're often struck by a sense of culmination, a feeling of imminent change. Like romance and our relationship with the Inner Beloved, this entrance into the dark change-place is sometimes frightening, sometimes bewitching or enchanting, sometimes glamorous and calming.

Of the four seasons, autumn is the one associated with the west — the ending of summer being like the ending of the day. In the autumn, leaves fall, plants decay, and life energy begins to move down into the ground and into burrows and caves.

Resonating with all of these west associations, the West facet of the Self loves to descend into the depths, to stand beneath things (to under-stand them), to fall into ruin, to fall in love, to ponder the meanings and the symbols, to explore the unknown, to wander in wilderness, to be immersed in magic and learn how to attract it, to discover or uncover what has been hidden or rejected or banished, to say yes to darkness, to sink into dreams, to praise our mortality, to seek the doors to other worlds, to lift the veils, to be allured by crypts and the cryptic.

Given all these dark predispositions, it's not a surprise that the West facet is also our Guide to Soul, our usher to the underworld, where we — our Egos — become undone, decomposed, disassembled, so that we can, with good fortune, be reassembled in another, riskier, more potent, sleeker, and wilder configuration.

PRACTICES FOR CULTIVATING THE WEST FACET OF THE SELF

In egocentric cultures, like that of mainstream contemporary America, the Muse-Beloved and the Wild Indigenous One (West and South) are the two facets of our natural human wholeness most actively suppressed, the two facets most dangerous to patho-adolescent societies.[13] In chapter 3, we considered why this is true for the South. The reason the West facet is a threat to the Western world is straightforward enough: in order to function at all, military-industrial society, as I've been suggesting, needs at least half of its citizens to occupy the dull and offensive roles of consumer, worker bee, paper pusher, soldier, and tyrant — and to experience this desecration as merely normal, to relabel this travesty as simply what human life is like.[14] These conformist roles are mind numbing, soul violating, heartbreaking, people harming, and world wasting. In order to have a majority of people willing to sign up for such a colorless flatland, the innately lavish human imagination must be crushed with an array of blunt tools, including patho-adolescent television programming; teach-to-the-test "educational" methods; fearmongering religious indoctrination; and the widespread hawking of vitality-suppressing and creativity-crushing addictions to TV, computers, smart phones, and other screens, gadgets, shopping, junk food, pornography, insipid entertainment, and the modern human-diminishment pharmacy of alcohol, painkillers, tranquilizers, crack, amphetamines for children, and vastly overprescribed antidepressants for everyone.

Many people rightly decry the omnipresence today of war — military interventions for the purposes of plutocrat profits and the pilfering of limited natural resources at the expense of everybody and everything, especially Earth and the poor, and at the cost of the innocent lives of young soldiers and civilians of all ages. But such wars wouldn't be possible — or even thinkable — if it weren't for the pervasive suppression of the human imagination. A nation with ample and authentic creativity (and compassion) would never choose or tolerate imperial resource wars and would be fully capable of generating and implementing a great variety of inspired strategies for creating a world that works for all people and species. As contemporary American poet Diane di Prima rants, "THE ONLY WAR THAT MATTERS IS THE WAR AGAINST / THE IMAGINATION / ALL OTHER WARS ARE SUBSUMED IN IT."[15]

It is our vibrant imaginations that we so urgently must resurrect, that we must protect and encourage in our children, champion and cheer in our teenagers, and consciously cultivate in ourselves, as if our lives and the lives of all other species with whom we share this planet depend on it. (They do.)

Where to begin? With our children and teenagers, and with our families, schools, religious organizations, and cultural pastimes. And with ourselves.

How might you begin? Accessing and cultivating the Muse-Beloved is easier than you may have (so far) *imagined*. The primary means of doing so is to simply envision that this bundle of resources is waiting within you. It is! Remember, then, to call on it, and then call. When you need to make a pivotal decision, like who you'll spend your life with, or what career you'll choose, or how to creatively respond to the opportunities of our precious twenty-first-century global moment of environmental-economic-cultural collapse, choose first to call on your Muse-Beloved or Guide to Soul. But also with more immediate yet still significant decisions — like how you'll respond to a loved one's feelings, how you'll approach a creative project, or what you'll write in the next sentence — ask the West facet of Self to share its deeply imaginative counsel.

This may take some practice before it comes easily. You may first need to slow down, clear at least an hour or two of uninterrupted time, step into a quiet room or a private outdoor space, and begin with a few deep breaths. It may help to remind yourself that your human psyche naturally incorporates a deep creativity distinct from your ability to willfully figure things out, an ingenuity that is not controlled by your strategic mind. You can't force the Muse (or the Dreamer) to perform on demand, but you can remember that she exists and has come to your aid many times in the past, in your dreams, for example, and when insights have arrived "out of nowhere." Breathe into these memories. Feel your gratitude for the innate capacity your psyche possesses to imagine wildly, profoundly, and wisely. As you do so, an image of your Muse might arise — a human figure, perhaps, or some other creature, or a spring, tree, or stretch of wild coast. Maybe you'll simply feel the

Muse's presence in your body. How does it feel to be alive in an animate and evolving world that includes hummingbirds, rain forests, symphonies, and spiral galaxies? What's it like to feel within you a creativity that is "your own / way of looking at things" (as Stafford puts it)? To feel how "every / glance at the world around you [can] be / a sort of salvation"?

As soon as you make experiential contact with your Muse — even tentatively — ask her for support. Let her know what decision you need to make, what question you're sitting with, or what opportunity you have. (Try not to phrase it as a "problem.") You may imagine yourself walking into a sacred chamber, an inner sanctum (let yourself see, in your mind's eye, the fine points of this space — the color of the walls, the arch of the ceiling, the quality of the light), bringing with you a question that you want to offer to the Muse as a gift. (Perhaps: What in my current life seems like an obstacle but, if I surrender to it, could in fact hold the key to transformation? Or: How might I begin writing about the Muse?) Present your question and then wait for a response. Your versatile Muse might reply in any variety of ways: with an image, insight, feeling, a somatic sensation, your body spontaneously moving or dancing, a thought out of nowhere, a memory of a dream or waking experience, or something you see or hear in the world around you. Be sure to offer gratitude for whatever happens, keeping in mind that she might not respond right away. Allow what you receive to inform and shape the actions you take in response to your question.

Another way to develop the West facet of your Self is to cultivate a relationship with your Inner Beloved — a type of courtship. We're longing for the Beloved, yes, but the Beloved is also longing for us. The Beloved is patient and willing to wait. As we court the Beloved, we must be patient ourselves. Demanding a response is not helpful. What's your best way of courting? Is it through poetry, writing, singing, dancing, or another art form? Whatever means of expression we choose, the creative embodiment of our longing for the Beloved is our most powerful means of inviting the Beloved's presence and the gifts the Beloved brings.

Cultural support in developing the West facet of your Self is easy to find on the edges of contemporary society. There are likely to be a variety of groups or practitioners in your area with whom you can immerse yourself in Westerly disciplines such as dreamwork; deep interactive imagery; the artistic or creative process; the study of myth, ritual, mystery traditions, or depth and archetypal psychology; or the practice of poetry, dance, music, and (of course!) soulcraft.

Voice Dialogue, Four-Directions Circles, Dreamwork, and Deep Imagery with the Muse-Beloved

Imagine yourself turning to the appendix to wander through these four core practices for cultivating the Muse-Beloved.

West Walks

Ideally, undertake these walks in late afternoons or early evenings (the West time of day) and especially in autumn. Wander in wild or semiwild terrain till you find a place or a thing (on the land, in the sky, or in water) that resonates with your Inner Beloved, that mysterious Other with whom you long to merge and that you have for too long, perhaps, projected onto other humans. You'll recognize such a thing or place by your strong attraction to it, as well as by your sense of it as at least a bit dangerous, psychologically or spiritually. You're not looking for a place or thing that feels comfortable or familiar or very much like you, the sort of place you might normally end up on a hike. When you happen on a Westerly thing or place, it will surprise you, and you may feel a sense of fate that you arrived there — or misfortune, or luck, or both. Under ordinary circumstances you might never have chosen it or even noticed it. Your imagination is stirred there. And memories. There's a sense of possibility, of mystery, of perhaps discovering something that could change your life. While there, you might be troubled by the sort of questions that, as poet David Whyte says, "can make / or unmake / a life, / questions / that have patiently / waited for you."[16]

　　If and when you find such a thing or place — on some walks, even long ones, you might have no success — practice courting the Inner Beloved there: Speak aloud directly to the place or thing that drew you, and tell it what you're experiencing, what qualities you feel or sense or imagine there, and how it seems to resonate for you with the Beloved. Then — this could be a stretch for you (actually, it's best if it is) — write a love poem to this place or thing, or to your Animus or Anima in the way you find it embodied there. Recite the poem. Perform a dance for the Beloved. Or simply move in a way that this place seems to invite or that embodies how you're feeling. Spontaneously generate a Calling Song, the song that calls your Beloved to you, and then sing it. Or you might hear the Beloved singing his or her call *to you*. Sing with it. Express your deepest longings to encounter the dark alluring mysteries of this place. Open yourself to the possibility of being changed there — not just passively but by what you find yourself doing there, what is drawn out of you, what you overhear yourself saying or singing.

Go for West walks often.

Anima/Animus Walks

Walk as the feminine woman of yourself (if you're masculine) or as the masculine man of yourself (if you're feminine). Walk not like your culture's concept of a stereotypic man or woman but in the way that the healthy, exemplary man or woman of you would actually walk — or does walk. It can take a little while for you to make imaginative, emotional, and sensory contact with the fully fleshed-out man or woman of you. Take your time. Experiment. Move as this Other. Move toward that which the Other finds alluring. Experience your body and emotions as those of the Other. Imagine as the Other. Sense in the way the Other does. Take in the world as the Other. Greet the creatures and things of the world as would the Other.

Record in your journal what you discover through your emotions, imagination, and senses as well as with your heart-centered thinking. Describe your experience to yourself in terms of the Anima or Animus or the powers of the dark West.

Muse Art

Tune into your Muse and ask her to move your paintbrush, crayon, or colored pencil on a large sheet of paper. Don't try to create anything in particular. Let yourself be surprised by the colors, shapes, and movement she forms.

Or, on a walk, collect small natural and/or human-made things that look or feel Westerly to you (do this without harming anything). Later, throw them together on a bedsheet. What shapes or forms get created? What mysterious tales do they whisper to you? What love story or shadow figure emerges? What meanings do you imagine among these objects and the way they arranged themselves on the sheet?

The West Facet of the Self
and the Descent to Soul

As we've seen in the previous three chapters, if a person is to succeed at entering the underworld of Soul and return with a mythopoetic boon for her people, she's going to need, before embarking on the journey, the well-honed capacities and sensibilities of the North, South, and East facets of her Self. Yes. But this leaves the question, Who in the world would *want* to embark on such a descent in the first place? And why?

Enter the Dark Muse-Beloved, who knows precisely why one would want to descend and is, quite frankly, immoderately enthusiastic about it. This explains why one of the Muse's nicknames for herself is the Guide to Soul. She's a lover of mystery, a devotee of the fecund dark, an aficionado of profound change, a freakish fan of fearsome affairs, and an enthusiast of symbolic significance. The West Self loves nothing more than to wander, hopelessly lost, in the romantic and alluring (to her) dark waters of the underworld. There a person can undergo a transformation considerably more profound than what the West can work in the middleworld, and this is something the Muse-Beloved loves.

There, in the underworld, you can glimpse and be shattered by the revelation of the myth, story, name, poem, or song you were meant to live in this lifetime. This shattering — this "decisive defeat," as Rilke puts it[17] — enables your reconfiguration, your reshaping, into a means of expression for your true identity. And this reshaping allows you to make, as David Whyte puts it, "a promise it will kill you to break,"[18] a vow to manifest the mysterious, metaphoric truth at the hub of your psyche, to carry this truth, as a gift to others, in what you do and how you be.

It's the Muse-Beloved, then — or the Anima or Animus, the Wanderer, the Magician, the Psychopomp, the Guide to Soul, by these or any other names or images — it's this West facet of the Self, that most desires to descend to Soul...when, that is, the Ego is ready for the journey. This can be as early as a person's late teens but, in the contemporary Western world, more likely decades later, if ever.[19]

But your Guide to Soul doesn't merely carry your desire to descend; this facet of Self also possesses the knowledge and the skills to do so. Your Guide to Soul has an innate understanding of what the underworld is and how to maneuver in it, like a seasoned wilderness guide prepared for the constantly unexpected — indeed, one who lives for it — and has the instincts to adapt to almost anything that shows up. Your Guide to Soul comprehends what is being sought — the largest conversation you're capable of having with the world — and how to track such a treasure in the wilderness of Soul. Your West Self will not be appalled or repelled should you stumble into one of your core wounds, or personal demons (disowned Shadow figures), or unacknowledged addictions, or inner critics. These are all welcome and honored guests in *its* world, grist for the mill of Soul encounter. And your Guide to Soul is entirely comfortable with states of nonordinary consciousness (in fact, craves them); knows how to operate when the rules, norms, and frames are incessantly shifting; and knows how to recognize symbols encountered and how to surrender to and be changed by them. Your Guide to Soul loves to deconstruct, to disassemble things, even to help you (your Ego) disintegrate, which, of course, is the necessary precursor to imaginative reassembly.

In short, when you're venturing down, the Dark Muse-Beloved is your most indispensable facet of the Self.[20]

The West facet of the Self is essential, too, on your return from the underworld, because now you're faced with the daunting question of how to manifest the unearthed myth or mystery in the middleworld of your everyday life. This is the 3-D Ego's work, not the Soul's. But this work of manifestation is going to require an impressive affinity for the deep imagination, because discerning the means to manifest mystery is not something the Ego is simply going to figure out. Rather, your delivery system for soul-suffused passions must be discovered, revealed, intuited. And this, of course, is a specialty of the West in its Muse or Dreamer dimension. In order to "carry / what is hidden / as a gift to others"[21] — Whyte, again — you must call on the Muse's mastery for imagining both the aim and the means to it, to dream or envision one or more ways to make it real. The Muse holds "your own / way of looking at things" — Stafford — and this way of looking is something you discover and are blessed by, not something you make up.

THE WEST FACET OF THE SELF
AND THE ASCENT TO SPIRIT

If by Spirit you mean — as I do — the vast consciousness or imagination that infuses and animates everything in the Universe, then the ascent to Spirit refers to the cultivation of a personal relationship with this original intelligence (through, for example, the practice of meditation, prayer, or contemplation). By virtue of the ascent, you may be blessed by a conscious merging with Spirit, experiencing the world from a vast, ultimate perspective. In such extraordinary moments, your Ego expands to encompass all things. Alternatively, it could be said that in such moments your Ego disappears entirely but temporarily, and yet you remain conscious. Whether or not you experience such a numinous moment, the path of ascent refines your capacities for full presence, acceptance, nonattachment (not to be confused with *de*tachment), and service.

Given that the West facet of the Self specializes in the descent, what good is it on the other half of the spiritual journey, the ascent to the upperworld?

First of all, as we've seen, the West facet enjoys nothing so much as change. While rooted in your Muse-Beloved, you won't flip out when shapes begin to shift or when the ground falls out from beneath you. Change like this happens on the ascent as well as the descent (and often enough in everyday middleworld life). As your consciousness begins to expand toward Spirit, your Ego, in its protective mode, might very well become alarmed and try to steady itself, potentially causing a crash. Steadied by your West, however, you're more likely to feel: "Oh, now *this* is interesting. Let's explore it." Relative to your Ego's everyday middleworld domain, the upperworld is a wilderness as much as is the underworld or the untamed expanses of a remote mountain range. The West affords you a certain existential courage that complements and amplifies the openness to experience carried by your East's Innocent and Fool.

Second, as we've seen, the Muse-Beloved is a devoted student of allurement and romance. The desire for a personal relationship with Spirit springs as much from a capacity for spiritual romance as it does from a desire for transcendence. Christian nuns say they're spiritually wed to Jesus, surely intimating allurement and a variety of romance. But you don't have to be Christian or female to feel the romantic draw toward Spirit. Witness the spiritual love poetry of the ecstatic Persian mystic Rumi, for example, or the Hindu's devotional worship (bhakti) of Shiva or of Vishnu (in his incarnation as Rama or Krishna), as practiced by both men and women. The Inner Beloved adds spice, a fervent heat, a devotional swoon, a gravitational pull to the upperworld journey that might otherwise be characterized largely by the relative coolness, humor, and lightness of the Innocent/Sage. The West allows the ascent to catch fire. As noted earlier, the Inner Beloved is an extrahuman polyamorist, allured by the unique essence (or Soul) of each transient thing, yes, but also ignited by the eternal divine presence that animates *all* things.

Third, there's as much mystery in the upperworld as in the underworld. The treasuring of hidden meanings is one of the West's great talents. The Sage is not prone to dissection and analysis, without which Spirit could not be as fully appreciated. When we want to explore and cherish the symbols, myths, and motifs of the Divine, we need the Muse to take the lead. We need the Magician of the Depths to evoke holy wonder. We hope our Wanderer shows up so we can lose ourselves in the labyrinths of the Lord.

Fourth and finally, Spirit encompasses everything, and this includes the darkness as much as the light, the unknown as much as the known, the unconscious as much as the conscious, the depths as much as the heights, the devil as much as the god. Spirit cannot be celebrated in its fullness by that which is primarily light oriented (the East). The West's bent for that which lies below is of equal merit on the path to Spirit. Spirit, after all, is found not only in our daylight hours but also at night and in our dreams, in death and decay as much as in life and growth, and in the cryptic as much as in the crystal clear.

Rilke, for example, found his God in the depths of his own psyche, a God that is dark, subterranean, and wild:

> ...But when I lean over the chasm of myself —
> it seems
> my God is dark
> and like a web: a hundred roots
> silently drinking.
>
> This is the ferment I grow out of....[22]

The idea that we grow out of God is not at all unique to Rilke, but the image of God as being of the dark and rooted in the ground beneath us — this is rare. Only a person with a well-developed West could generate and venerate such an image of the Divine. Some adherents of contemporary mainstream religion might consider Rilke's image of God to be blasphemous;

but, to me, such an opinion would illustrate the consequences of religious perspectives deprived of the West facet of our human wholeness. The Dark Muse-Beloved has been swept out of the house of egocentric society (or into its basement), resulting in a literalized world, in which it's rare to find visionaries, deep creativity, or holistic spirituality.

Although his West facet was well honed, Rilke was as drawn by the upperworld as by the underworld:

> You see, I want a lot,
> Maybe I want it all:
> the darkness of each endless fall,
> the shimmering light of each ascent....[23]

Rilke is an outstanding example of a person blessed with access not only to the upperworld and underworld but also to all four facets of the Self — in other words, to both his vertical and his horizontal wholeness.

Part II

THE
SUBPERSONALITIES

As we saw in chapter 1, the four groups of subpersonalities (North, South, East, and West) consist of immature, wounded, or fragmented parts of our psyche, each of the four groups having a distinct set of strategies for self-protection. Beginning in early childhood, and usually outside our awareness, we invent these strategies with the goal of psychological, social, and physical survival and adaptation. You might say these are four wounded and immature "places" we might "come from," just as the Self incorporates four mature, wholeness-based places we might embody. When experiencing and acting within the framework or feeling of a subpersonality, our Ego is, during that time, identified with that subpersonality — perhaps "hijacked" by it.

The goals of psychological Self-healing include (1) cultivating awareness of our subpersonalities, employing the compassionate perspective of the Self, and (2) honing our ability to continue functioning from the Self when one of our subpersonalities tries to take over. In this way, we gradually cultivate a three-dimensional Ego (one with access to the fourfold Self as well as to Spirit and Soul) that can act and speak *for* our subpersonalities rather than *from* them.

What all the subpersonalities (from all four directions) have in common is that they strive to protect us from circumstances they deem to be threatening to our psychological, social, or physical well-being. They do this whether or not their efforts *really* protect us, whether or not some other form of protection would be more effective, and, for that matter, whether or not we really *need* protection. The odds are that in childhood we really did need these forms of protection, and these strategies worked well enough. But at some point in life, most people, even if they would still appreciate this wholeness-diminishing security in some ways, no longer truly need it, and their lives are unnecessarily restricted and dulled because of it. Generating subpersonality survival strategies early in life appears to be an unavoidable feature of being human; learning to grow beyond these protected zones later in life enables us to become *fully* human.

As we'll see in the next four chapters, each of the groups of subpersonalities can be further differentiated by distinguishing those that identify (1) self-impeding ways in which we relate to and experience ourselves (the intrapersonal perspective) and (2) relationship-stifling ways we interact with others (the interpersonal perspective). See maps 1 and 2 on pages 22 and 23 for a bird's-eye view of all the subpersonalities.

In the next chapter we'll explore the varieties of North subpersonalities, and in the following three chapters we'll consider those of the South, East, and West.

Chapter 6

North

LOYAL SOLDIERS

There's a boy in you about three
Years old who hasn't learned a thing for thirty
Thousand years. Sometimes it's a girl.

This child had to make up its mind
How to save you from death. He said things like:
"Stay home. Avoid elevators. Eat only elk."

You live with this child, but you don't know it.
You're in the office, yes, but live with this boy
At night. He's uninformed, but he does want

To save your life. And he has. Because of this boy
You survived a lot. He's got six big ideas.
Five don't work. Right now he's repeating them to you.

— ROBERT BLY, "ONE SOURCE OF BAD INFORMATION"

The Inner Critic: Wayne, an amateur singer-songwriter who works as a software engineer, has always dreamt of a career as a recording artist, but he's never managed to send a demo to even a single agent or recording company. When he considers it, an inner voice snarls that his lyrics are dull, his melodies uninspired, and his voice grating.

The Inner Flatterer and Caretaker: Rod, a marine, has a good deal of pride in his physical strength, cunning, and courage, both on and off the battlefield. Others notice he has no close friends or any real intimacy with women. When someone comes in too close emotionally, he always seems to remember he's needed elsewhere to save the day. In his mind, there are few people in the world who can do what he does as well as he does it.

The Codependent: Rhonda's husband is an alcoholic, often misses work, has frequent affairs, and gets into fights with his friends. She covers for him, calling his boss to say he's sick again or informing his friends that he really does love them but is so stressed from work. She does her best to be indispensable to him because she secretly fears no one else would want to be with her.

The Robber Baron: George makes lots of money. Lots. He operates several sweatshops in cities where it's easy to find workers because many have only two options: work long hours in miserable conditions for pitiful wages or starve. He doesn't have any real friends, but people treat him with great deference. They're afraid of him or need a job.

The Tyrant: Ruth never felt loved or socially accepted as a child or youth. She learned that the only way to get what she wanted was to have power over others. Now she's a high school principal who terrorizes her faculty as well as the students. She commands a bitter obedience.

Keeping Ourselves Safe

The approach to self-protection (physical, psychological, social, and/or economic) that the North subpersonalities have in common is to get us to act small (either beneath our potential or one-dimensionally) in order to secure a safe place of belonging in the world. They achieve this by avoiding risk, by rendering us nonthreatening, useful, or pleasing to others, or by urging us into positions of immature power over others (dominator power).

Loyal Soldiers is the general term I use for the intrapersonal varieties of North subpersonalities. We'll see why in just a bit. *Rescuers* and *Pseudo-Warriors* are my general names for the interpersonal varieties.

Map 1 shows, in the north quadrant of the inner circle, three of the most common versions of Loyal Soldiers. The first two (Lion Tamers and Inner Critics) help us secure a safe place of belonging by provoking us to feel and act small (unimportant, inferior, unable), as we can see with Wayne, the singer-songwriter. The Inner Flatterers, on the other hand, strive for a safe place by making us feel "big," even though the result is that we behave in small ways, emotionally or socially, as does Rod, the marine.

Map 2 shows, in the corresponding location, six designations for the interpersonal varieties of the North subpersonalities (the Rescuers and Pseudo-Warriors). All six secure a safe place of belonging by shaping us to be useful to others while also having power over them. The first three (Caretakers, Codependents, and Enablers) are the Rescuers, who specialize in appearing useful but turn out to be controlling as well, as in the case of Rhonda, the codependent wife. The final three (Robber Barons, Tyrants, and Critical Parents) are the Pseudo-Warriors, who emphasize the power-over aspect; but by exploiting and controlling people and "resources," as George and Ruth do, they're also useful to egocentric collaborators and to egocentric society more generally.

People who find it easy to embody the North facet of their Self, their Nurturing Generative Adult, are also likely to rely on the survival strategies of their North subpersonalities, their Loyal Soldiers, in part because the South facet of their Self, their Wild Indigenous One, tends to be underdeveloped and relatively unavailable to provide its emotion-and-body-rooted experience of belonging as a counterbalance for the North subpersonalities' ungrounded and abstract fear of abandonment. As we'll see, the resources of the South facet of the Self are key to healing the North subs (and to complementing the strengths of the North Self).

LOYAL SOLDIERS

Most Loyal Soldier subpersonalities form in early childhood in response to physical, psychological, or social woundings. We may have been criticized or punished for simply being our naturally exuberant, untamed selves, or perhaps someone took advantage of our innocence or vulnerability. The mission of Loyal Soldiers is to develop childhood survival strategies that minimize the chance of additional woundings or abandonments.[1]

Loyal Soldiers see their task as protecting us — and they do, especially in childhood. But at a certain point in our personal development, their strategies impede our growth far more than they provide a genuine service.

The symbol of the Loyal Soldier derives from actual events of World War II. During the war in the Pacific, many Japanese marines and soldiers found themselves stranded on deserted or sparsely settled islands after surviving shipwrecks or plane crashes. Some of them managed to endure, alone or in small bands, under primitive conditions and in total cultural isolation. Several were discovered alive many years after the war — some more than thirty years later. The astonishing thing is that each of these men retained an extraordinary loyalty to his military mission. Unaware that the war had ended, each one, upon being found, was keen to return to combat. They were told, of course, that the war was over, and that Japan had lost. But defeat was unthinkable. To them, the war could not be over because their loyalty to that cause was the psychological anchor that had kept them alive. Being a soldier was their only place of belonging in the world.

Upon returning home, however, they were held in no less esteem for upholding the by-then-discredited aspirations for military empire. The Japanese people highly value the capacity to sacrifice personal agendas for a greater cause. So these loyal soldiers — unlike America's Vietnam-era veterans, for example — were welcomed home with great honor and public displays of gratitude and hailed as heroes. After some months of being appreciated and loved in this way, these loyal soldiers gradually reintegrated into society as esteemed and contributing members.

Each one of us has subpersonalities that are Loyal Soldiers: courageous, competent, stubborn, and self-sacrificing versions of ourselves committed to assertive and sometimes drastic measures to survive the realities of our families and communities, which, in egocentric societies, are often dysfunctional. Their most common strategy when we were children was, and now continues to be, a sort of psychosocial downsizing, suppressing our natural exuberance, emotions, and desires so that we become more like what our parents and others want, or so that we become less vulnerable to others' hurtful opinions and behaviors.

Loyal Soldier childhood survival strategies include harsh self-criticism (to make the Ego feel unworthy and less likely to make enthusiastic choices that could provoke criticism, punishment, or abandonment); certain kinds of self-flattery (to motivate the Ego to adopt and maintain an agreeable but one-dimensional role such as heroic rescuer or brilliant confidant); placing one's own agenda last (in order not to displease anyone or arouse anger or envy); and other codependent behaviors (a focus on meeting other people's needs). Strategies also include self-imposed "rules" designed to keep us out of trouble (as in Robert Bly's droll poem that opens this chapter: "Stay home. Avoid elevators. Eat only elk"); partial or complete social withdrawal (to minimize hurtful contacts); efforts to protect ourselves from criticism by adopting an unpleasant or downtrodden appearance; and the suppression of our intelligence, talent, emotions, wildness, or enthusiasm. Whatever the strategy, the Loyal Soldier's adamant and accurate understanding is this: if you're forced to choose, it's better to be suppressed or inauthentic than ostracized or emotionally crushed — or dead.

Inner Critics

As you can see from this list of Loyal Soldier survival strategies, the Inner Critic is one form that Loyal Soldiers can take. You might even have a great variety of Inner Critics, each with a distinctive style and method for addressing different domains of danger. You could, for example, have a Cleanliness Obsessive who won't let you leave a single item out of place or a dish uncleaned for fear of what others might think. Or perhaps, like Wayne, you have your own onboard Music Critic who instantly slams any attempts at songwriting that could result in crushing rejection letters or, possibly worse, great success that could require you to risk disgrace in flubbed public performances. Or maybe it's a Social-Fault-Finder who deems your every interpersonal gambit to be awkward if not retarded and who will rarely let you out of the house for fear of total social self-mortification. Or maybe you have a Body-Image Griper, who...well, you know.

Inner Flatterers

Self-flattery is another common way for Loyal Soldiers to operate and, perhaps surprisingly, can have the same outcome as self-criticism. If your Inner Flatterer can get you to puff up in a social role that actually cuts you off from your greater potential or true magnificence, then you'll be less likely to take social, economic, professional, or artistic risks that could render you vulnerable to failure, humiliation, ridicule, rejection, or jealousy. Loyal Soldiers often use false flattery to keep you safe from the hazards inherent in your own brilliance and promise.

There are stereotypical masculine and feminine versions of such self-flattery, although each version is available to both women and men. Some men, like Rod, the marine, might hear an inner voice that tells them: "When the going gets rough, *you* don't sit and cry like a girly girl; you take action!" or "Feelings are for women, achievement is for men. *Real* men. Like you." This sounds like flattery — and feels like it to some men sometimes — but in truth it's one way Loyal Soldiers in a patho-adolescent world keep a man safe from the risks and challenges of his full humanity (and genuine masculinity).

The stereotypical woman's Inner Flatterer is more likely to say things like: "You are so extraordinarily skilled at taking care of others — look, for example, at all the cooking and housework you do. Your entire family would probably starve to death or catch fatal diseases if it weren't for you." Again, it sounds like flattery, but it's actually the sound of the prison walls being fortified, protecting you from the genuine risks of living your real life.

Lion Tamers

Much of what gets us into trouble with others, especially in the first half of childhood, is our innate wildness — our uninhibited emotionality, our instinctive sensuousness, our utterly innocent exuberance, our uncensored belief in what we want, our natural desire to love and be loved and to take the world into our arms. As children, we are untamed human animals. Our families and teachers tend to see themselves as agents of our domestication, as Lion Tamers. Some part of our psyches recognizes early on that if we continue much longer in our unrestrained natural ways, we may sustain some serious emotional injuries, perhaps physical ones, too. Consequently, we learn to incorporate within ourselves the strategies of our outer Lion Tamers so that we can do this to and for ourselves, rather than continue taking the risks and paying the price exacted when others do this to us. Better to be self-restrained than restrained by others. What we lose in authentic wildness, we gain in psychosocial safety.

Our inner Lion Tamers de-wild us with strategies such as self-criticism, rule imposing, obsessions, fear of rejection, and spurring us to develop personas and routines that are inoffensive, entertaining, or helpful to others, such as clown, perpetual hostess, serious professional, flatterer, flunky, harmless lunatic, or handyman.

"If You Only Stop Singing I'll Make You Safe"

Poet David Whyte offers a startling image of the Loyal Soldier — a dark presence who alleviates our fears in exchange for the suppression of our authentic voice:

> …you made that pact
>   with a dark presence
>   in your life.
>
> He said, "If you only
>   stop singing
>   I'll make you safe."…[2]

The grave problem with having made such a pact in childhood is that, once adopted, it becomes a bedrock layer of our personalities. Achieving liberation from our Loyal Soldier survival strategies is one of the most challenging and long-lasting tasks of the individuation process, requiring a good deal of courage, discernment, and endurance even into genuine adulthood and elderhood.

Our juvenile survival strategies of self-diminishment form the core of our most self-defeating patterns: those that disparage our dreams, our potentials, and our healthy wildness, or that aggravate low self-esteem and troubles with intimacy. And, most irksome, these strategies are often on automatic pilot, launched outside our awareness and without our consent or control. It's as if they were being masterminded by someone else. Sometimes, we feel victimized by our own psyche.

The Loyal Soldiers' ongoing efforts to protect us from our early childhood wounds and fears eventually become more of an obstacle to our growth than the original wounds themselves.

RESCUERS

Turning now to the interpersonal strategies of the North subpersonalities, let's first consider the Rescuers, who secure for us a safe place of belonging by prodding us into small social roles that are useful to or enabling of others. These include our Caretakers, Enablers, and Codependents.

Rescuers manage other people not from the position of organizational boss or supervisor but from the role of helper or servant. From a distance, it looks as if they're contributing to their families and society — and they are in some ways — but on closer inspection it turns out that they take as much as or more than they give.

Rescuing is common in egocentric society. In one version, a person serves others with the hidden agenda of carving out a place of acceptance and belonging for herself, a place where she'll be safe from abandonment. She accomplishes this by making herself indispensable, as Rhonda has with her alcoholic husband. This kind of Rescuer believes she has little inherent worth and fears that nobody would really want to be with her if they didn't need her.

In another variation, the Rescuer does not consciously question his worth but believes he won't get what he needs and deserves unless he sees to it himself, which he does by indulging others until he's made them dependent on him. Then, to get what they need from him, they provide him with what he wants — social or economic security, or a blind eye turned toward his addictions, or perhaps simply deference or flattery. At this point, he's in control. If he encounters resistance, he can blackmail them, either emotionally by evoking guilt, shame, or fear, or materially by withdrawing money or privileges.

With the Caretaker variation of the Rescuer, the individual achieves a safe place by providing for others, but her "care" comes at a high price for both the recipient and the provider. The recipient pays with his guilt for taking so much and with his consequent lack of development and loss of autonomy. The Caretaker (also sometimes known as a Giving Tree) pays by never truly feeling loved or worthy. She feels needed for what she does, not loved for who she is. Every act of caretaking digs her hole of low self-esteem a spadeful deeper. She also pays by enslaving herself to a life of service from which she derives little fulfillment. She's buying superficial acceptance, not true belonging. The Caretaker is in fact more a taker than a (care) giver.

Enablers are Rescuers in relationships with alcoholics or other chemically dependent persons. The Enabler enables the addict by supplying him with substances or covering for him when he's too wasted to meet his obligations — again, like Rhonda.

A Codependent, too, is often partnered with an addict, whether the addiction is chemical or behavioral. More generally, a Codependent forfeits his authenticity in order to obtain social acceptance. In the most dysfunctional codependent relationships, two people are enmeshed in an emotionally abusive alliance. They stay together because it gives each of them a place, even though it's often a miserable one.

By whatever name, the Rescuer substitutes his or her real self and his or her authentic relationships for a place of temporary, precarious belonging.

PSEUDO-WARRIORS

Pseudo-Warriors are those North subpersonalities that attempt to keep us safe by confining us to interpersonal or vocational roles that feel more or less invincible, or to positions of egotistic and exploitive control over other people. These are not the roles of mature, spiritual, or authentic Warriors.

On the surface, people in Pseudo-Warrior roles might appear to be successful. As businesspeople, Pseudo-Warriors often generate fantastic profits. As teachers, they sometimes pioneer new educational methods. Others might have passed consequential legislation, raised money for worthy causes, or accomplished significant medical or technological advances. As parents, they might have raised impressively high-achieving children.

But the Pseudo-Warrior's intentions and labors are not rooted in the Soul's desires or in service to the Earth's unfolding. Her career choice derives not from her depths but from family pressure or inheritance, unimaginative vocational guidance, financial or social ambition, or arbitrary life circumstances. And whatever her career may be, she uses her position primarily to generate and maintain security for herself.

At the end of the day, the Pseudo-Warrior sometimes experiences emptiness or despair. Despite her achievements and good intentions, her labors — especially if she's employed by a large corporation or by government — often cause significant harm to individuals, communities, or environments. But she's not aware of alternatives for herself or the world. She's embedded in an egocentric and anthropocentric system like almost everyone she knows.

Other Pseudo-Warriors, those with limited moral development, experience no guilt for how their efforts plainly damage the world. Foremost for them are personal pleasure and security in the form of wealth and power.

Three versions of the Pseudo-Warrior are the Robber Baron, Tyrant, and Critical Parent.

The Robber Baron is an unethical capitalist, a captain of industry who achieves success at the expense of humanity and of the environment shared by all species. Sometimes he's a sociopath (has no conscience), but other times he's simply unaware of the consequences of his actions or he's stuck in a role he understands all too well but is unwilling to change. The Robber Baron, like George the sweatshop owner, exploits the labor of poor and oppressed people at home and abroad. He assaults the Earth to extract and use or sell the planet's "cheap" (to him) resources. He peddles toxic or exploitative products and services such as high-sugar soft drinks, baby formula, contemporary television programming and advertising, child pornography, consumer goods made with sweatshop labor, junk food, heroin, oil from tar sands or natural gas extracted by fracking, genetically modified organisms, or chemical pesticides and fertilizers.

Despite his company's constant marketing efforts to generate public desire for such products, he'll tell you it's not his fault that people want and buy these things. And what egocentric person would blame him for doing what pays so well in dollars, prestige, or power? In the end, what motivates the Robber Baron is his longing to be accepted, even admired, and to have a comfortable and secure place in society. He doesn't want to be alone or to have to risk his security by embarking on the adventure of authentic self-discovery. He is, in essence, a conformist doing what he's been taught. Perhaps he's simply pursuing his nation's version of the American Dream, which, he imagines, is what everyone wants.

Owing to the way egocentric society functions, it's difficult for any one of us to completely avoid occupying the role of the Robber Baron — or his customer. At least at times. At least unconsciously.

While the Robber Baron is bent on profits, the Tyrant is hooked on power, like Ruth, the ruthless high school commandant. The Tyrant leads in a harsh and oppressive manner. Her primary interest is not service or leadership but domination or personal triumph (or revenge). Beyond reaping whatever material rewards she can, she wants to safeguard her insecure place in the world. She acquires her safety by force; she cannot be thrown out unless she's overthrown. Instead of gaining her place by pleasing the authorities (as do Rescuers), she *becomes* the authority. She winds up isolated in her fortress and soon enough realizes she has lots of power but no friends.

The Tyrant has plenty of opportunities to act out his anger at the early abandonments and betrayals he suffered as a child. He can show the world (and especially his parents) that he will no longer be pushed around, that others can no longer control his place in the world. He will do the deciding now. With sufficient military power at his command, he can enjoy the perverse catharsis of acting out his childhood rage through state-perpetrated terrorism (perhaps deceitfully labeled "liberating the oppressed and exporting democracy"), unprovoked invasion of sovereign nations, genocide, or world war.

Egocentric societies also generate countless *Petty* Tyrants, who possess relatively little destructive force but whose tyranny or bullying can be devastating nonetheless. None of us are immune to acting as Petty Tyrants when something triggers our fear and anger over real or imagined abandonments or humiliations.

A Critical Parent is a Petty Tyrant who generates and sustains a secure social place by dominating and controlling other people, usually his own children, but sometimes students, employees, friends, or a spouse. The Critical Parent also protects himself from experiencing his own feelings of grief, guilt, shame, or hurt — psychologically overwhelming to feel — by keeping his emotions restricted to the much safer anger channel. But by avoiding his more tender feelings, he also bans himself from experiencing love, either as a recipient or as a giver.

The Critical Parent criticizes other people in a way similar to how the Inner Critic self-restrains and the Lion Tamer self-domesticates. The odds are that a person who often adopts the Critical Parent role, in which he controls and restricts others, possesses some very active and dominant Loyal Soldiers with which he controls and restricts himself. And he probably learned both strategies by having suffered his own parents' undermining criticism and oppressive control.

CONSCIOUS AND UNCONSCIOUS FUNCTIONING OF THE NORTH SUBPERSONALITIES

Loyal Soldiers, Rescuers, and Pseudo-Warriors can operate both unconsciously (independently of the Ego) and consciously (when the Ego is identified with or merged with one of these subpersonalities).

When Loyal Soldiers operate unconsciously, we (our Egos) simply feel diminished — or flattered in a way that in fact diminishes us. When an Inner Critic, for example, is operating outside our awareness, we notice only how bad we feel about ourselves, which we probably attribute to the fact that we must objectively be deplorable or inadequate. We passively accept our deficiencies or even our contemptibility, as does Wayne, the singer-songwriter. Or when a Lion Tamer is working behind the scenes, we're likely to feel bored and uninspired and probably not know why. Similarly, when an Inner Flatterer is engaged in his covert mischief, we might simply be puffed up and feel lucky, blessed, or favored by the gods, like Rod, the marine.

Compare this with a Loyal Soldier's strategies when we know that's what we're doing: When we're Ego-identified with an Inner Critic, we consciously choose to dress ourselves down, to read ourselves the riot act, to royally perform a degradation ceremony upon our very own poor selves. We know we're doing it and feel we deserve it. Perhaps we've just caught ourselves in the act of a grave transgression or a humiliating display, and we want to be sure we don't take another risk like that any time soon.

When we unconsciously engage in the roles of Rescuer — when we don't know we're doing it — we probably feel something like heroic, compassionate, or self-sacrificing, even though we're actually undermining the authenticity and well-being of both the other and ourselves. Likewise, the unconscious Pseudo-Warrior mostly feels courageous, virile, effective, righteous, or victorious, despite the fact that she's actually more likely to be cowardly, destructive, immoral, or tragic — while nevertheless succeeding at maintaining her shaky security and power.

On the other hand, when *consciously* adopting a Rescuer role, such as that of Enabler, we're likely to feel ashamed for doing so, or feel trapped, not seeing any viable alternative, not seeing any other way to survive. The Self sees a way out, but the wounded subs do not. As long as we're consciously identified with — merged with — the Rescuer role, we're likely to be stuck there.

Conscious identification with a Pseudo-Warrior role — *choosing*, that is, to be cruel, controlling, or critical — is also a sad and desperate position to be in. Few people would want to think of themselves as a Robber Baron, Tyrant, or Critical Parent. If they did experience themselves this way, most people would want to find an exit, an alternative. Again, the Self knows several possibilities, but people stuck in the wounded North might see only addiction or suicide, in this way turning the cruelty, control, and criticism onto themselves.

The North Subpersonalities as Immature Versions of the Nurturing Generative Adult

There are some commonalities as well as obvious differences between the North subpersonalities and the North facet of the Self.

As we saw in chapter 2, the cardinal direction of north is linked with the generative personal qualities of intelligence, leadership, competence, endurance, and strength, and it is these very qualities that enable us to care for, protect, and nurture self and others. Loyal Soldiers, too, care for, protect, and nurture us, especially in childhood, but they do so in a much less mature and effective manner than the Self.

Loyal Soldiers are pseudo-adults who attempt to protect us from psychological, social, and physical harm, but they do this by making us small, invisible, or limited (they narrow our horizons). In contrast, our Nurturing Generative Adult protects and nurtures us by encouraging adequate preparation and conditioning, offering helpful suggestions and guidelines, self-care when things go adversely, and skills for improving less-than-optimal circumstances for both self and others. Healthy, mature parents help their children in these same ways. Children without mature parents must fend for themselves.

Our Inner Flatterers, like our Adult, encourage us to be active and in service to others, but our Flatterers choose roles and arenas that are socially safe and relatively easy, and that ultimately undermine our greater potential and our full humanity. In contrast, our Adult always encourages us to take whatever risks we're sufficiently ready for. From the perspective of the Self, failures are perfectly okay as long as they're authentic failures. Humiliations, too, are entirely acceptable as long as they result from attempts at authenticity and as long as we learn something from them; and for the Adult, humiliations, although perhaps excruciating, are entirely survivable.

Both our Rescuers and our Nurturing Generative Adult intend to be helpful to others (in a Northerly way), but the Adult is care*giving*, soulcentric, and ecocentric, while our Rescuers are care*taking*, rescuing (as opposed to truly and deeply helpful), egocentric, and self-protective.

HEALING OUR RELATIONSHIPS
WITH OUR NORTH SUBPERSONALITIES

The protection provided by our North subpersonalities ultimately subverts the opportunities to grow into our innate potential, our true destiny. The life that ensues may be safe in many ways, but the lack of meaning and fulfillment — the unrealized experience of truly participating in and contributing to our world — leads to depression, anxiety, and despair. And then we might attempt to alleviate these vexations with behavioral and substance addictions, obsessions, meaningless and destructive risk taking, bullying, or suicide, none of which make us any safer or more secure. And as we get older and our influence and power increase, we're increasingly liable to wreak havoc upon our world while occupying the interpersonal roles of the North subs.

So what can you do when one of your North subpersonalities shows up or even takes over — and you, through your 3-D Ego, notice? If you have sufficient access to the fourfold resources of your Self, you'll most likely be able to do much of this work independently (although everyone can benefit from some help, at least sometimes). If, on the other hand, you're not sufficiently healed — likely the case for virtually all teenagers and the majority of young adults in America, for example — then assistance is necessary from a skilled therapist or a mature parent or mentor, someone who is trustworthy, fiercely loving, and supportive of your deepest potential.

The goal of the healing work described in this book is to learn to embrace and heal your subpersonalities from the compassionate and mature perspective of your Self, as opposed to having someone else or another one of your own subs prop up a wounded sub.

As we heal our relationships with our subpersonalities, essential support comes from the facet of the Self in the opposite direction of the sub in question. So, for example, the Wild Indigenous One holds an indispensable key to healing our Loyal Soldiers. Why? Because what our Loyal Soldiers most fear is that we'll have no place in the world, that we'll be kicked out, shamed, or shunned — left with nowhere to belong. And belonging is precisely the strong suit, the forte, of our Wild Indigenous One, who has absolutely no doubt about our deep belonging in this world, a confidence no social static could ever begin to shake. A vital step, then, in healing our North subs is to call on the South facet of our Self to help us feel — emotionally and somatically — all the ways we truly do belong and our unconditional kinship with all beings, human and otherwise, of the greater Earth community.

Self-Assessment: Is the War Over?

The preliminary step in cultivating a healing relationship with your North subs is to determine if the "war" of childhood survival is really over, as discussed earlier, in the story of the Japanese soldiers. This is the war your Loyal Soldiers have been fighting on your behalf all your life. You need access to your Self in order to make this assessment.

The war of psychological survival ends when you have sufficiently developed your inner and outer resources for mature self-care. Your outer resources are, for example, healthy friends, mentors, and a dependable social network — people who really care about you. Your inner resources include your authenticity; your skills in emotional integration, conflict resolution, self-sustenance, and social-life management (including your ability to choose wisely which people to invite into which social roles in your life, and which roles you will occupy with them); and your skills in generating emotional safety, intimacy, and belonging — all capacities possessed by the Self, especially your Nurturing Generative Adult.

The war is over, in other words, when you have cultivated the emotional and social skills to nurture yourself in the face of harsh criticism or rejection by someone who matters to you, when you know you'll survive the very things your North subpersonalities have been protecting you from.

If you have not sufficiently developed these inner and outer resources or don't have the awareness to apply them to yourself, the war is not over for you, and you really do still need the Loyal Soldiers' old strategies for protection. You also need help — from a psychotherapist, mentor, coach, or elder — in cultivating your Nurturing Generative Adult and in developing your social network.

Learning to love your Loyal Soldiers is key to healing your relationship with all of the North subpersonalities, both the intrapersonal and interpersonal varieties. Rescuers and Pseudo-Warriors, after all, are the interpersonal roles we take with others when our Loyal Soldiers have succeeded in convincing us of our smallness or vulnerability.

Once the war is over, you can begin the same sequence of four steps with your Loyal Soldiers that the Japanese took with their loyal soldiers, which we'll explore in greater detail shortly: they (1) welcomed them home as heroes, (2) thanked them deeply and sincerely for their loyalty, courage, and service, (3) told them, gently and lovingly and repeatedly, that the war was over, and finally, (4) helped them find new societal roles for employing their considerable talents.

It's essential to understand that it's not possible to stop your childhood survival strategies by ignoring your Loyal Soldiers or by rebuking them or by attempting to banish them. Any of these reactions will only make things worse: your Loyal Soldiers, fearing all the more for your safety and security, will regroup, enlist new recruits, and return as vast armies.

1. Welcoming Home Your Loyal Soldier as a Hero

This first of the four steps requires that you identify your Loyal Soldiers' childhood survival strategies — the means by which they've been embodying their heroism, the things they've been doing to keep you small (and "safe") — and what it is they've been protecting you from. You detect their strategies in what you (as 3-D Ego) hear them saying to you — the criticism, flattery, and suggested actions — and in what they've gotten you to do, whether or not you've heard their "voices." Whenever you catch yourself having employed a Loyal Soldier survival strategy, use your capacity for creative visualization to compassionately turn toward that Loyal Soldier and, rather than criticize or reject him, welcome him "home" as the hero of your childhood that he truly is. The most effective times to welcome him home are the moments when he's active, but this requires you to be in your 3-D Ego at the time. Most often we do this work sometime after a Loyal Soldier has been activated, once we're re-centered in the Self.

For example, say you recently caught yourself turning down an attractive but risky social invitation because you didn't believe you could survive the potential humiliation if you came off as a fool. Begin by recognizing — from the perspective of your Nurturing Adult — that your esteemed Loyal Soldier of Social Isolation has been successfully protecting you from criticism and rejection. Instead of berating him or yourself for this defensive strategy, welcome him home as a hero. Let him know you understand he's still using this strategy in an attempt to keep you safe. Give him specific examples — this is an essential part of this first step — of your childhood circumstances in which you really did need such strategies to avoid criticism, rejection, punishment, or abuse. Show him, in other words, that what he did during your childhood was absolutely good and right under the circumstances.

2. *Offering Your Sincere Gratitude*

The second step is to deeply thank your Loyal Soldier for the intention, skill, and love behind his strategy of keeping you safe in your *current* life by, in this example, advocating social isolation in order to evade criticism. Let him know how much you appreciate his courage, his tenacious loyalty, and the intention behind his survival strategy. You don't have to love his strategy, only the intention behind it. Specifically name for him this intention, so that he knows you know. When you find tears of gratitude rolling down your face, you know you've completed this second step. It can take weeks or months before you first succeed in this all-out way, but it's essential to reach this milestone of falling in love with your Loyal Soldier. This can be difficult and counterintuitive, because often your reflex reaction is to wallop him or get rid of him. Don't wallop. Love.

A healthy sense of humor (East) can make all the difference in working with your Loyal Soldier. It often helps to banter with or tease your Loyal Soldier in a genuinely loving way, if, that is, you feel ready and able to do this and you can do it from your Self.

3. *Telling Him the War Is Over*

Third, gaze inside yourself, see your Loyal Soldier, and tell him the war is over. Merely saying the words, however, is not enough. You must inform your Loyal Soldier as specifically as you can what the exact war conditions were during your childhood (for example, perhaps he chose social isolation for you because of a jealous, controlling, and critical older sibling who turned all the kids in the neighborhood against you) and in what sense you're no longer subject to those conditions.

Then, to drive home the point that the war is over, describe for your Loyal Soldier the relevant resources for relationship building and self-care that you now possess but didn't in childhood (for example, assertive self-expression, emotional-access skills, the ability to laugh at yourself, listening skills) and also your social resources (name your existing true friends, guides, and mentors). And here is where the perspective of your Wild Indigenous One is especially helpful, perhaps necessary: with all the embodied emotionality and healthy wildness of the South facet of your Self, remind your Loyal Soldier of your deep and unconditional embedment in your human and other-than-human worlds.

As you enact these first three steps, it helps to remember that your Loyal Soldier has been functioning admirably for a very long time with extremely limited resources and information. He needs to be shown repeatedly that you — with the fourfold resources of your Self — are strong enough to take over his job. He's not going to turn over his post to just anyone. Even if the war is over, the subpersonality he's been protecting — one of your Wounded Children (to be explored in the next chapter) — is likely to be fragile, not tempered or strengthened or skilled. Your Loyal Soldier needs to know that you can protect this tender part of you, honor it, and allow it space to grow and develop. Your psychological integrity in the face of fear (of criticism or of your own strong emotions) needs to be confirmed to both your Loyal Soldier and yourself. The unconscious repetition of dysfunctional family patterns is not easily overcome.

These first three steps constitute the primary work of retiring your childhood survival strategies. Whenever possible, enact this sequence as soon as you recognize the occurrence of any of your old defensive patterns, either in the moment (this is more difficult) or as soon as you've returned to your Self. This takes a good deal of courage, effort, and time.

Remember, these steps will work only if your War of Childhood Survival is truly over and if you're able to access the full self-compassion of your 3-D Ego.

4. Reassigning Your Loyal Soldier

After many months, perhaps years, of this practice, you may be ready for the fourth and final step of Loyal Soldier rehab. This is when you'll reassign your Loyal Soldier to tasks that promote intimacy, service, and fulfillment, in this way preserving and integrating his skills in a growth-promoting way. One person might, for example, ask one of her Loyal Soldiers (all of whom have a legendary capacity for vigilance) to watch for any and all opportunities to genuinely express love to new and old intimates, a tried-and-true (and positive) way to deepen relationships and make one's world safer and more gratifying, an intention any Loyal Soldier can fully get behind. Another person might ask one of his postwar Loyal Soldiers to help him distinguish between people or situations that are truly dangerous emotionally and those that are safe enough and yet risky enough to animate personal development.

It's important to not begin this fourth step too soon. Otherwise, your Loyal Soldier might fawningly pretend to be reassigned while redoubling his behind-the-scenes efforts to keep you safe by making you small. Never underestimate the allegiance and cleverness of your Loyal Soldiers.

It's also important to remember that, whether or not you succeed at reassigning them, your Loyal Soldiers never go away. In fact, as we individuate and take new risks, they're likely to be reactivated, even using the old strategies you thought you had outgrown. But it gets easier to recognize your old veterans and to welcome them home again.

Much of the best of contemporary psychotherapy is a collection of methods for helping people identify their Loyal Soldiers' strategies, retire them, and develop a new set of Self-derived practices for fully feeling, imagining, and sensing, and for generating interpersonal intimacy and belonging. In the process, the war of emotional survival ends (if it hadn't already). Good therapy like this develops the resources of the fourfold Self.[3] If your social environment is not healthy, then effective therapy includes helping to make it so or, if that's not possible or likely, abandoning your former scene and creating a healthier one. In early childhood, you couldn't have done either of these things on your own, which is why you developed your Loyal Soldier strategies in the first place.

I can't overemphasize that, in doing this healing and wholing work of self-care and self-compassion, it's essential to never reject, criticize, or attempt to banish your Loyal Soldiers. When your Loyal Soldiers' original purpose of self-preservation and survival is recognized and honored, you can begin to live increasingly beyond that purpose, shaping a life of greater imagination, courage, heart, and service to your people and the world.

THE ABILITY TO GRIEVE

In welcoming home your Loyal Soldiers, don't be surprised if you encounter a great deal of sadness. As you identify and gradually retire your childhood survival strategies, you'll recognize and feel how much you've lost or postponed — relationships, creative expression, personal fulfillment, inspired service — as a consequence of those strategies employed so many years beyond their need. This grief can be so intense, so fearful in itself, that you might find yourself backing away from your Loyal Soldier rehab work. Indeed, your Inner Critics might appear in droves in an attempt to steer you away from this grief, which is terrifying to them, too. You may even be tempted to keep the war going — or convince yourself that it's still being waged when it's actually over — in order to avoid facing the damage done.

Life is full of inevitable losses, including the lives of our loved ones and, eventually, our own bodily vitality. The ability to grieve, then, is one of our most important psychological skills, and it's best cultivated sooner rather than later. When encountering the grief evoked by your Loyal Soldier work, you might remind yourself that within each loss are the seeds of a new life, just as, after a devastating forest fire, the seeds of a new forest wait in the soil. It helps to remember the archetype of destruction/creation: new life arrives only after the end of the old way, and grief is a necessary part of any deep transformation.

ADDITIONAL PRACTICES FOR HEALING OUR NORTH SUBPERSONALITIES

Voice Dialogue, Four-Directions Circles, Dreamwork, and Deep Imagery with Loyal Soldiers

Turn to the appendix for these four ways of enhancing your relationships with your Loyal Soldiers.

A Loyal Soldier Exercise

- Go to a place, indoors or out, that feels sufficiently private to you. Bring your journal and perhaps some crayons, pastels, or colored pencils and, if you'd like, a handful of modeling clay. You'll need a minimum of an hour — two or three being much better.

- If you're not already in it, evoke the compassionate perspective of your Self (see chapters 2–5) — all four facets. It's important that you not continue this exercise until you're confident you're in the consciousness of your Self, which is to say, your 3-D Ego.
- From the vantage point of Self, identify one of your Loyal Soldiers and one or more of the childhood survival strategies that he (or she) employed recently in your life. Give your Soldier a name based, perhaps, on his survival strategy (for example, Wayne might name his "Demon Music Critic"). Record in your journal the specific strategies he uses and the sort of life circumstances during which he uses them.
- Ask your Loyal Soldier to appear in your imagination. Close your eyes if this helps. Observe carefully what he looks like, what he's wearing, what he's doing or saying, what mood or condition he seems to be in, and how you feel about him (remembering to sustain your Self perspective!). Let yourself be surprised at what you discover. Make some journal notes. (Optional: sculpt him with clay; sketch him in your journal; give voice to him in chant, song, words, or sound; and/or assume his posture or movements.)
- From the consciousness of your Self, wholeheartedly thank your Loyal Soldier *out loud* for his years of devoted service in keeping you safe by keeping you small. In doing this, call on your Nurturing Adult's compassion, your Wild Indigenous One's capacity for full-bodied and animated emotions, your Innocent/Sage's vast perspective and sense of humor, and your Muse-Beloved's deep imagination and treasuring of dark mysteries.
- More specifically now, inform your Loyal Soldier out loud that you see how the survival strategy he recently used was cleverly employed by him to protect you from being laughed at, losing a relationship, feeling stupid, failing, or some other social or psychological risk. Drawing on all the resources of your four-faceted Self, explain this to him with gratitude so he knows you truly appreciate his efforts on your behalf. Make some notes.
- Tell him a story, out loud, from your early personal history that illustrates why, when you were young, this sort of strategy was in fact necessary, or at least effective, to keep you safe(r). Refer to your family, school, church, or community dynamics; injuries, illnesses, vulnerabilities, sensitivities, traumas, abuse, and so on.

- Look him in the eye with gratitude and appreciation and tell him the War of Childhood Survival is now over (if it is). Tell him about the inner and outer resources you possess now but didn't at the time he invented his strategies. (Acquiring these resources is what ends the war.) Give him an example or two of what you would now do — anchored in your fourfold Self — if you were to be criticized, rejected, fired, abandoned, and so on.

- Speak to him, from the experience of your Wild Indigenous One, about your unconditional belonging in the more-than-human world (which includes the human world).

- Using the resources of your Self, thank him again — out loud — and remind him the war is over.

- Let him know that while he's still a valued part of your psyche, you now possess more mature means of protecting and comforting yourself. Tell him he can continue using his old strategies if he insists, but that you'll be protecting yourself in more effective ways, so his old strategies are actually unnecessary now.

- Design and enact a simple ceremony to honor and thank your Loyal Soldier. You might, for example, invite him to stand proudly in front of the full community of your psyche (all the facets and fragments) and then recite for all to hear some examples of the courageous actions he has taken on your behalf, especially in childhood. You might pin a medal on his shirt. You might salute him. Or bow to him. Or embrace him. Let him know that he's welcome to retire his old strategies any time he wishes, and that he'll receive a full and honorable discharge. Thank him again. Welcome him home. Gently whisper in his ear that the war is over.

- Record in your journal what happened, what you felt, what you learned.

An Introduction
to Advanced Subpersonality Work

Cultivating a relationship between the Self and your wounded subpersonalities (of any of the four directions) is not merely an exceptional means for middleworld (everyday) healing and wholing, although it's certainly that. It can also provide a path to Soul discovery and initiation, an underworld way to be with your woundedness that I call *advanced subpersonality work*. It's "advanced" in two respects. First, this work is rarely possible and certainly not recommended until you've reached the stage of development I call the Cocoon (when the Wanderer archetype is most active in your psyche), the stage in which you're fully prepared, psychologically, to ask life's deeper existential questions, including "Who am I really?" and "What is the unique, mythopoetic gift I was born to carry to others?" During this period of life, your foremost yearning is to explore the mysteries of nature and psyche, and you're willing to risk almost anything to make possible an encounter with Soul.[4]

Second, Soul-oriented subpersonality work is advanced in the sense that it's not likely to go well without a solid foundation of healing and wholing. Success with Soul encounter necessitates considerable immunity from being hijacked by your subpersonalities, which in turn requires dependable access to the resources of the Self. To say yes to advanced subpersonality work is to invite the toppling of the applecart of your everyday life. Your belief in the story you've been living, no matter how wholesome or fulfilling, must erode before you're able to glimpse the larger and deeper story of Soul.

Although advanced subpersonality work is by no means the only path — or even the primary one — to Soul encounter,[5] it seems to be an inevitable, hazardous adventure along the way.

The central principle of advanced subpersonality work is that our psychological wounds provide portals into the very depths of our psyches. Our wounds are not merely — or even primarily — things to heal and overcome. They're also, *when we're developmentally prepared*, something to reopen, explore, learn from, and be transformed by. When we're ready for the descent to Soul (beginning in the Cocoon), we're not so much interested in working on our wounds; we'd rather have our wounds work *on us*. We ask not to be healed but rather to be torn open so that we may remember who we were at the start and who we can yet become. From the wholeness of Self, we invite ego-death or psychospiritual dismemberment, without any knowledge of or guarantee of outcomes.

For advanced subpersonality work, it's strongly recommended that you have the guidance of someone who knows the terrain well. For this reason,

I offer in these pages only the bare outlines of what this work looks like. *Caveat emptor.*

ADVANCED NORTH SUBPERSONALITY WORK: LOYAL SOLDIER WORK AS A PATH TO SOUL

Your Loyal Soldiers, in all their diverse intrapersonal and interpersonal guises, have been doing their best, for longer than you can remember, longer than you've been conscious, to protect you from harm, mostly psychological injury and social loss. They do all they can to stand between you (your Ego) and what they fear to be grave danger. Imagine looking at them and seeing, immediately behind them, an immense fire, a conflagration they fear will consume you. They want to keep you from stumbling into that fire, and for the most part they've succeeded.

The advanced work with your Loyal Soldiers consists of simply this: marching right past your faithful guardians and directly into the fire. And doing this repeatedly and as unconditionally as you can.

This fire is the collection of social, psychological, and spiritual opportunities your Loyal Soldiers fear will expose you to the possibility, if not likelihood, of criticism, ridicule, humiliation, ostracism, job loss, relationship loss, financial ruin, spiritual crisis, and so on.

Why in God's name would you want to walk into that fire? Well, to further emphasize the point I've been belaboring, you *wouldn't* want to until you've reached a certain point in the Cocoon stage (or later). Why would you *then?* Because you know that on the other side of that fire a terrible and ecstasy-igniting secret awaits you. Ecopsychologist and poet Anita Barrows knows this secret well:

> You will come at a turning of the trail
> to a wall of flame...
>
> ...all that stands between you
> and everything you have known since the beginning
>
> is this: this wall. Between yourself
> and the beloved; between yourself and your joy,
> the riverbank swaying with wildflowers, the shaft
>
> of sunlight on the rock, the song.
> Will you pass through it now, will you let it consume

whatever solidness this is
you call your life, and send
you out, a tremor of heat,

a radiance, a changed
flickering thing?[6]

Assuming you're ready to walk into this flame, how do you identify what it represents in your life? How will you find your fire? Simple, really. This is where all your previous Loyal Soldier work, explored earlier in this chapter, comes in handy and is indeed necessary. In cultivating your relationships with your Loyal Soldiers — learning to thank them, love them, and welcome them home from the War of Childhood Survival — you've learned what sorts of circumstances they consider dangerous for you. You've been identifying the patterns, the sorts of life situations during which your Loyal Soldiers show up, the moments when your Inner Critics, Flatterers, and Lion Tamers suggest an immediate downsizing. What have you learned? What are the particulars they deem precarious and that lead them to come to your "rescue"? Is it when you're about to take a certain kind of social risk, like singing onstage for the first time, leading a controversial community project, or broadcasting your contentious political passions? Or maybe you're about to tell your lover or friend a difficult truth, or publicly announce your expertise and availability in a new (for you) arena that will test everything you're made of, or acknowledge a not universally accepted sexual orientation. What about "inner" psychological risks, like fully feeling a grief you've managed until now to keep a lid on (or maybe it's a longing), or allowing yourself to fully feel loved by another? Or an artistic or professional risk, like Wayne the singer-songwriter finally sending off that demo? Or maybe it's a spiritual risk, like cultivating your own relationship with God regardless of what the church or the priest might say, or questioning, for that matter, whether there's one god or many gods — or any gods at all.

Whatever it is that your Loyal Soldiers have been trying their best to protect you from, this is what you will now choose to dive into, with full consciousness.

When you do, will you in fact be humiliated, ridiculed, fired, or abandoned? Will you end up triggering a spiritual crisis, a dark night of the soul, or a divorce? Maybe, maybe not. But you won't step into that wall of flame until you're confident you have the inner and outer resources to survive precisely these sorts of experiences — and, in the worst-case scenario, just barely surviving could be what happens. You want to be prepared for such outcomes, but they are not, of course, why you're doing this.

What you can be fairly certain of is that the fire will change you, although not in a way you can accurately predict. Venturing into these unknown precincts, you'll have experiences that might be ecstatic or harrowing and painful, or both, but either way they're likely to alter you at your core, to reshape what you know as the world, and to provide you with psychological and spiritual opportunities you wouldn't have had otherwise. Emerging on the other side of that wall of flame, you might find yourself standing before a mysterious and ominous door and choose to walk through, leading to a series of additional thresholds that could in time afford an encounter with the mysteries of your destiny.

You had thought your Loyal Soldiers were trying to protect you from ruin. They were. And did. But they — like all your other subpersonalities from all four directions — were also protecting you from experiencing certain mysteries before the time you were psychospiritually prepared to understand them and to act responsibly in relation to them. In a sense they were protecting the world *from you*. Because on the other side of that wall of flame, you might have access to certain powers (abilities or knowledge) that can be used for good or ill. These are Soul powers, like the ability to generate perception-expanding images, to make friends with enemies, to weave cocoons of transformation, or to sing the beauty, grace, and grief of our world; or like the knowledge of how to shape-shift, of how to see into the depth of hearts, or how to perform antistructural magic. Your Loyal Soldiers kept you from going there until you had sufficient maturity to use these considerable powers in service to the whole, the interdependent community of life.

So you can see that the advanced form of Loyal Soldier work goes well beyond the garden variety in which we "merely" welcome home our faithful protectors. The latter is foundational to healing and growing whole. The former can open doors to spiritual transformation and power.

Chapter 7

South

WOUNDED CHILDREN

> Sometimes, when the light strikes at odd angles
> and pulls you back into childhood
>
> and you are passing a crumbling mansion
> completely hidden behind old willows
>
> or an empty convent guarded by hemlocks
> and giant firs standing hip to hip,
>
> you know again that behind that wall,
> under the uncut hair of the willows
>
> something secret is going on,
> so marvelous and dangerous
>
> that if you crawled through and saw,
> you would die, or be happy forever.
>
> — LISEL MUELLER, "SOMETIMES, WHEN THE LIGHT"

The Conformist: Conrad, a midlevel executive at a midwestern insurance company, is married with three kids and a suburban country-club membership. He votes middle-of-the-road, is a big football fan, and attends church most Sundays. As a child, he had a great fear of criticism and, more than anything, just wanted to fit in. He does.

The Victim: Vickie, a sullen thirty-something, is currently a clerk at a department store but doesn't expect to hold on to her job for long. She broods about how things always go wrong for her: layoffs, difficulties maintaining a relationship, frequent health problems, car breakdowns. Her parents often come to her rescue, or a friend, or the pastor at the church, or the social worker at the health center.

The Rebel: Reggie is a street musician in the city. He joins street protests at every opportunity — almost doesn't matter what they're about. He's simply "against it" and knows that no one in the establishment can ever be trusted, like his dad, for example, who abandoned him when he was six.

The Princess: Priscilla is a rock-and-roll superstar who's often in a bad mood. She regularly fires people in her entourage who do not serve her every whim. She never felt loved by her parents, despite all the music teachers they hired for her and all the exotic vacations they bought for her and her friends.

Getting Our Basic Needs Met

All living things have needs. We're no exception. Our most basic human needs are what psychologist Abraham Maslow referred to as physiological necessities (including food, shelter, and sleep), safety needs (including physical security, moral order, and economic and family stability), and basic social acceptance from at least one other person. The approach to self-protection shared by all our South subpersonalities is the attempt to get our basic needs met through emotion-fueled strategies — and the only such strategies available to them are immature ones.

Immature survival strategies are, of course, most common in childhood, but they linger far into later developmental stages and probably never completely disappear for anyone. Part of the process of psychological healing and wholing (one-quarter of it) is learning to meet our basic needs in more mature fashions. Our immature South strategies are often on "automatic pilot" and might be deployed any time the 3-D Ego doesn't show up with the Self's more effective resources.

And yet, childhood is not simply a survival struggle. Even in our early wounds there is something mysterious — "something secret...going on," as poet Lisel Mueller puts it. The wounded elements of our psyches do their best to protect us not only from avoidable harm but also from what the poet calls the "marvelous and dangerous," the knowledge of which we may not be emotionally ready to bear until we reach a certain milestone of psycho-spiritual development. Upon reaching the life stage of the Cocoon (when our feelings open to the enigmas of our own depths), we find ourselves, astonishingly, intrigued by our old wounds and able to penetrate "behind that wall," where we might chance upon invaluable clues to our mythopoetic identity. We'll explore such mysteries and such opportunities at the conclusion of this chapter.

VARIETIES OF SOUTH SUBPERSONALITIES

Map 1, on the south side of its inner circle, indicates *Wounded Children* as the name for the intrapersonal versions of our South subpersonalities, the unripe parts of our psyches that are prone to feeling hurt, angry, afraid, sad, guilty, jealous, or ashamed and that often act out these feelings in impulsive ways. (To "act out" is to express our emotions indirectly or symbolically through our actions.) We learned these patterns of behavior in childhood and continue them as long as they're sufficiently successful in meeting our basic needs. Sometime after our early teen years, for most people, they don't work nearly so well. Indeed, they often backfire.

Our Wounded Children are the parts of ourselves that are, well, wounded. They've been injured, traumatized, or rejected — by others, by ourselves, or by our life circumstances. Some of our Wounded Children — the Outcasts — are not only inventors and bearers of survival strategies but also the *casualties* of the survival strategies of our other subpersonalities.

Map 2, at the inner south, shows four interpersonal versions of our South subpersonalities, ways we act with others when stuck in a South rut: Conformists, Victims, Rebels, and Princes/Princesses. When we enact these social roles, we're attempting to get our basic needs met in immature emotional ways. These four roles are all versions of the archetype of the Orphan.

People born with an ease in cultivating the capacities of the South facet of the Self, the Wild Indigenous One, might also be predisposed to use the survival strategies of their South subpersonalities, their Wounded Children. This is because the North facet of their Self, the Nurturing Generative Adult sitting across the circle, tends to be underdeveloped and mostly unavailable to provide its mature caregiving skills to counterbalance the South subs' immature tactics for meeting basic needs. The North Self holds the key to the healing of the South subs (and to complementing the strengths of the South Self).

WOUNDED CHILDREN AND OUTCASTS

It's natural, human, and unavoidable to react emotionally to the events of our lives. If we know how to listen to them, our emotions inform us (and others) about the state of our current relationships with others and with ourselves — and with our world, more generally. Among other things, our emotions inform us about our physical, psychological, and social wants and needs — including our basic needs.

We're emotional no matter how mature or individuated we become. Emotionality is no more a sign of immaturity than steel-hearted imperturbability is a sign of maturity. The incapacity to emote is a severe disability, rendering a person effectively inhuman. Our emotions are a fundamental dimension of our aliveness and communion with the world.

In chapter 3 — on the South facet of the Self (the Wild Indigenous One) — we explored the nature of healthy emotionality, what we can learn from each kind of emotion, and the four steps of emotional assimilation. We saw that when children are tenderly taught how to embrace their emotions as an invaluable resource, they develop a high capacity for bringing their outer world of relationships into alignment with their inner world of experience, and vice versa.

But even when our emotional education goes well, it never goes anywhere close to "perfect." And to the extent that our childhood families and communities were less than healthy and mature, the development of our "emotional IQ" might be correspondingly limited, in which case we'll have some catch-up work to do later in life. Each one of us in childhood, even if from a healthy family, had to fend for ourselves emotionally to some degree — some of us only minimally, but others, extensively or entirely.

The immature ways we emotionally fend for ourselves constitute the strategies employed by our Wounded Children subpersonalities. When we feel hurt, for example, we might act out the role of the victim with the hope of being rescued or being given what we want. Sometimes this works. Other people, when hurt (and hijacked by one of their Wounded Children), will act primarily on their anger, threatening others or exacting revenge. If this strategy works — if it gets their basic needs met — they're more likely to use it again. Yet others, when hurt, will learn how to act more pleasingly and submissively, and this might get them what they want. In general, our Wounded Children want others to meet our basic needs. They don't believe we can do this directly for ourselves (which was true in early childhood).

But not all of our Wounded Children are trying to help us survive. Some, as I say, are simply casualties of our other subpersonality survival strategies or of the unkind actions of others. These are our Outcasts, elements of our psyches we rejected in order to survive, in order to be accepted by others. These are the versions of ourselves of which we are ashamed — perhaps our gentleness or fierceness, our sexuality, our anger or sadness, our fear or embarrassment, our love of dance or poetry, our joy or vivaciousness, or our need for touch or compassion. Once we reject these Wounded Children and label them bad or worthless, they exist in a marginal, banished state within our psyches. Nonetheless, we live every day with some awareness of their pain and heartache.[1]

For children, conscious self-rejection is less harmful than being rejected by others, even if it's no less painful. By restraining ourselves from acting in ways that lead to being shamed, we're less likely to be abandoned. The price we pay is *self*-shaming, resulting in Outcasts within us we're not willing to love, who we've neglected and exiled. Although our Outcasts persist as pockets of pain within us, they embody great gifts — strengths and sensibilities not deemed worthy by others in our early lives, but gifts we can reclaim when we're psychologically ready to do so.

The reclamation process usually begins with grief. We must mourn our psychological woundings by others, our consequent self-woundings, and the loss of joy, aliveness, and relationships that resulted from all our self-diminishments. Then, with the self-development that comes from cultivating the resources of the Self, we must learn to embody again these banished versions of ourselves. We must welcome home our Wounded Children Outcasts, embracing them as essential dimensions of our wholeness. The perceived defect is redeemed as the virtue it originally was. We'll explore in greater detail this aspect of Self-healing.

Subpersonality Conspiracies

Our subpersonalities often collude with one another in their attempts to protect us. Sometimes, for example, our Loyal Soldiers (North) accurately recognize the vulnerability of our Wounded Children (South) and attempt to shelter us from being further wounded or rejected. Our Loyal Soldiers might blame or shame us (when we're identified with a Wounded Child) to get us to act submissively or to go invisible — so that we're less likely to be attacked or abandoned by others. With ample experience of wrongdoing (guilt) or wrong-*being* (shame), we're less likely to get into social trouble.

But this emotional burden of shame or guilt can be so debilitating to our Wounded Children that our Addicts (East) provide anesthesia, or our Escapists (East) an emotional furlough. Or our Shadow (West) shoves these disturbing feelings underground like nuclear waste, taking the "out of sight, out of mind" approach, even though it's always the case that the guilt and shame (and nuclear poisons) continue wreaking their havoc. Our Shadow could also protect our Wounded Children by repressing the memory of experiences that would be emotionally incapacitating if recalled.

If we had parents or siblings who harshly criticized us, our *Inner* Critics (North) might now rush in to preemptively censure us when we even think about taking a social risk or acting exuberantly. Or our Pseudo-Warriors (also North) might fight fire with fire, turning *us* into a Tyrant, Bully, or Critical Parent, in this way scaring off any further hurt or criticism.[2]

When our Wounded Children are angry about having been hurt, ignored, or spurned, and if acting out this anger doesn't result in our needs being met — and it often doesn't — then our other subpersonalities might recognize this immature fury for the potential catastrophe it is and attempt to douse the fire with, for example, Loyal Soldier self-criticism (North) or Addict-inspired self-numbing (East).

Often our subpersonalities work together to "protect" us from grief. When identified with any subpersonality, we don't have the maturity or wholeness to understand that grieving is natural and healthy and often the threshold of healing. Nor, at such times, do we have access to the abilities and knowledge we need to grieve effectively. Deep grieving, like all fully felt emotions, is a capacity and gift of the fourfold Self, and it is further enabled by the wholehearted support provided by the communal grieving practices found in healthy communities.[3]

DEPRESSION

Our subpersonalities of the North, East, and West may be able to "manage" the somatically and psychologically undigested emotions of our Wounded Children of the South — to suppress, deflect, or defuse these emotions. The catch, however, is this: Managed emotions are not digested emotions, and emotional digestion is what we need in order to continue developing psychologically. Managing an emotion can temporarily shield us from the pain of experiencing it or from the wrath and rejection of others reacting to how we might otherwise act it out, but this "protection" disqualifies us from benefiting somatically from the emotion or from learning — through the four-step emotional digestion cycle — about ourselves, our relationships, and our world. In contrast, the 3-D Ego, by way of the resources of the Self, possesses all the capacities we need to maintain good relationships with our own emotions and with other people (and other species and the animate Earth more generally).

The essential point is this: *managed emotions result in depression.*

For me, the most precise definition of depression is a bad case of suppressed emotions, emotions that have been managed instead of being felt, digested, understood, assimilated, and acted on in a way that preserves and improves our relationships. When a person is depressed in this way, she has a significant backload of undigested feelings piled up behind an inner dam, blocking the natural flow of her psyche and her life. If this blockage becomes severe or prolonged, her physical and psychological vitality will grind to a halt. She'll become sluggish, "vegetative," and quite possibly suicidal.

What the depressed person needs is to feel more, not less. This highlights the disastrous consequences of thinking of depression as a bad case of sadness, with the implication that the cure is to feel less sad. Such a prescription is exactly wrong. If a person is depressed because of a backload of unassimilated sadness (it could be a backload of any number of emotions), then what she needs is to fully feel her sadness, to grieve wildly. Any "psychotherapeutic intervention" that would try to talk her out of her grief, distract her from it, or suppress it with psychopharmacology would just make her depression worse, and certainly would not be therapeutic. Rather, it would result in the same sort of emotional suppression or repression that her subpersonalities have been employing all along. This kind of "therapy" perpetrates an iatrogenic (doctor-caused) depression on top of her intrapsy-chic one.[4]

Affective depression is, at root, the suppression of the South facet of the Self, the blockage of the wild, indigenous, emotive, erotic, and fully embod-ied dimension of our human wholeness.[5] The best therapy for depression begins with the resuscitation, animation, and liberation of the Wild Indig-enous One. Wholing supports the deepest and most effective healing.

ORPHANS:
CONFORMISTS, VICTIMS, REBELS,
AND PRINCES AND PRINCESSES

Most of us were not literally orphaned, but all of us experienced, early in life, psychological abandonments — cataclysmic moments of realizing we must fend for ourselves emotionally, socially, or physically. Even if we were adored and well sheltered within a loving family, we experienced ourselves, at times, as alone in the world. What five-year-old hasn't realized there isn't anyone who can perfectly protect him from pain, embarrassment, loss, ill-ness, accidents, or the occasional cruelty of other children?

The Orphan archetype begins to take hold the first time we feel let down by caregivers who have been less than perfect in their caregiving. In that moment, we feel forsaken. This is one of our first conscious experi-ences in life: being split off, tossed out of paradise, suddenly separated and needing to make independent decisions for our own welfare. Aghast, we re-alize we understand our needs better than our caregivers do, that on some level we're fundamentally on our own. Orphaned.

The archetype of the Orphan is a living presence within each of us, tak-ing the form of our South subpersonalities using their immature strategies to create the kinds of relationships that might meet our basic human needs.

The four main forms of the Orphan archetype — Conformists, Vic-tims, Rebels, and Princes/Princesses — correspond to four interpersonal styles. The difference between them concerns their primary emotional reac-tion (fear or anger) to having been wounded in childhood and their status (insider or outsider) relative to mainstream society or a desired community. Conformists are fearful insiders. Victims are fearful outsiders. Rebels are angry outsiders. Princes and Princesses are angry insiders.

Conformists

The Conformist's biggest fear is that he'll be abandoned again. He does whatever is necessary — submission and subservience — to meet the membership requirements of whichever group grants him the most desirable social status. Most Conformists adopt the values and roles of mainstream society, like Conrad the insurance executive. But others conform to the behavioral code of a gang, an ashram, or a personal-growth program. The more pleasing and impressive the Conformist's self-presentation, the better the place and rewards he'll be granted.

The Conformist is the most popular Orphan option in egocentric middle-class society, because, if the Self-animated path to authenticity and wholeness is unavailable, the most attractive alternative way of life is one with egocentric rewards — security, comfort, money, consumer products, professional prestige, and power over others.

Everywhere we turn in mainstream Western society, we run into the same materialistic message: Life is about maximizing monetary wealth, possessions, physical attractiveness, and dominator power. A person's goodness or popularity is a matter of how much he owns, how good he looks, and how much he controls. This is the most common message in contemporary politics, business, education, and much of egocentric religion, as well as in Hollywood movies, mainstream books and magazines, TV programming, and other forms of culture-degrading advertisement. And this is the subtext in a large percentage of conversations people have every day in egocentric society.

Victims

Like the Conformist, the Victim subpersonality is motivated primarily by fear of future abandonments but has little hope of obtaining socioeconomic rewards. Victims present themselves as being injured, incapable, or unlucky and, consequently, needing to be rescued. Victimhood is a common outcome for oppressed and poverty-class people in an egocentric society, but it occurs in middle- and upper-class families, too.[6] Victims, like Vickie the clerk, believe themselves to be ineligible for social or economic success either because of their class membership (in which case, it is often the egregious reality) or because of their self-image as loser, misfit, or oddball (possibilities for people of any socioeconomic class).

The interpersonal role of Victim, however, is not as bad as it perhaps sounds. There are, after all, many Rescuers in egocentric society.[7] A Rescuer is someone who combines a North, Loyal Soldier, subpersonality (who feels unworthy of truly belonging) with a South, Conformist, subpersonality, someone who secures an accepted place in a community by rescuing its Victims. When you're in the Victim position, there are many kinds of rewards you can receive from a Rescuer. (Those oppressed by racism, sexism, and classism often have little choice in the matter.) Victim rewards include excessive sympathy from Rescuers; release from responsibilities; disability and workers' compensation without having to be truly injured (as long as a good semblance can be managed); underdog-type manipulative power over others; and, for Victims who successfully sue the right person or organization, money.

Rebels

The Rebel is primarily angry about the childhood abandonments he's suffered and doesn't believe he's eligible to acquire the rewards of mainstream society in any of the "legitimate" ways. (As an outsider, he's usually correct.) His anger inclines him toward coercion, aggression, and theft. Like Reggie the street musician, he rebels against almost everything his parents, schoolteachers, religion, and culture stand for. He might even rebel against some of his peers, for they, too, might have abandoned him. Rebellion is a common Orphan choice for angry people in the oppressed and poverty classes of egocentric society. It's also widespread among the angry middle class.

At his depths, the Rebel feels something like this: I don't have a clue who I really am, but I'm not going to act or be anything like *them* — those corrupt sellouts with privilege, conventional power, or money. I'm going to be whatever they're not. And in spades.

Again, occupying such a place is not all bad. The Rebel has a good deal of energy, self-respect, and freedom — certainly more than what he sees as the helpless Victim or the chump Conformist. He's not a slave to a paycheck or "the man." He has his fellowship with other Rebels. He knows how to party and have a good time. He's eligible for rewards, such as special status within his clique or gang; opportunities to act out his anger in cathartic and violent ways against imagined or real oppressors and convenient scapegoats; a shadow form of notoriety and respect; a heady better-than-thou feeling; and all the loot he can steal or swindle, usually without guilt, especially if his victims are Conformists or Princes or Princesses in the wealthy mainstream.

Like Rebels, Conformists also don't know who they are, but they know how to act on the basis of what's acceptable — a solution opposite to that of the Rebels. Most Conformists acquire an insider pseudo-identity by mimicking the styles and behaviors of the mainstream. Rebels achieve an outsider pseudo-identity by adopting styles and behaviors that mock, negate, counter, or deconstruct the mainstream and, ironically, by conforming to the styles and behaviors of their fellow Rebels.

Princes and Princesses

In common with the Rebel, the Prince or Princess is angry about childhood abandonments but, unlike the Rebel, is fully eligible to obtain and enjoy the material and social rewards of his or her community. The Prince or Princess in fact feels entitled to those rewards and uses condescension, intimidation, and control to get them, like Priscilla the rock star. Princehood or Princesshood is a common Orphan subpersonality in the upper-middle and upper classes, but an attitude of entitlement is entirely possible in the lower classes, especially among those who, as children, were treated by their families as little Princes or Princesses.

In essence, the Prince or Princess feels: I don't have a clue who I really am, but I'm angry and deserve benefits. I'm pissed off about my parents' attempts to get me to perform in humiliating ways [to be the cute or sexy Princess, for example, or the clever, on-the-make Prince]. This is not really how I wanted to be, but the impressive bribery made it worthwhile, and so I played along. Now I'm entitled to all I've been promised and then some. So whatever I'm going to be or do in life, I'll have plenty of privilege and power, money and possessions.

Being a Prince or Princess is clearly not so bad. Yes, they had to betray themselves to reap all those spoils, but as far as they can see, there wasn't a better option. In egocentric society, most people, if they had the option, would exuberantly embrace the bounties of fake royalty (sweepstakes winner, millionaire captain of industry, heiress, movie star). Whether or not they feel angry or entitled, they're likely to feel lucky.

———

For any given person, all four Orphan roles are available. It's entirely possible to be a Rebel in one social scene (politically, for example — perhaps as a Tea Party candidate), a Conformist in another (with a high-paid corporate job, for instance), a Prince in a third setting (perhaps among one's friends, family, and political supporters), and a Victim in a fourth (maybe as a plaintiff in a million-dollar lawsuit against a resort that failed to provide a high-quality vacation experience).

People who've gotten mired in life as Orphans have all unintentionally betrayed themselves — their authenticity — in order to gain some degree of socioeconomic security (or excess) and some amount of social acceptance, both of which are aspects of basic needs. They have little or no idea who they really are or how to find out: they're merely going through the motions. In contrast, people who have cultivated their 3-D Egos are always deepening their authenticity, which they do in part by experimenting with a variety of social roles and styles congruent with their true character.

Conscious and Unconscious Functioning of the South Subpersonalities

When one of our Wounded Children or Orphans is functioning unconsciously — independently of our Ego — we might notice only a background sensation of emotional reactivity or perhaps an occasional impulsive behavior that takes us by surprise (and probably disturbs others, too). We're likely to not know what we're feeling, why we're feeling it, or why we're acting the way we are.

For example, say in the course of a pleasant conversation with a friend, you learn something that, by implication, dashes a hope you'd been semiconsciously harboring. You might notice only a vague sensation of disappointment without being able to put your finger on what's troubling you, if anything. But, beneath your awareness, one of your Wounded Children noticed right away and reacted immediately with some combination of sadness, hurt, and anger, and perhaps some jealousy or shame. You (your Ego) didn't notice — at least at first — in part because the interaction was warm and agreeable. But as the exchange continues, you find yourself, out of the blue, saying something a tad spiteful or unkind, and it surprises you as much as your friend. You feel a bit flushed and confused. Perhaps you apologize and say you don't know what came over you (which is true). But this gets you wondering. Perhaps later, after the encounter, the emotion rises to the surface and bursts into awareness. Maybe you even recognize what triggered it: what was said and how it implied that your barely conscious desire was not to be realized. Now you have the opportunity to fully experience the emotion, knowing that in the end you (your 3-D Ego) will act on behalf of your Wounded Child's feelings, not *from* them.

On the other hand, this Wounded Child might hijack your Ego right in the midst of your conversation with your friend. (When this happens, a psychoanalyst would say you're in the grip of a complex.) If you're Ego-identified with your Wounded Child, you're feeling its emotions fully — you're consumed by them. You've lost your larger perspective (that of your 3-D Ego), if you ever did have it. You're feeling snubbed or rejected and tempted to vindictively act out your hurt.

The goal in healing and wholing is to cultivate the capacity to function from the perspective of your 3-D Ego, which draws freely on the resources of the Self, Soul, and Spirit, and which understands the real needs, deep longings, and protective intentions of your subpersonalities. Your subpersonalities are not wrong or shameful. Rather, they draw on a narrow and immature perspective, and their emotion-digestion skills are limited. When you're in the grip of a Wounded Child emotion, you have the opportunity to move through the four steps of emotional assimilation, all accomplished from the perspective of the 3-D Ego, utilizing the fourfold resources of your Self.

"Freudian slips" are well-known instances of a South sub acting independently of our Ego. You're at the proverbial family dinner and intend to say, "Pass the salt, please," but instead, to your and everyone else's horror, it comes out something like: "The hell with you, Paul!" A Wounded Child you hadn't even been aware of has suddenly and momentarily grabbed the internal microphone. There you sit with a rather raw emotion exposed — one you didn't even know you (still) had — and it's not going to be easy to sweep this gaffe under the dining room rug. Paul is sitting there fuming and glaring at you, warming up his lips for a peppery rejoinder. It won't do much good now to protest, "What I *meant* to say was..."

Our Outcasts, too, can act up outside of Ego awareness. Our Outcasts' pain and sense of inferiority and defectiveness can be a chronic condition, zapping our confidence, energy, spontaneity, and joy. A lot of psychic energy is required to sustain the banishment of our Outcasts, and so much vitality is sequestered in their domain. The good news is that when our Outcasts are welcomed home, all this aliveness is again available to us.

At other times, we might be thoroughly Ego-identified with an Outcast long ago labeled as shameful or worthless. We sink into despair, write ourselves off, feel humiliated, and perhaps act out self-destructively by, say, turning down a great job offer or social invitation or physically harming ourselves.

Orphans, too, can act both independently of our Egos and by way of them. When one of your Rebels, for example, is unconsciously active, you might cheerfully agree to a chore assigned by your boss but find yourself performing it poorly or too late "without meaning to." If, on the other hand, you were at the time Ego-identified with your Rebel, you might have instead responded to your boss's request with a dismissive laugh, or, if that would have been too dangerous, you might have begun creatively planning a way to passive-aggressively foil her project without being caught. In either case, your Rebel has found a way to act out your anger, get even, and assert your autonomy, although in ways that undermine your relationship with your boss (and perhaps your job), as well as your own integrity.

Our inner Victims can also act out independently of our awareness. You might, for example, be involved in a team project, and a Victim subpersonality begins to feel it's being overlooked or unappreciated. But all you notice, at first, is that your energy and motivation have flagged and that you seem to have little to contribute. Perhaps the others begin to notice, too. If one of the others happens to be identified with one of her Tyrant subpersonalities (North), she's likely to snap at you. Now you feel hurt and are fully merged with your Victim. You slink off somewhere to wallow in self-pity. Or, if the Tyrant's retort provoked an angry Rebel in you, all the ingredients for an emotional brawl are present.

This same team-project scenario could begin with you unconsciously acting out a Prince or Princess subpersonality, perhaps feeling inadequately revered by the others and finding yourself making subtly snide remarks about the progress of the project. Suddenly someone snaps, "Who the hell do you think you are, Your Highness?" But you don't realize what your Prince or Princess has been doing! The retort drops you into a Victim sub. You've been hijacked. You slip away to lick your wounds while, within you, behind the curtain of consciousness, an ad-hoc merger of a North Tyrant and a South Rebel is crystallizing, and they're beginning to plot revenge. And so on.[8]

Our Conformist subpersonalities, too, can show up subconsciously. When one of your Conformist subs is seeking social acceptance at any cost, you could find yourself, to your bewilderment, agreeing to opinions at odds with your own impassioned beliefs. At other times you might, with conscious deliberation, choose to fall into step with social pressure in order to avoid conflict. Sometimes we submit ourselves to *inner* conflict and choose to compromise our integrity rather than risk outer conflict and social rejection.

THE SOUTH SUBPERSONALITIES AS
FRAGMENTED VERSIONS OF THE WILD INDIGENOUS ONE

Our Wounded Children and Orphans are immature versions of the South facet of the Self. Our South subs and our South Self are, for example, equally emotional and vulnerable; but our Wild Indigenous One is emotional in a proactive, compassionate, and ecocentric way, while our Wounded Children and Orphans are emotionally reactive, self-protective, and egocentric, sometimes even narcissistic.

To be ecocentric is to hold the ecosystem in which one lives as the primary value, the most sacred context, and the foremost framework for evaluating what is good and what is to be defended or enhanced. Sometimes a species — even the humans — within an ecosystem must endure some losses or diminishment for the sake of the long-term vitality of the whole. When an ecosystem begins to unravel, all its species are endangered.

The Wild Indigenous One, being Southerly, is fully emotional, but emotional primarily from an ecocentric perspective. When we are in our Wild Indigenous consciousness, our joy derives from the astonishingly synergistic interactions of species, habitats, waterways, soils, and air; and our grief and anger are most powerfully evoked by losses to ecosystem vitality. Our Wild Indigenous One defends the rights of all species and habitats to survive and flourish.[9]

The South Self is also worldcentric: Despite honoring people of all races, religions, and sexual orientations, the South places a higher value on the well-being of humanity as a whole than on that of any particular group, including one's own, in those rare instances when one might have to choose between the whole and one of its parts. And, last, the South Self is sociocentric, placing a higher value on the well-being of its community or family than on the health of any one its human members, including oneself.

In contrast, our Wounded Children and Orphans are emotionally egocentric and reactive. They hold the needs and desires of our individual, isolated self as most important, and their emotions tend to be reactions to actual or perceived threats to fulfillment of those needs and desires. The primary (and appropriate) mission of our South subs is *self*-protection.

The difference between our Wounded Children and our Wild Indigenous One is not the degree of emotional vulnerability but rather what events in our world evoke this vulnerability. Our Wild Indigenous One is anguished by climate disruption, nuclear poisoning of vast areas, biodiversity loss (twenty-seven thousand species going extinct every year),[10] and the suffering of billions of humans from state oppression and the terrible poverty it engenders. Through the emotionally alive perspective of the South facet of the Self, we can discover what the diminishment of our world tells us about ourselves and the psychological vulnerabilities of our species. And it is from this perspective that we can take courageous corrective action before it's too late.

HEALING OUR RELATIONSHIPS WITH OUR SOUTH SUBPERSONALITIES

Our Orphan strategies — our interpersonal South strategies — for meeting our basic needs become less effective as we get older simply because fewer people in our lives are willing to indulge us when we act as a Conformist,

Victim, Rebel, or Prince or Princess. At least this is true in a healthy society. The more immature the society, the more our Orphan strategies get results throughout life. Orphan strategies work best when employed in relationships with people who are also in Orphan roles. This is what traps people in codependent relationships.

Conformists generally reinforce the roles of other Conformists. Consumer societies, for example, are sustainable only when there are enough people willing to support each other (socially, psychologically, and economically) to enact dreary and deadly Conformist roles when they have a choice to do otherwise — roles such as bureaucrat, desk jockey, casino zombie, TV junkie, junk salesman, or shopping-mall-junk consumer, and even immoral and death-dealing versions of these roles, such as junk-food-ad designer, Wall Street toxic-asset broker, inventor or manufacturer of weapons of mass destruction, military contractor in empire-building wars, economic hit man, or corrupt politician.[11]

Conformists and Victims generally defer to Princes and Princesses (entitled people, including the wealthy, bosses, politicians, royalty, and celebrities), and this deference enables the latter to get away with their entitlements. Rebels couldn't be Rebels without Conformists and Princes or Princesses to rebel against. Victims, as we've seen, require Conformist-Rescuers in order to meet their basic needs (and often vice versa).

Our inner Orphans might succeed at meeting our basic needs, but they do so in ways that significantly limit our capacity to meet our higher needs, such as love, integrity, authenticity, meaning, fulfilling participation, self-actualization (individuation), Soul encounter, and Spirit realization. Orphan roles are a means to an end (survival). They're not rooted in the authentic qualities of our personalities (our real desires, attitudes, and interests) or of our Souls (our mythopoetic identities), or of our upperworld identity as embodiments of Spirit. The eventual result of Orphan inauthenticity is depression, addiction, or suicide, all of which end up undermining — or precluding — fulfillment of our basic needs.

So what to do about our Wounded Children and Orphans?

As we saw with our Loyal Soldiers, the following advice is likely to work only if the War of Childhood Survival is over (see pages 141–42) and if you have a solid preestablished rapport with the fourfold resources of your Self. After all, which parts of you have the capacity to heal your wounds? Certainly not your wounded subpersonalities. Our challenge and opportunity is to use our horizontal wholeness to compassionately embrace our woundedness.

When responding to your Wounded Children and Orphans, it's especially important to do so with the perspective and resources of the facet of your Self on the opposite side of the circle — namely, from the compassionate consciousness of your Nurturing Adult.

When you become aware of the emotional tenderness and vulnerability of one of your Wounded Children, you can "sit with" and empathically embrace him or her. Most people find it easy to imagine their Wounded Children as little boys or girls. The way to tend to your emotional woundedness is essentially the same way you'd care for an actual little boy or girl. Imagine how you — when feeling centered, calm, and capable — would respond to a small child who's feeling mad, bad, sad, or scared.

Whether the emotional undercurrent within you is subtle or a five-alarm fire, listen fully and deeply to what your Little Boy (or Girl) has to say, with the goal of understanding what happened and how this constitutes some kind of misfortune, danger, or crisis for him. Again, it's essential that you do this with the resources of your Nurturing Adult.

Don't try to talk your Wounded Child out of her feelings! Your opportunity is to talk her further *into* them. Your emotions don't go away when you ignore them; they just go underground. By empathically talking your Wounded Child into the depths of her emotions, you'll give her the experience of being understood, and this by itself will open the emotional gates further and be deeply comforting. Whether she's feeling angry, hurt, guilty, ashamed, sad, scared, hopeless, jealous, or envious, talk her into it. Legitimize her emotions.

Here are four components: By listening to her story from the perspective of your Nurturing Adult, you'll be able to identify soon enough (1) what emotion(s) your Little Girl (or Boy) is feeling, (2) what happened (or what she thinks happened) that elicited the emotion, (3) how it makes total sense that she'd be feeling precisely those emotions under those circumstances, and (4) what this tells you about her (which is to say, you). Basically, as you become aware of each of these four components, you're going to explain it to her in language she can understand. By doing so, you're legitimizing her emotions.

In the Western world, many people believe emotions don't make sense — that they're irrational. But in fact there's nothing irrational about emotions. Also, rationality is only one feature of our multidimensional human psyches, and to promote rationality above all other qualities is to promote intrapsychic and interpersonal imbalance and decay — and ultimately cultural collapse.

Let's say your Little Boy is hurt and angry because you felt criticized for something you felt you had actually done well. Shifting your consciousness to your Nurturing Adult, begin by encouraging him to tell you the whole story. Don't interrupt except to ask questions that draw out additional elements. As he recounts his tale, empathize with his experience and respond in ways that show you understand. This will enable him to feel more fully. Let him know, specifically, what you understand about his feelings. This corresponds to the first three components of legitimizing. For example, you might say, "You're feeling deeply hurt because you just finished weeding your wife's garden, which was very kind of you, and then, instead of being thanked, you got royally chewed out by her because apparently some of the 'weeds' turned out to be flowers she recently planted. Well, of course you're feeling hurt! You put aside your own cherished plans for the day to surprise your wife with something you knew she'd appreciate." If you were in fact listening well and communicated what you understood, you ought to be getting a big yes response from your Little Boy, who's feeling his hurt all the more fully now. After a while, you might continue: "And you're probably feeling angry, too, because she yelled at you, not at all taking into consideration your completely good intentions. Yes?" "Yes." "And maybe you're feeling a bit guilty, too, in that you did in fact, although totally without knowing it, ruin a lot of flowers. Yes?" "Yes." And so on.

Then, component 4 makes explicit what's been discovered: "This reveals some really good things about you: You want to be helpful to those you love. You want to increase the warmth and harmony between you and your loved ones. You want people to know this about you, even when your attempts at loving backfire. And you also want to get it right — to actually be helpful when you intend to be. The fact that you feel guilty about pulling the flowers demonstrates this — you unintentionally acted in conflict with your own desire to please your wife."

Although we don't consciously choose our emotional reactions, this doesn't make them irrational; it only makes them nondeliberate. When we have an emotion that seems irrational, we're revealing our current identification with a subpersonality that would have preferred we felt some other way or that doesn't understand our feelings. Attempting to suppress or discount an emotion by calling it irrational reveals a lack of self-compassion.

All emotions are based on nondeliberated appraisals of our circumstances, such as "This is dangerous" (fear), "I'm being treated unfairly" (hurt or anger), "I've lost something precious" (grief), "I've wronged somebody" (guilt), or "This is what I've been hoping for!" (happiness). Sometimes our appraisals are mistaken, but this doesn't render our emotions irrational.

After legitimizing your Wounded Child's emotions, the next step — which is essential — is taking action. Make a plan for how you (your 3-D Ego) will act on those emotions and what they reveal about yourself. Let your Wounded Child know what you plan to do on his or her behalf (and then do it). For example, you might plan to apologize to your wife, plant new flowers for her, and let her know you hadn't been aware you were "weeding" some of her flowers. If she doesn't apologize for yelling at you, you might let her know why it hurt when she did, telling her in a way that communicates your desire for mutual care.[12]

Another example, this one with shame: Let's say that for many years you've been the executive director of a nonprofit environmental organization that has been accepting large donations from corporations that engage in mountaintop-removal coal mining or clear-cutting of forests, and that you've tended to look the other way when it comes to these destructive practices. You justified this to yourself and your board by insisting it was a necessary evil and pointing out the great preservation work your organization does in other arenas. But one day you wake up and realize you've hypocritically contributed to environmental degradation. Suddenly you feel intense shame. Part of this shame is healthy, mature, Self-rooted shame that suggests how you've violated a genuine and deeply held value. But you also have an activated Wounded Child who feels completely worthless and suggests the only way out is resignation, maybe even suicide.

Shame is even bigger than guilt. Wounded Child shame does not suggest merely that you're a good person who did something wrong, but that you did something so wrong your entire being must be flawed. If, however, you can evoke the consciousness of your 3-D Ego, you can sit with your ashamed Wounded Child. He tells you his story. You legitimize his feelings by noting that the values of environmental protection are core to him (and you), and that it now seems to him you've been violating these values, so of course he feels ashamed. Although you had never intended harm, he now feels the extent of the damage done and senses that you-he should have seen this earlier, and that perhaps you were even blindsided by your ambition to make your organization financially secure and to have your employees be grateful for their ongoing jobs. His shame actually reaffirms his core values (and yours). The shame is understandable and makes sense, and now it guides you to plan acts of restitution as a way to both recommit to those values and make amends. You let your Wounded Child know what you plan to do in this regard. You won't let your Wounded Child act on his shame on his own. You'll do it yourself with the resources of your Self.

When loving our Wounded Children, we act for them, not from them. We devise mature means to meet their basic needs. Sometimes we take them for "walks," during which we listen, legitimize their emotions, and create resourceful, mature ways to act on those emotions. We utilize our North nurturing skills and generativity to act for them, our South emotive capacities to help them fully feel (both bodily and in full range), our East abilities to appreciate the bigger picture of our emotional lives, and our West's ability to look within and discover hidden meanings in our emotions.

Each time you catch yourself enacting an Orphan role, it suggests a basic need being inadequately met. Consider why you enacted that Orphan role in those particular circumstances. What basic need was your Orphan trying to meet? Why didn't you try more mature strategies? What were you afraid of? What skills are perhaps lacking? How can you meet those needs more maturely and effectively?

When you realize you've been enacting any of the four Orphan roles, you might call on the resources of your fourfold Self to

- discover more of your authentic nature (your genuine values, interests, feelings, desires, and attitudes) revealed through your Orphan reactions;
- access your deep imagination (your Muse) regarding authentic social roles you might live your way into (in work, love, and friendship);

- learn mature ways to protect yourself from other people's immature criticism, rejection, and so on;
- learn ways to respond effectively to criticism, to better understand
yourself and others and deepen your relationships;
- learn and practice anger-management skills and nonviolent communication;
- further hone your negotiation skills;
- develop your skills at community building; and
- take your next steps in cultivating physical, psychological, and spiritual self-reliance.

Good psychotherapy can help you identify your Orphans, embrace
them, and develop mature alternatives that employ the resources of the Self.
But if you already have sufficient access to your Self, you can do this on
your own much of the time.

ADDITIONAL PRACTICES FOR HEALING
OUR SOUTH SUBPERSONALITIES

Voice Dialogue, Four-Directions Circles, Dreamwork, and Deep Imagery with Wounded Children

Refer to the appendix for these four ways of nurturing your Wounded
Children.

A Wound Walk

- Venture out to a wild or semiwild place, at least a park, somewhere
few people congregate. Bring your journal and, if you'd like, some
crayons, pastels, or colored pencils and/or a bit of modeling clay.
You'll need a minimum of an hour — two or three will be better.[13]
- If you're not already in it, evoke the fourfold perspective of your
Self — the consciousness of your 3-D Ego. This step is essential
before proceeding.
- Wander until you find a thing or place that to you *feels* wounded. It
might be an empty animal hole, a mine shaft, a scattering of bones,
a gash in a tree, a bulldozed site, a pile of trash, or a place infested
with invasive weeds. Don't proceed to the next step until you've

found a spot or a thing that truly feels wounded to you (whether or not it's objectively wounded) and that evokes from you an empathic emotional response of sorrow and/or compassion.

- Sit with that thing or place, open all your senses to it, and tune into the emotions evoked in you. Fully take it in. Out loud, tell it what you observe, feel, and imagine it's like to be in its condition or to have suffered what it has or to represent what it does. Attend to the flow of your emotions. Make notes in your journal if this helps you feel more fully.

- Now, with the resources of your Self — especially those of your Nurturing Adult — speak out loud to this thing or place about your own woundedness, past or present, physical, psychological, social, or spiritual. On behalf of your Wounded Children, tell a story or two about your wound(s), how it occurred, and what it's been like to live with it. Be sure to speak to the wounded thing or place. Take the time you need to do this thoroughly. Make journal notes if it serves you.

- With the consciousness and resources of your Self, feel, sense, imagine, and/or embody (through gesture or movement) your wound or woundedness. Take your time.

- Next (only after completing the above) fill the space in which you sit with this question: How does my wound grant me authentic, life-serving power? Don't try to answer it. If your strategic mind generates an answer, congratulate it, and then, evoking the resources of the Self, keep filling the space with this question, not trying to get an answer. With the awareness of your Self, attend carefully to what happens — both in the world around you and within your emotions and imagination. There's no need to receive an answer... but one might arrive on its own. More likely and better than an answer, however, is a response: something curious you observe in your surroundings, or a feeling, an image, a memory, an insight, a revelation.

- Employing the resources of your Self, embody, express, and/or respond to what happens within or without, using words, gestures, movement, verse, song, chant, drawing, or clay.

- Record your discoveries in your journal.

ADVANCED SOUTH SUBPERSONALITY WORK:
THE SACRED WOUND AS A PATH TO SOUL

As discussed in chapter 6, learning to embrace our wounded subpersonalities with the consciousness and resources of the Self can morph into a means of Soul encounter, but only for those people — relatively rare in contemporary Western societies — who are developmentally and spiritually prepared for the spiritual descent. This journey is always risky, and for many it's particularly so when entered by the gate of the wounded South. Before reading on, you may want to review the overview and cautions offered in the introductory section on advanced subpersonality work, on pages 148–50.

The Core Wound

When we've made significant progress with the task of welcoming home our Loyal Soldiers (see previous chapter) and have eliminated all substance addictions and other notable dependencies (see next chapter), we might find a branch of memory particularly and uniquely painful. We might begin to reexperience psychological woundings so distressing we formed our primary survival strategies in reaction to them, so hurtful that much of our personal style and sensitivities have their roots there.

This is what I call the *core wound*, something deeper and more painful than the ordinary hurts and injuries of everyday life. Some of our Wounded Children and Orphans have their origins in this wound.

People who grew up in the most egocentric settings, in which family dysfunction is common, often have core wounds that originated in emotional abuse or neglect. Perhaps as a child, a woman was blamed by her alcoholic father for his own misery, or her father acted as if she were his girlfriend, or her insecure and jealous mother saw her as a threat to her marriage. Maybe an older stepsister tormented her, or a strict and demanding grandparent told her she would never measure up.

To be wounded, however, you need not come from a dysfunctional family. Your core wound might stem from birth trauma or a birth defect, or the death of your mother when you were three, or a pattern of innocent but shattering betrayals at the hands of your older brother. Maybe it was your father's absence due to illness, or your guilt for surviving the car wreck that claimed your younger sister, or your own childhood bout with a potentially deadly fever.

Although personal histories often include injurious events such as these, the core wound rarely stems from a single traumatic incident. More often it consists of a pattern of hurtful events or a disturbing dynamic in one or more important relationships.

We all have a core wound. From a spiritual perspective, this isn't an accident, nor is it unfortunate.

The mysterious nature of the core wound can best be appreciated by understanding that it results from the convergence of one or more wounding events with a preexisting Soul-devised vulnerability. *Core wounds are not caused merely by our woundings.* Each one of us is born with a physical, psychological, and/or spiritual vulnerability — a susceptibility arranged by the Soul itself, which renders us woundable in a particularly painful way by a certain variety of wounding events. Most kinds of wounding events would result in a core wound in only a small percentage of people. Other people, if they were to experience the same event, might feel hurt or injured, but the wounding would not penetrate all the way to the core of their psyche.

The Soul (or Mystery, more generally) orchestrates our core wound because the experiential encounter with Soul would be unlikely or impossible without one. An impeccably assembled Ego, one that never encountered a moment of supreme self-doubt, would be invulnerable to falling apart. Soul encounter requires that we first die to who we thought we were and then be plunged into a period of not knowing, during which we might uncover a mystery. A seamless Ego that in no way doubted itself would never be motivated to leave the "home" of its adolescent story, would never second-guess its conventional life trajectory, would never wander off into the mysteries of nature and psyche, and would, consequently, never reach true adulthood. Mystery, then, sees to it that we are born with a core vulnerability, one that will be actuated or precipitated by certain kinds of wounding events.[14]

As singer-songwriter Leonard Cohen suggests in "Anthem," "There's a crack in everything; that's how the light gets in." The Navajo people of the American Southwest have a related belief. They say that perfection keeps Spirit from entering a thing. In their masterful weavings, they incorporate a deliberate irregularity, an errant line or color that looks like an unintended flaw but is actually a purposeful deviation called a "spirit line," the place where Mystery might enter.

Our core vulnerability — and by extension, our core wound — is the spirit line in the work of art called a human psyche.

Our Soul-contrived core vulnerability might be an unusually great sensitivity to the mere gaze of other humans, or to being physically touched (lovingly or otherwise), or to the suffering of nonhumans, or to the astounding wonder of the night sky. Or it might be a predisposition to feel like a stranger in a strange land, to be shamed easily, to cry at the drop of a hat, to swoon from the unutterable beauty of music or blossoms or stone, or to have wildly strong empathic responses to almost everything. Or it might be an inexplicable need to always be right, the best, the worst, or invisible, or to always be seen, sought after, or seeking. Or it might be an absolute inborn yearning and necessity to dance, to design, to sing, to worship.[15]

These and other core vulnerabilities virtually assure that one or more events will occur in our lives, usually in childhood, which we'll experience as exceptionally traumatic or damaging.

Imagine a girl who is regularly brought to tears by the wonder and sublimity of music but has been forbidden to sing or to play an instrument. Or imagine a boy of unusual emotional sensitivity who constantly worries about his psychologically unstable mother and then has to endure her loss when she suddenly flees the family without warning.

After letting this idea of the core wound sink in, we may find ourselves pondering whether we ourselves, or our Souls, have a certain kind of responsibility, in a transpersonal, spiritual sense, for our core wounds — responsibility, not blame. Yes, we suffered one or more wounding events in the form of an accident, a disease, a loss, or abuse, but the effect of those events was amplified by our core vulnerability. The core wound is an opportunity for the Soul as much as it is a liability for the Ego.

The Sacred Wound

When you're sufficiently mature psychospiritually, it's possible to experientially reenter and explore your core wound, which can serve as a portal to the discovery of your Soul's purpose and destiny. By entering that portal with the resources of your fourfold Self, you can transform your core wound into a Sacred Wound.[16]

If and when you're able to surrender to the grief, frightful memories, and bodily residues you encounter at the heart of your core wound, no longer distancing yourself from what awaits you there, your psyche is in this way torn open so that new questions can be asked about who you are at your roots. These fomenting questions enable you to discover and understand the nature and spiritual purpose of the core vulnerability with which you were born, as well as the terrible wounding events of your life (without ever condoning acts of child abuse, war crimes, cultural oppression, or other depraved actions). These questions, experiences, and insights facilitate the relinquishment of your old, smaller story (your middleworld, adolescent life) and the embrace of a larger story, a Soul story, one partly revealed by the wound itself. Your core wound becomes sacred when you're ready to release your attachment to your small story and become the vehicle through which your Soul story can be lived into the world.

As Lisel Mueller suggests in this chapter's opening poem, your core wound becomes a portal through which you might discover "something secret is going on, / so marvelous and dangerous / that if you crawled through and saw, / you would die, or be happy forever."

With access to the fourfold resources of the Self, you can experientially dive into your core wound, revisiting your memories of the wounding events, and discover how they affected your psyche, your relationships, and your life. You can feel, in a way you never have before, the vulnerability built into the core of your psyche. By courageously and patiently allowing the associated suffering to do its work, neither indulging nor repressing the pain, you reach the bedrock of your psyche, where the most profound truths of this lifetime await.

To reach such a place, you must avoid making sense of your pain too soon or finding relief too quickly (Escapist), blaming someone for your anguish (Victim), or seeking revenge (Rebel). Beware, also, of other subpersonality reactions, such as caving in and seeking refuge in self-blame, self-pity, or playing the role of the martyr; or in denial, cynicism, abandonment of your own dreams and values, or paranoid confidence in a never-ending series of further woundings. With 3-D Ego consciousness, you must allow the reexperience of the wound to do its work on you even if you descend into despair. If you remain there long enough, you'll be shorn of the personal patterns and attachments that must die so you can be reborn into a greater life.

Sacred Wound work should not be attempted before the Cocoon stage, and most people would want or need some support and guidance in the process from mature adults or elders who've successfully traversed such terrain themselves.

In the contemporary West, conscious investigation of the core wound, when attempted at all, most commonly takes place in those rare psychotherapies that journey deep into the psyche to encounter the demons and monsters of our greatest fears and hurts. These wounds can also be approached through exceptional forms of bodywork or through ceremonies that welcome our grief and allow its full experience.

In a Soul-centered setting, the elders and the adult initiators, who know we all carry core wounds, offer rituals and nature-based practices that help us uncover and assimilate the lessons and opportunities, the sacred treasures, hidden in our wounds.

In whatever way we go about it, cultivating an intimate relationship with our core wounds loosens our attachment to our former identity and becomes a potent doorway to the metamorphosis that occurs within the Cocoon and beyond.

Chapter 8

East

ADDICTS AND ESCAPISTS

I will not die an unlived life.
I will not live in fear
of falling or catching fire.
I choose to inhabit my days,
to allow my living to open me,
to make me less afraid,
more accessible;
to loosen my heart
until it becomes a wing,
a torch, a promise.
I choose to risk my significance,
to live so that which came to me as seed
goes to the next as blossom,
and that which came to me as blossom,
goes on as fruit.

— DAWNA MARKOVA

The Escapist: Steven is bored by his cubicle-bound desk job at a mega-corporation; he spends hours each day playing a video game featuring an apocalyptic battle in which angels and demons unite against humans.

The Addict: Joan's only child died at age three, and her husband left her soon after. She drinks too much most days after work.

The Blisshead: Moonbeam (née Ethel) grew up in a midwestern, hail-and-brimstone fundamentalist family. When she was seventeen, she escaped to Santa Cruz, California, fell in with the New Age crowd, and learned how to bliss out with the help of crystals and cross-dimensional chanting.

The Puer: Peter enjoys playing almost any game or sport and is good at it. He's also a pilot and loves flying small, experimental aircraft, soaring high over the workaday world of responsibilities, relationship conflicts, and commitments.

Another Escapist: Right now, curiously, I'm finding it rather difficult and uncomfortable to write about the East (no surprise, given how West I am). Come to think of it, I'm feeling a strong impulse at the moment to discover what last night's snowfall feels like beneath my skis. I'll be back in a few hours. Maybe. Stay tuned...

Evasion

The method preferred by our East subpersonalities for keeping us safe (physically, psychologically, socially, economically) is evasion — rising above traumatic emotions and circumstances and sidestepping distressing challenges and responsibilities. East subs evade through psychological strategies such as addictions, obsessions, dissociations, self-numbing, and escapist fantasies, and through social maneuvers such as vanishing acts, delinquency, recklessness, flightiness, flippancy, and mischievousness.

Beginning in early childhood, our faithful East subs defend us from overwhelming emotions and intolerable or painful bodily states. Later in life, they also attempt to shelter us from more existential hazards such as "falling or catching fire" or risking our "significance," as Dawna Markova puts it in this chapter's opening poem. They might, for example, try to protect us from the psychospiritually perilous descent to Soul or the equally precarious ascent to Spirit, or from falling in love again, breaking out of whatever social or vocational cage we've trapped ourselves in, recklessly risking some wild new life adventure, or fully feeling our grief, rage, or despair about what our lives have become or what has happened to our formerly flourishing world.

The broad-spectrum names I use for the intrapersonal versions of the East subpersonalities are *Escapists* and *Addicts*, as you can see in map 1. These are the versions of ourselves adept at extracting us from situations we find threatening to our self-image or that we experience as physically or emotionally overwhelming — beyond what we feel we can tolerate. And, when our Addicts and Escapists aren't able to extricate us physically or socially from ordeals or nightmares, they have a backup plan borrowed from the proverbial ostrich: they can, at least, block our awareness or memory of trauma.

The interpersonal versions of the wounded East are the escapist social roles we play. These are the ways people are likely to see us when we're using our East survival strategies. Map 2 suggests Blissheads, Addicts, and Puers/Puellas as representative labels; variations include Obsessives, Junkies, Fanatics, Rogues, New Age Flakes, and Spiritual Materialists.

As we've seen, the cardinal direction in which we're most at home tends to be opposite our least-developed facet. People naturally strong in the East facet of the Self, the Innocent/Sage, are prone to heavy reliance upon their East subs, their Escapists and Addicts, in part because the West facet of their Self, the Muse-Beloved, is underdeveloped and unavailable to provide its darkness-savoring appetite to counterbalance the East subs' inclination to escape into the light. As we'll see, the West Self provides an essential key to the healing of the East subs (and to complementing the strengths of the East Self).

ESCAPISTS

What recourse did our psyches have, in early childhood, when faced with circumstances that threatened to psychologically devastate us, torments from which our Loyal Soldiers and Wounded Children — our North and South subpersonalities — weren't able to preemptively protect us? What happened, in other words, when our Loyal Soldiers, through their acting-small gambits, failed to dodge trials and tribulations, and our Wounded Children's Orphan routines didn't sufficiently secure our essentials or our social safety? When our North and South subs don't do enough to protect us, our psyches do what they can to free us from the intrapsychic mess we're in. Enter, from the East, our Escapists.[1]

When the going gets rough, our Escapists swoop in to get us the hell out of Dodge. Often they simply remove us physically from social scenes our Wounded Children consider menacing, but if that doesn't work or isn't possible, they safeguard our psyches by extracting us experientially — they prevent us from registering, remembering, or fully feeling traumatic events (as with Joan, the alcoholic who has not yet grieved the loss of her child and marriage). Maybe they let us witness the events themselves but, through self-numbing, spared us the conscious experience of the emotions evoked by those events. Or they might have completely separated our consciousness from the events (dissociation) to prevent or delay knowledge of a trauma. "I left my body while it was happening," we might say sometime later. Perhaps our Escapists got really good at fantasizing, so good that it felt as if we were somewhere other than where we were, a strategy employed by Steven, the cubicle-caged video game addict.

Our current menace might be our own emotions: grief, hurt, anger, fear, guilt, or shame so intense we're not able to endure it. Or it could be a betrayal by a friend or family member, or the burden of too many responsibilities, or the threat of failure, humiliation, or condemnation, on the one hand, or of too much success, visibility, or praise, on the other.

You might think that the protective strategies our subpersonalities used in childhood — or still use — are unfortunate, ineffective, or damaging. But this is not necessarily the case. Our subpersonalities are to be praised for enabling our survival. Sometimes their strategies are the best we could have hoped for. For example, in the moment of severe physiological injury, shock (the acute medical condition associated with a fall in blood pressure) supports our survival by decreasing our ability to feel the excruciating pain of physical injury. Likewise, *psychological* shock protects us from fully feeling an overwhelming loss too soon. ("When they told me she was dead, it didn't even register.")

Starting in middle childhood, we also devised a variety of behavioral routines to escape emotionally intolerable situations. We may have developed an extraordinary interpersonal sensitivity to individuals or circumstances that felt dangerous to us, enabling us to slip out the back door before an encounter or use social gambits that enabled escape ("Excuse me, I've got to go see a man about a horse").[2] Or we may have simply not shown up in the first place or learned to sidestep any attempts to corner us. When such maneuvers enabled us to avoid truly harmful encounters, this may have been our Nurturing Generative Adult coming to the rescue. But when we were "protecting" ourselves from socially risky but potentially growth-enhancing experiences, it's more likely that our Escapists were at work, perhaps in cahoots with one or more Wounded Children or Loyal Soldiers (for example, "I'm afraid of people!" or "You'll make a fool of yourself," respectively). Agoraphobia (fear of crowded spaces or of panicky feelings) can be all three acting together, in extreme cases resulting in an unwillingness to leave home.

As long as the War of Childhood Survival rages, our Escapists might be essential to our existence, but we pay a high price for their services: arrested development, social isolation, ruined relationships, missed opportunities, and — if it's the experience of our emotions we've been escaping — depression (unassimilated emotions).[3]

ADDICTS

Addiction, a special case of psychological escape, is a common form of evasion in patho-adolescent societies. Here I mean the negative addictions — dependencies (on substances or behaviors) that undermine or restrict our vitality and potential.[4]

Through addictions, we distract ourselves or numb out in order to avoid the emotionally painful precincts of our lives. The most damaging and difficult-to-kick addictions are chemical; they create a physiological dependency, a neurological impairment of our capacity to feel, and a secondary behavioral impairment — by altering what we attend to and how we spend our time.[5] But there are many other addictions, such as those focused on food, shopping, impersonal sex, TV and other screens, gambling, and work, and these, too, by distracting and deadening us, can effectively cut us off from our full range of feeling, sensing, remembering, imagining, and acting.

In addition to extricating us from the experience of intolerable pain (physical, emotional, or spiritual), addictions can generate a kind of bliss or joy — maybe a much-needed calmness or peace or a fuller sense of belonging or presence.

Perhaps most addictions do both: grant us relief from pain as well as access to ecstasy, at least temporarily. The question that lingers, of course, is what price we pay.

It seems that with any addiction, as time goes on, the ecstasy gradually diminishes and the pain relief does as well. This seems to be especially true with substance addictions characterized by physiological dependence. The avoidance of the psychological and physical horrors of withdrawal can become a new and ample motivation for maintaining a chemical addiction — and eventually the sole (and dwindling) benefit.

Some addictions can truly serve us, at least temporarily, perhaps even save our lives. Some traumas, for example, simply can't be survived by young or fragile psyches. And some torments provoke reactions from us that can further jeopardize our safety — say, a relationship ordeal that provokes a hazardous escape, suicide, or lethal aggression. Although sometimes lifesaving, the strategies of our Addicts significantly limit our options and retard our individuation.

What to do? Later in this chapter, we'll explore how the 3-D Ego — by way of the Self's perspectives — can learn to love and liberate our Addicts (and Escapists).

But it must be emphasized that addictions can be exceedingly difficult to kick. People with substance addictions especially need help — from friends and family, psychotherapy, twelve-step and other recovery programs, acupuncture, or other mainstream and alternative health-care approaches. More on this later.

WE'RE ALL IN RECOVERY FROM WESTERN CIVILIZATION

Sooner or later, we each must address the paramount addiction in the Western and Westernized worlds: our psychological dependence on the worldview and lifestyle of Western civilization itself.[6] The Western worldview says, in essence, that technological progress is the highest value, and that we were born to consume, to endlessly use and discard natural resources, other species, techno-gadgets, toys, and, often, other people, especially if they're poor or from the global South. It's a world of commodities, not entities; of consumers, not human beings; and economic expansion is the primary measure of progress. Profits are valued over people, money over meaning, our national entitlement over global peace and justice, "us" over "them." This addiction to Western civilization — especially now that the Chinese, too, are hooked — is by far the most dangerous one in the world because of how rapidly and extensively it's undermining the natural systems of Earth.

Addiction to Western civilization protects us from seeing and feeling the staggering price all Earthly life pays for our consumer habit. And it protects us from having to make any radical changes in lifestyle,[7] or from having to grow up, leave the "home" of our adolescent comforts, and embark upon the hazardous journey of initiation that leads to an existence that's life enhancing, meaningful, and fulfilling.

The more we live in a materialistic flatland, the more we need it in order to keep from experiencing the agony of our alienation. Each of us has the opportunity to carefully examine our lives, uncover the ways in which our addiction to Western civilization operates, and make the biggest, most courageous changes we're capable of.

Blissheads

Turning now to the interpersonal strategies of our East subpersonalities, let's begin with our friends, the Blissheads, who, as their name suggests, help us escape intolerable realities — or merely unpleasant ones — through social personas suffused with ecstasy, rapture, or euphoria.

"What's wrong with that?" you might ask. Well, nothing's wrong with ecstasy — *real* ecstasy — as long as it doesn't keep us from intimacy, authenticity, personal development, or our full participation in the world. And this is precisely what we sacrifice when we rely on a Blisshead sub to evade the painful or risky emotions or realities of our lives.

When hijacked by a Blisshead, we take flight into the light, often into a superficial and immature belief in the Divine that leads us to profess and act as if everything in the world is perfect just as it is, God would never let anything bad happen to us or our world, and, if we simply pray enough, love enough, or think positively enough, all problems will be solved.

If a Blisshead sub were to get its way, we would, like Moonbeam of Santa Cruz, skip through life with a perma-smile, always looking on the bright side, and in this way be forever psychically protected from harsh realities and from our own deeply troubling wounds, traumas, and unassimilated emotions.

One variation of the Blisshead, ungenerously labeled the New Age Flake, believes, for example, that if we would simply think positively enough, we would all be fabulously wealthy, healthy, and happy.[8] Someone abducted by her inner Blisshead might believe such "secrets" for fear of what lies hidden beneath the surface of her everyday awareness. Blisshead positive thinking can be delusional and dangerous because it ignores the real source of problems and encourages complacency. The 3-D Ego embraces neither magical thinking nor doom and gloom but, rather, full feeling and belonging (South), deep imagination and meaning (West), wisdom, nonattachment, and contemplative communion with Spirit (East), and careful observation and engaged action (North) to cocreate with others a better world.

Our Blissheads — like our Escapists and Addicts, more generally — are terrified of the dark (the unknown), our wounds, undigested emotions, loss, death, decay, the unconscious, and the descent to Soul. These are, of course, the realms of life unconditionally celebrated by the facet of the Self on the opposite side of the circle from the Blisshead: namely, the Muse-Beloved in the West, happily surrounded by corpses, nightmares, and sacred scars (as well as Eros, romance, and deep imagination). The Blisshead is not interested in heading West (exactly what it must do to be healed). Dwelling in the light is its idea of a great solution. This isn't bad policy — if, that is, the War of Childhood Survival is still being waged *and* we lack more mature strategies.

FLYING BOYS AND FLYING GIRLS

A second interpersonal strategy of the wounded East takes the form of the *puer aeternus* or *puella aeternus*, Latin for "eternal boy" and "eternal girl," a.k.a. flying boys and flying girls. A person in the grips of a Puer or Puella subpersonality attempts to live an endless sequence of marvelous adventures, like Peter the playful pilot, revealing both an addiction to shallow ecstasy and an aversion to real responsibility. Puers and Puellas covet independence and freedom and chafe at all boundaries and limits. They fear and avoid situations from which escape isn't easy, finding any restrictions intolerable. Sometimes known as Peter Pans or Wendys, people whose Egos are primarily identified with these East subs are the child-men and child-women who refuse to grow up and courageously face the challenges of life, waiting instead for their ship to come in and solve all problems.

With their fear of falling, Puers and Puellas prefer to "fly above" difficult emotions, relationship responsibilities, and the demands of life. Sometimes they manage to get away with this for extended periods, especially if they're in partnership with a Caretaker, Enabler, or Codependent.

One variation of the Puer and Puella is the Spiritual Materialist, a subpersonality who avoids emotional pain and the challenges of life by a flight into shallow versions of spiritual practice. For the Spiritual Materialist, the primary (but usually unrecognized) benefit of meditation, prayer, or yoga is the evasion of everyday difficulties and of the dark realms of the West quadrant of the psyche.[9]

Other interpersonal versions of the Escapist with some family resemblance to the Puer/Puella include the Fanatic or Obsessive (so focused on one thing that she can conveniently overlook almost everything else) and the Rogue (flawed and often puerile, but attractive and charming nonetheless).

CONSCIOUS AND UNCONSCIOUS FUNCTIONING OF THE EAST SUBPERSONALITIES

Like our North and South subpersonalities, our Addicts and Escapists can function either consciously (when our Ego is hooked by them) or unconsciously (flying beneath Ego radar, but flying nonetheless).

Many addictions and escape routines operate unconsciously. We can be completely unaware that a habitual evasion is in progress while, for example, drinking ourselves into a stupor, or suddenly finding ourselves with a splitting headache, or on the way to the ski slopes, or love-struck yet again by a passing stranger. If so, we're not aware at the time that we're avoiding anything. When functioning unconsciously, our East subs are on automatic pilot, deployed without Ego choice or awareness. At such times, we're obviously not capable of intervening on our own behalf. With the 3-D Ego unavailable, the addiction or escape unfolds unimpeded (unless someone *else* intervenes).

Unconscious deployment of an East sub is most likely when we haven't yet begun our recovery process, especially when an East sub employs an addiction with strong somatic cravings, such as substance dependency, chronic hunger, or sex madness. Such urges can be so strong we're simply carried away by them.

Another variation involves traumas that occurred in early childhood before we possessed conscious self-awareness, wounding events such as physical or sexual abuse. When memories of such wounds are triggered by current circumstances, our East subs often come to our rescue and deflect our awareness to other realms — to keep us from being retraumatized. The 3-D Ego is capable of remembering and metabolizing these traumas, but this won't happen until we *have* a 3-D Ego.

When an Addict or Escapist is operating unconsciously, we can't stop them on our own. We either need help from others or need first to access our fourfold Self (and consequently our 3-D Ego), through which we can become conscious of our Addict or Escapist and then stop their evasion. Or we need both a 3-D Ego and help from others. Because the power of addictions can be so immense, we often need the support of others in a nonshaming environment — hence the great value of recovery communities such as twelve-step groups. Other great resources to remember when we get retriggered by early childhood woundings are body-centered psychotherapy and other somatic therapies that help us fully reinhabit our bodies and liberate the emotions entangled in our flesh.

Once we're centered in our 3-D Ego or once the addictive behavior is stopped long enough, conscious access to the East subs becomes possible. Then we can gradually discover what our Addicts and Escapists really wanted, beneath their cravings.

A true and lasting recovery process requires us not only to stop our addictive patterns but also to cultivate access to the resources of the Self. This second, essential dimension is usually absent from the recovery agenda of addiction therapies and support groups.

We can gradually become conscious of our automatic-pilot Addicts and Escapists. We can begin to recognize our repetitive, compulsive behaviors. As we cultivate our 3-D Ego, we get better at noticing when an evasion routine is about to be launched or is already operating. We may or may not yet have the ability or the willpower to stop it, but at this point, at least, our Ego is conscious of, or even partially identified with, the East sub. We know what we're doing and know it isn't valid or consistent with who we really are. This is a major step in the recovery process. It requires the conscious cultivation of the 3-D Ego.

How does our 3-D Ego support the recovery process using the fourfold resources of the Self? Here are some examples: Our Nurturing Adult comforts our Wounded Children when they regain consciousness of the emotions and bodily states associated with our original woundings. Our Wild

Indigenous One reclaims full somatic experience of our emotions and of our sacred kinship with all members of the Earth community, including human society. Our Muse-Beloved dives for the dark treasures and meanings waiting within our wounds. Our Innocent/Sage cultivates an expanded awareness of the wounding events, placing them in a vast, consciousness-shifting context, and also brings an innocent nonattachment to outcome that enables the 3-D Ego to act in the world in ways our Addicts-Escapists had previously blocked. We'll explore all this in greater depth later in this chapter.

The East Subpersonalities
as Fragmented Versions of the Innocent/Sage

The cardinal direction of east is, of course, where the Sun rises, and so east is universally associated with light and ascension and, by association, with joy, lightheartedness, and rising above. This suggests what the East subpersonalities and the East facet of the Self have in common. Both are oriented toward the light — toward, for example, ecstasy, joy, and the Divine — and with rising above our everyday preoccupations with rules, norms, and the practical.

But whereas the East facet of the Self rises toward innocence, present-centeredness, and wisdom, the East subpersonality settles for simply getting high. While the East Self proactively reaches toward illumination and enlightenment, the East sub reactively flies above and beyond troubling emotions, relationships, and realities. The East Self transcends; the East subs escape. The East Self helps us see the bigger picture; the East subs just want a *different* picture (preferably one that feels happier, invulnerable, or at least safe). The East Self enables us to expand perception and understanding, while the East subs mostly want to alter, limit, or distort perception and understanding. The East Self possesses a mature and healthy sense of humor about the human condition, whereas the East subs display a giddiness, flippancy, or frivolity that betrays its fear or grief.

While the East facet of the Self spurs us toward greater consciousness, our East subs function by restricting consciousness. But here's the commonality: in both cases, everyday consciousness is temporarily altered, we're liberated from self-obsession, and the boundaries that separate and contain us are dissolved.

HEALING OUR RELATIONSHIPS
WITH OUR EAST SUBPERSONALITIES

The childhood survival strategies of our Escapists, Addicts, Blissheads, and Puers/Puellas do in fact protect us, to some degree, from intolerable emotions and Ego-devastating perils, and these strategies are certainly better than nothing. But they do only so well, and the price of employing them is great. When we escape the realities of our lives, we're at the same time forsaking our potential — our destiny and greatest contributions to a world in need, and consequently our personal fulfillment as well.

To make matters worse, the evasion tactics of our Addicts and Escapists often result in additional woundings of the very parts of our psyches these tactics were designed to protect: our Wounded Children. These fragile flames may have been comforted and safeguarded by the initial respite from overwhelming emotion or threatening circumstance, but our East sub evasions eventually give rise to substance addictions, for example, that lead to social rejection or medical disability; or our evasions bring about relationship failures that lead to grief and/or shame, or they result in depression and anxiety that lead to more addictions and relationship failures, and so on, all of which compound our Wounded Children's experience of vulnerability and deprivation.

So, what can you do when you have one or more East subpersonalities running much of your life?

The preliminary question, as always, concerns the War of Childhood Survival: is it over? (See "Self-Assessment: Is the War Over?" on pages 141–42, in chapter 6, for a reminder of what this means.) Do you have adequate access to the fourfold resources of your Self (explored in the first half of this book)? Do you have a sufficient social support network? If the answers to these two questions are something other than a confident yes, you'll want to seek help from someone (or an organization or community) with well-honed expertise in helping people skyjacked by their Escapists or Addicts. In the contemporary Western world, these helpers include psychotherapists (but only if they have specific training in addictions), addiction counselors, and twelve-step groups; and, if trained in the process of recovery, somatic and bodywork therapists, acupuncturists, herbalists, and spiritual advisers. You'll want to avoid any "helpers" who are Rescuers or Conformists or whose approach entails trading in your addiction or escape routines for new ones, such as alternative addictive substances (prescribed or otherwise) or the regimens of cult membership.

On the other hand, if the war is over for you, then you can be much more self-sufficient in your healing and growing. But, it must be emphasized, you'll still experience great benefit from the support of friends, mentors, professionals, and support groups.

If and only if the War of Childhood Survival is over for you, then here are seven steps I suggest in your work with your Escapists and Addicts (and their interpersonal manifestations as Blissheads and Puers/Puellas), and which I will describe in greater detail shortly:

1. Recognize that you are or have been using an Addict or Escapist strategy, name it, and make amends.
2. Abstain from the behaviors involved in your addictions and escape patterns.
3. Further cultivate the resources of your fourfold Self (develop or strengthen your 3-D Ego).
4. Experience, explore, and heal the emotions, memories, and realities your Addicts and Escapists have been helping you to avoid, and learn to respond to them from the perspective of your 3-D Ego.
5. Offer your sincere and profound gratitude to your Escapists and Addicts for their services.
6. Replace your old routines with positive habits of presence, self-encounter, and mature action.
7. Uncover, reclaim, and act on the deep longings beneath your former escapes and addictions.

The order of these steps is somewhat flexible, but generally they're best enacted as shown here. Some people will need more time or more help with some steps than with others.

1. Recognize and Name Your Addict or Escapist Strategy

The first order of business is to render fully conscious the strategy your East subpersonality has been using. (There can be more than one strategy and quite possibly more than one East sub.) Name the strategy — video games, for example, or alcohol, puer or puella high-flying, or compulsive shopping. Acknowledge how it has functioned in your life, what the price has been, and how it has affected your relationships, your job, your health. If others have suffered from your addiction or escape routines, make apologies and amends if doing so will not cause more harm. This first step begins the process of enabling your Ego to identify less with your East sub(s) and more with the Self: You affirm that you (the maturing Ego) are not the Addict or Escapist, that your East sub is part of your psychological makeup, and that you have used its strategies. And you can now choose to do otherwise.

2. Abstain from Your Addictive and Escape Patterns

Choose, then, to do otherwise. Abstain from the behaviors involved in your addiction and escape patterns. This is much easier said than done. Here, too, you may very well need help from others, especially with substance addictions, the latter being sustained in part by somatic compulsions and cravings. You must be resolved to completely cease the strategies of your East subs, not merely reduce then. You must discontinue your substance use, disable the television, delete the video game app, surrender your credit card, quit gambling, and so on. *This does not end or cure your addiction; it only stops the behaviors.* The compulsions will diminish only gradually as you continue with the following steps. If you have a relapse in this step, don't panic; instead, continue with the first two steps while you add the third (and seek help with this step).

You might find it relatively easy, or at least possible, to stop the addictive behaviors for a few weeks. But stopping for much longer than that might be somewhere between difficult and impossible, unless you have some success with further cultivation of the Self, which is the goal of the next step.

If your patterns of escape do not involve addictions to substances or activities, but are ways of directly avoiding responsibilities, emotions, conflicts, or intimacy, then your task in this step is to intentionally confront what you have been avoiding: Risk real intimacy. Surrender to the depths of your own emotions. Act on your genuine responsibilities.

3. Further Cultivate the Resources of Your Fourfold Self

Now is the time to further cultivate the resources of all four facets of your Self well beyond what you previously accomplished. When addressing your East subs, it's especially important to develop your West Self, your Muse-Beloved. (See chapter 5.)

Cultivating the fourfold Self has its own intrinsic value, of course, but you're also going to need these resources in the following steps. This work develops or strengthens your 3-D Ego. Seek help from guides, mentors, coaches, and therapists as needed.

4. Experience, Explore, and Heal the Emotions, Memories, and Realities Your Addicts and Escapists Have Been Helping You Avoid

As you leave behind the substances, activities, flights, and vanishing acts that have distanced you from yourself, others, and the world, you'll notice that the emotions, memories, and realities you've been avoiding reenter your awareness. You will, of course, be tempted to run. But you won't. This time, you won't hide behind the tried and true "solutions" of your East subs or any new substitutes. Instead, you'll call on your fourfold Self to embrace whatever appears. Again, you may need help in doing this, but if you have the capacity to remain in your 3-D Ego, your human helper(s) will primarily be supporting you in sustaining that 3-D awareness. Embracing whatever appears in your 3-D awareness means you experience the previously banished emotions, memories, and circumstances from the perspective of the Self.

Let's say, for example, that it's the experience of low self-esteem that your East sub has been protecting you from, which is to say you have a prominent but previously censored Wounded Child who feels utterly unworthy, unwanted, shameful, or defective, in part because you have Loyal Soldiers who've been criticizing you from an early age in an attempt to keep you safe from taking any significant risks. Ask your Nurturing Generative Adult to embrace your Wounded Child, as we discussed in chapter 7, fully acknowledging and empathizing with the pain of the latter's emotions and drawing out his stories. Your Nurturing Adult will also help welcome home your Loyal Soldiers, as we saw in chapter 6.

Invite, too, your Wild Indigenous One to assist you in fully feeling all your emotions and then to help you and your Loyal Soldiers experience the sacredness of this world and the truth of your belonging here.

Your Muse-Beloved can facilitate your exploration of what lies beneath your Wounded Child's feelings of worthlessness. For example, ask yourself how you were treated as a child, and what you were told about yourself. How did it serve you then to believe these things and to learn to perpetrate this emotional abuse against yourself? And then, and most essentially, what did you most long for as a child and teenager, for which you were shamed and for which you still long?

And your Innocent/Sage can help by, for example, suggesting the humor or perhaps the poetic justice in all this, or the opportunity here to heal a generations-old wound, or how your story is an instance of the pathos of the human species and that your experiencing this fully could contribute to our collective evolution, not merely your individual healing.

As you learn to use the resources of your fourfold Self to sustain awareness of your previously banished traumas, you'll notice a corresponding lessening of the compulsion to engage in your old evasion routines. Fewer circumstances will trigger these habits. This reduces the likelihood of relapse.

Although all four facets of your Self are of great benefit in embracing and healing your East subs, let's focus a bit more on your Muse-Beloved, who faces your East subs from across the circle and has both the desire and the ability to look into the dark (unknown) precincts of your life, to dwell there indefinitely, indeed to make its home in precisely those places your East subs have so carefully avoided. Your West Self can help your East subs grow roots and sink them into dark, fertile soil. In this way, you gradually become more real, like Pinocchio, the wooden puppet of the nineteenth-century children's novel. When you've been waylaid by an East sub, you're prone, like Pinocchio, to telling lies, exaggerating, and creating tall tales. Your Muse-Beloved is your onboard Blue Fairy (Pinocchio's enchanted adviser, who eventually grants him life as a real boy), your maestro for approaching and assimilating the truths of your psyche and of your world. There are treasures of insight and meaning waiting in those troubling emotions you've been sidestepping, and the relationships and circumstances you've so assiduously avoided are the ones holding the greatest opportunities for the enrichment of your everyday life. This enrichment is a big part of what your East subs have wanted all along but did not know how to achieve.

5. Offer Your Sincere and Profound Gratitude to Your Escapists and Addicts for Their Services

About here (or earlier) in your recovery process would be an excellent point at which to thank and praise your Escapists and Addicts for all the real benefits of their survival strategies. This step is similar to what you did with your Loyal Soldiers in your North sub healing work. (See chapter 6.) Your East sub survival strategies were certainly not the most mature, and you did pay a heavy price for them, but they may have saved your life psychologically or physically in one way or another. Let your East subs know what you were facing when you were younger — the traumas, the overwhelming emotions, the unrealizable and unbearable longings — and thank them for helping you to escape these experiences with the strategies they used until you were psychologically ready to assimilate them, as you are now.

6. Replace Your Old Routines with Positive Habits of Presence, Self-Encounter, and Mature Action

Now you can move on to the work of replacing your old escape routines with positive habits of presence, self-encounter, and mature action. Again, your fourfold Self is your primary resource. Here are a few examples: Your Muse-Beloved is ready to help you cultivate a wholehearted and passionate curiosity about all that is hidden, dark, or decaying in your life and the world, enabling you to discover things you would have previously experienced as horrors but now find endlessly intriguing and precious — the nightmare character, for example, becomes a vital ally to your creative expression; death becomes the wisest of spiritual guides. Your Nurturing Generative Adult is now engaged to meet your basic needs in a mature, effective, and equitable manner. Your Wild Indigenous One coaches you in the somatic and psychological ecstasies of fully experiencing your emotions and your kinship with all life. Your Innocent/Sage helps you cultivate a big-picture awareness of the circumstances you once found so threatening, along with a nonattachment to outcome as you courageously act in more mature ways. Your Self as a whole enables you to participate more fully in the world in meaningful, creative, and fulfilling ways; confront your fears; ask and offer forgiveness; deepen relationships; love more boldly; and risk offering your most precious gift to a world so much in need.

What additional ways can you imagine the fourfold Self supporting you during your process of recovery from and growing beyond escapes and addictions?

7. Uncover, Reclaim, and Act on the Deep Longings beneath Your Former Escapes and Addictions

This is the advanced work with your East subs. We'll explore this final step later in this chapter, but first some practices that will support you in the above steps.

ADDITIONAL PRACTICES FOR HEALING OUR EAST SUBPERSONALITIES

Voice Dialogue, Four-Directions Circles, Dreamwork, and Deep Imagery with Addicts or Escapists

See the appendix for these four practices for uncovering the meaning of your addictions and evasions.

An Addict/Escapist Exercise

- You'll need a minimum of an hour for this — two or three or more would be better. Bring your journal and perhaps some crayons, pastels, or colored pencils and, if you'd like, a handful of modeling clay.
- If you're not already in it, evoke the fourfold perspective of your Self (see chapters 2–5). This is essential before continuing.
- Go out and wander in a wild or semiwild place until you come across a place or a nonhuman thing with which you can fall utterly in love. To truly benefit from this exercise, you really need to find such a thing or place. You might think of it as a sacred Other. Sit there. Out loud, praise that place or thing, letting it know the ways it allures you.
- Then, in that place, fearlessly review the addictions and escapes of one of your East subs, one that is still active in your life. In your journal, describe these escapes and addictions; identify under which life circumstances they seem to be most active (what triggers them?) and what draws you to these particular strategies.
- Continuing with the perspective of your 3-D Ego, write about all that this Addict or Escapist seems to fear — what he's been trying to avoid by using the addictions and escapes you just reviewed.

- Now allow a picture of your Addict or Escapist to form in your imagination. Draw a portrait of him or, with clay, fashion a representation.

- From the consciousness of your 3-D Ego, tell your Addict or Escapist what you believe he fears and wants to avoid...and why. Tell him some relevant stories that illustrate his survival strategies that, in the past, estranged you from self, others, and the world. Thank him sincerely and deeply for his invaluable assistance in helping you survive.

- Then, let him know that you (the 3-D Ego) are choosing to be utterly present to the world because it's made of countless beguiling mysteries and numinous miracles, such as the sacred Other (the thing or place) you happen to be currently sitting with or in. Tell your Addict or Escapist why you've fallen in love with this particular Other. Let him know you've made a commitment to be available to the world as fully as possible, just as it is, despite the inevitable pain and troubling ecstasies of doing so and the unavoidable metamorphoses of an unprotected life, many of which you would not have chosen. Recite aloud for him the poem by Dawna Markova that begins this chapter. (Perhaps you'll even memorize this poem.) Let him know what resources you (the 3-D Ego) have that enable or empower your mindful and wholehearted presence to and in this world. Make a list of these resources and read them out loud every day for the next week. Your goal is to strengthen these resources, not merely end an escape pattern or addiction.

ADVANCED EAST SUBPERSONALITY WORK:
ADDICTIONS AS A PATH TO SOUL

Our Addicts and Escapists have been protecting us from experiences they imagine to be intolerable or unsurvivable, but they've also been offering us some comfort and transcendence from the humdrum. They're not only escaping *from* but also reaching *toward*. They're reaching toward something bigger, deeper, and more meaningful than ordinary, mainstream, everyday life. They're doing what they can to break into a more mystical or spiritual realm. But they don't really know how — and certainly not in a sustainable and life-enhancing way. Our addictions and escape routines are, paradoxically, both an attempt to find some sort of transcendence and a defense against truly succeeding. As strategies they are substitutions for something spiritually real, the path to which has been lost or never found by the Ego.

For example, an addiction to alcohol ("spirits") can be a substitute for cultivating a relationship with Spirit. Soldiering — escaping into the military — can serve as a life-and-death surrogate for the death-rebirth process of authentic adult initiation. Compulsive eating can stand in for the satisfying of genuine spiritual hunger. Obsessive gambling can be a better-than-nothing alternative to risking everything for the chance of a meaningful and fulfilling life. We might deceive ourselves into believing we're after a high, heroism, hunger satiation, or hard cash, but at some hidden depth of our psyches we really want to become fully human, to participate unconditionally in the world, and to offer our singular gifts to our people.

There's something we each utterly long for but are also deathly afraid of, what Rumi calls "a passion, a longing-pain."[10] We fervently yearn for an expansion of consciousness but are also terrified of obliteration. We want to transcend the small self — but without ruining it or losing it entirely.

The strategies for transcendence employed by our Escapists and Addicts may ultimately be unsuccessful and self-defeating, but these subpersonalities are at least asking the right questions. They're at least seeking something real. And when we're developmentally prepared for genuine spiritual adventure, the transcendental longings of our East subs can be an invaluable aid.

Before we consider how, I must pause again to emphasize that advanced subpersonality work can be utterly dangerous for those not psychologically and spiritually prepared. It's essential that you've cultivated dependable access to your fourfold Self before attempting the work described here. Please see the overview and cautions offered in the introductory section on advanced subpersonality work, on pages 148–50.

Advanced work with your East subs also requires that you be in a stable and dependable recovery from your addictions, especially any involving substances, which means you haven't had a relapse for at least several months, and that your former compulsions are minimal to nil.

Advanced East subpersonality work ushers you into the heart of the longing-pain your Addict-Escapists have been failing to find or perhaps avoiding even while seeking it. One approach is to sit with the following question while centered in your 3-D Ego: "What is the deeper longing from which I protected myself through my addiction, or that I *thought* I was satisfying through my addiction?" Hang out with this question as often as you can, at different times of day, in all seasons, while walking or sitting in a variety of landscapes. Don't try to figure out the answer. (It'll be the wrong one.) Instead, *invite* your longing-pain. Your goal is not an answer to a question but to fully feel your deepest longing and to let that longing happen to you. Risk the obliteration, the annihilation of your familiar sense of self. Your Muse is essential in this practice because, being the West facet of the Self, the Muse is what the East sub needs in order to realize its aspiration. Invite your Muse to respond to this question about your greatest longing-pain, offering her the opportunity to communicate through expressive arts such as watercolors, clay, collage, poetry, music, rhythm, or dance. Allow these expressions to emerge not from your strategic thinking mind but from the Westerly romantic depths of your longing. It doesn't matter if you understand what you're expressing. (It's probably better if you don't.) The important thing is to feel it and to let it have its way with you (your Ego) so that you are directly altered by the experience.

A practice likely to help is to attend your bodily sensations associated with your addictions or escapes (which you're now solidly recovering from, if you're doing this advanced work). These somatic experiences might be cravings for certain substances or activities, or they might be the somatic dimension of emotions you've avoided through addictions and escapes, or they might be bodily states you experienced when you went through withdrawal. Get to know these physical sensations without attempting to label or interpret them. Breathe into them and with them. Welcome them. Be curious about their precise sensory and kinesthetic qualities, their raw physical features. Your experience of these bodily states will begin to shift. Let this happen. Deepen your curiosity. Track the sensations as they change. Ask your Muse to help you with metaphors that capture your experience of the sensations. If strong emotions arise, let them happen to you and to your body without attempting to suppress them, hurry them, or interpret them. If memories appear, track them; record them in your journal.

If, while in the midst of advanced East sub work, longings appear for experiences of the sacred, mystical, or spiritual, feed these longings. Encourage them. Let the longing-pain happen to you. Let it transform you. This is the yearning of your Self and Soul to burst out of the limiting shell of the everyday persona or Ego. As India's mystic poet Kabir says, "It is the intensity of the longing...that does all the work."[11] Let it.

As these deeper longings emerge into consciousness, reclaim each one fully. Take it back into your body and into your life, learn to trust and believe in it again. And, finally, act on it: live your longing, boldly and wildly. Fill any emptiness inside you with this longing. This is a radical act leading to deep fulfillment, an ecstasy that only now can you bear to experience and live. Your true longings will usher you into the sheer beauty and frightening consequences of your Soul's passions, an experience that would previously have terrified you — perhaps driving you to addictions and escapes.

Advanced East sub work breaks you out of the flatland of a middle-world-only life and into the underworld of Soul and the upperworld of Spirit.

WALKING INTO THE FIRE

With advanced East subpersonality work, if it goes well and deep enough, you'll discover something about your Soul gifts, gifts that are sometimes entangled in and partially hidden or obscured by your deepest and earliest (and often preconscious) emotional wounds and their somatic expressions.

A sixty-year-old woman — I'll call her Wendy (as in Peter Pan's sidekick) — had been sober and in recovery for twenty-one years. She wondered if there were aspects of her early wounding, previously covered up by her alcohol use, that she had not explored and whether this might be inhibiting her full engagement with Self and Soul. Her underworld guide — I'll call him Peter — suggested to her that her alcoholism might not be an either/or thing, not just wound-evasion — that there might be hidden dimensions and gifts in it, maybe some archetypal potentials. Peter invited her to take a long, wandering walk with her Addict, to get to know this East sub and what she, the Addict, really wanted. At first, this invitation terrified Wendy, who feared endangering her long-running sobriety. But she also suspected her fear might be illuminating exactly what she needed to do. This realization tipped the scales. Through her Self-awareness, Wendy understood that one of her Loyal Soldiers was trying to keep her from getting to know her Addict, and that, after so many years of sobriety, she was actually fully prepared to walk into the fire.

Grounded in her fourfold Self, Wendy wandered out into the desert and invited her Addict to walk with her. In Wendy's deep imagination (roused by the West facet of her Self, her Muse), her Addict appeared in the form of a drunken hag. Wendy sat down with her journal:

> I began writing what the Drunken One of Me had been like and out poured all the negative, unattractive behaviors: out-of-control, demanding, critical, unreliable, self-absorbed, full of self-loathing and shame. But as I listed these traits, a shift came: The Drunken One of Me loves drama and intensity, longs for more of everything, longs for love. I began to uncover a deep longing under the numbing of alcohol. I found myself writing, "Rumi calls himself a drunk — the one intoxicated on God." In that moment, an unexpected link was forged from my East Addict to my West Guide to Soul. I wrote: "The Drunken One of Me is drunk on wildness, thirsty for the fires of mystery, thirsting for the touch of the Wild Beloved." A few more lines and then an image of Baubo emerged — the erotic, sensuous hag of the Demeter myth. Shocking, dancing with her big boobs rocking, her hips rolling, her dirty bare feet pounding the sweet earth. "Yes!" I wrote, "This is the wild kind of drunkenness I don't let myself get close to or allow others to see in me."
>
> Later, I went looking for images of the Drunken Hag and collected photographs of beautiful, strange, old women from cultures around the world. Flamboyant old women smoking cigars.

Wendy was discovering her Drunken Hag to possess an unsuspected resource of the greatest value — a wild, exuberant, and embodied freedom of expression, a natural capacity of her Wild Indigenous One, the South facet of her Self. This exuberant self-expression was a key to her deepest longing. She began to fall in love with her "strange, scruffy old Hag." Some months later, in a redrock canyon in the American Southwest, she writes,

> I walked alone among voluptuous stones with my Drunken Hag and also my Loyal Soldier, who so wants to keep her out of sight. I wanted to get naked in the Hag's body and dance in the open under that wide sky. To my Loyal Soldier, I said: "Thank you for all the ways you've

clothed me over the years, helping me to belong in human company. You've taught me how to follow the rules and wear the right face. But I seek a new kind of belonging now, with the Earth and wildness and a true self. I need you to be my guardian warrior. Warn me of real dangers, not false ones. Help me know how to take care of myself." I danced. And, afterward, I proclaimed aloud, "I take you in, Old Drunken Hag of a Woman of Me! Let your fire break loose in me!"

Wendy discovered an extraordinary depth of authenticity in her Addict, as if her capacity for wild and embodied expression had been stowed away for years (perhaps in her Shadow) and was now reclaimable.

But the story goes deeper yet: Wendy's cultivation of her Wild Indigenous One enabled her, in turn, to develop a relationship with her Muse and eventually with her Inner Beloved — two aspects of the West facet of her Self:

> The more I went out onto the land, taking all of me into conversation there, making ceremony again and again, grieving, playing, relishing the beauty of wild nature, feeling my embodied self against the sweet, often difficult body of Earth, the writer of me was deeply nourished and inspired. The Muse became more insistent and visible. I began to put my writing out into the world — a gesture of offering to the Universe, of taking this part of myself earnestly, of claiming the gift.

But Wendy was still unclear about who her Inner Beloved might be or what her Soul gifts were. Some months later, she camped alone in the red-rock desert as a ceremonial invitation to her Inner Beloved.

> When I awoke the sky was pale. The birds were singing off someplace amid the scrub. I sat up, leaned into the wall of stone, and wept. Suddenly [I was] flooded with longing and grief for all that had not come in the night...for the Beloved, for the dreaded Shadow, for the terrible transformation I'd come for and feared to find. I cried out to my Beloved whoever this one might be. I cried out to the Shadow hiding between the rocks. Oh, Beloved, Beloved, come!...
>
> Then, amid the tears, I knew the one I had been seeking, I knew the one they call the Inner Beloved. For the first time, I knew the one I have for so long called The Poet. The Poet! The one who gives me eyes to see the world, who gives me language for the beauty and

terror, the one who connects me to the sacred depths of things, of myself. Suddenly this One, so loved, so little known!

There would be rain later and deep tears of wonder and gratitude. But in those early moments of the day I felt fresh, spare, welcomed. The Poet is with me. Holy Grace. I didn't know!

A person with a 3-D Ego eventually chooses such a courageous encounter with her Addicts and Escapists simply because she refuses to "die an unlived life," just as Dawna Markova refused. The poet chooses to no longer live in fear of falling, but, instead "to loosen [her] heart / until it becomes a wing." She chooses to step beyond her fear of catching fire and to instead allow her liberated heart to become a torch. She "risk[s her] significance" so that her Soul seed might blossom and be offered to the world as Soul fruit.

Chapter 9

West

THE SHADOW AND SHADOW SELVES

The range of what we think and do
is limited by what we fail to notice.
And because we fail to notice
that we fail to notice
there is little we can do
to change
until we notice
how failing to notice
shapes our thoughts and deeds.

— DANIEL GOLEMAN

Sinister Shadow, appearing in a dream: Harriet, a woman who never gets angry, dreams once again of being stalked by an ax murderer.

Sinister Shadow, projected: Jack, an antiabortion extremist who thinks of himself as "pro-life," gives serious consideration to terminating the life of an abortion-providing physician in his community.

Golden Shadow, projected: Rachel is waiting for her flight to board. A man sits down across from her. Their eyes meet. Her heart beats wildly. She's certain he must be the true love, her one and only soul mate. She nearly keels over with anticipation.

Shadow Self, acted out: Richard, a mild-mannered, middle-aged, teetotal, churchgoing, married accountant, awakens in an unfamiliar room with a bad headache. Then he remembers the party, the tequila, the nearly naked dancing, and what happened after. He's quite certain he must have been possessed, that this could not have been him, that the devil made him do it.

Sinister Shadow, projected: Donald, president of the United States, refers to the Soviet Union as "the Evil Empire"...and actually believes this is true.

What We Fail to Notice

The Shadow, one of the archetypes identified by psychologist Carl Jung, is composed of those elements of our own psyches that are unknown to us.

It's essential to understand at the outset that the Shadow is not what we know about ourselves, don't like, and keep hidden. Rather, the Shadow is what is true about us that we don't know — don't know at all — and, if accused of it, would adamantly and sincerely deny.

The purpose of the Shadow is to protect us from enacting personal characteristics that, if expressed, might land us in big trouble with others or ourselves. We stuff these forbidden parts of ourselves in a corner of our psyches where we can't find them, where we can "fail to notice" them, as Daniel Goleman describes it, writing in the form of a "knot," as originally developed by antipsychiatrist R. D. Laing in the 1970s.[1]

The aspects of ourselves we do know but keep hidden (whether we like these aspects or not) are not part of the Shadow. For example, if you're sloppy or cowardly, you might go to great lengths to appear neat or courageous, but neither sloppiness nor cowardice is in your Shadow. Rather, such aspects of your personality are well known by your Ego and consciously hidden, suppressed, or masked. Perhaps you're sloppy because you have a Rebel (a South sub) who resents all those childhood years when your military father enforced perfect order in your bedroom. You might now have, within your own internal military, a Loyal Soldier (a North sub) who fears you'll never make a friend or get a date unless you're immaculate. Or perhaps you're cowardly because of a Victim sub (South) terrified of experiencing more abuse like that which you suffered in childhood at the hands of your older brother, and now you have an Addict (an East sub) who gets you to drink whiskey until your fear is muted and you're able to take big social or physical risks that impress your friends with your heroism. These are not instances of Shadow.

Or maybe you live in California and love to hunt elk, but you keep this passion completely hidden from your local vegetarian, animal-rights friends. Once a year you go hunting in Montana, but you fib and tell your friends you're visiting your parents in New Jersey. This is not your Shadow.

The Shadow is what our psyches repress (render unconscious), not what our Egos suppress (consciously hide from others).

Many people think their Shadow is composed of their characteristics that are "dark" or "shadowy," in the sense of behaviors considered by many to be unacceptable, like adultery, gambling, vulgar language, or drug use. But if you know these things about yourself, they're not in your Shadow, and this is not the way in which the Shadow is dark, anyway. Whether or not the elements of your Shadow are socially unacceptable, they are dark simply in the sense that they're unknown (at least to you). They're hidden in the unlit recesses of your psyche.

Much of what's in the Shadow is in fact socially unacceptable, and that's likely why these things are there, but that's not what defines them as Shadow. Many other elements of the Shadow are entirely acceptable socially, but not personally acceptable to the Ego.

The Shadow is whatever the Ego isn't. The Shadow is what's true about who you really are, but you haven't a clue about it. The Shadow is the buried rage in a man who never met anyone he didn't love. It's the ax murderer in Harriet's dreams. It's the misogynist who might be secretly loitering within the psyche of a feminist. It's your own goodness and magnificence you don't see in yourself but do see in others. It's Rachel's own golden qualities she sees in the men she falls in love with. It's the killer in "pro-life" Jack. It's the Tyrant subpersonality within President Donald who perpetrates world-class terrorism (which he calls "waging a just war" or even "maintaining the peace") using carcinogenic depleted-uranium munitions and civilian-slaughtering drone assassins against a country he claims is harboring and supporting terrorists or that he believes to be an Evil Empire or part of an Axis of Evil. The Shadow is what you fail to notice about yourself.

This is difficult to accept and digest — that there are aspects or parts of ourselves we really don't know and that are completely at odds with who we think we are. Even when our other subpersonalities — those of the North, South, and East — act unconsciously (independently of our Egos), we still know them by how they affect our lives, thoughts, and deeds. Perhaps we don't acknowledge them to others, but we do know them. Not so for the elements of the Shadow. The Shadow is *always* unconscious.

There are at least three ways in which the elements of the Shadow can be true about you. One is that your eroticism, to take one example, is fully repressed. In addition to being totally unaware of your own erotic nature, it's also not expressed in any way in your behavior. Yet it's still part of who you are, and still waiting for you to discover and reclaim it someday, although this might never happen. A second way is that your eroticism is in fact expressed in your behavior, at least sometimes, but you're completely unaware of it and would deny it if accused (or complimented). If someone were to point out the erotic way you touch skin or silk or the seductive cut of your clothes, you'd sincerely believe they were mistaken, guilty in fact of wildly distorting reality. What they see as erotic, you understand as something completely different — say, as tenderness or a casual manner. A third possibility is that whether or not your repressed eroticism is expressed unconsciously in your behavior, when you observe others who are openly erotic in their personal style, you secretly wish you were like them, at least a little. Outwardly, you might approve of their eroticism or condemn it, but either way you have no doubt that you're not the least bit like them in this way.

Shadow characteristics can be either negative (what the Ego would consider "beneath" it) or positive (what the Ego would consider "above" it). We might call these the Sinister Shadow and the Golden Shadow, respectively.

The Golden Shadow contains traits our Egos regard as too positive to conceivably be ours, qualities we consider highly virtuous, elevated, or otherwise exemplary — selfless generosity, perhaps, or poetic eloquence, or creative urges like spontaneous public singing. Why does the Shadow contain positive qualities? The Shadow is always the opposite of the Ego, and the Ego includes some destructive, self-deprecating, and antisocial attitudes (especially when the Ego is identified with certain Loyal Soldier, Wounded Child, and Addict subpersonalities). We might have been abandoned or punished as children, for example, if we expressed positive qualities our parents considered inappropriate to their social standing or that made them uncomfortable or envious. The Shadow contains all aspects of the psyche inconsistent with the Ego, whether judged good or bad.[2]

When we suddenly fall in love, like Rachel, we're likely experiencing our Golden Shadow in or as another. When we experience a spiritual teacher as perfect and divine, we're probably projecting our own holiness. Our Golden Shadow is as dangerous to our Egos as is our Sinister Shadow. And when we project it on other people, our Golden Shadow can be as dangerous to them as it is to us, because they might assume it's actually true about them, leading to ego inflation and all the trouble they might float or fly into as a result.

THE SHADOW AND SHADOW SELVES

Our West subpersonalities try to keep us safe (physically, psychologically, socially, or economically) either by repressing (making unconscious) our unacceptable or inconceivable characteristics and desires (this is the function of the Shadow) or by briefly acting out these characteristics and doing so flamboyantly or scandalously, but without our being conscious of what we're doing. The latter are our Shadow Selves, which attempt to maintain some psychological stability by letting off steam as the only available alternative to complete self-destruction, as did Richard, the accountant, on his wild night, which he thinks of as his demonic dive into debauchery. Our Shadow and our Shadow Selves are the intrapersonal dimensions of our West subpersonalities, as shown in map 1.

Our interpersonal versions of our wounded West (see map 2) are the social roles we play (or are seen by others as playing) when we're possessed by our Shadow Selves. Common Western-culture versions of these roles include Sinister ones that might be identified as monsters, demons, perverts, satyrs, whores, vampires, and villains, but also Golden ones such as heroes, gods or goddesses, idols, and gurus. When possessed, we wouldn't identify ourselves in these ways — at least not at the time — but others are likely to experience us in ways that elicit these labels.

When possessed by a Shadow Self, we enact these roles without wanting to and without any clarity at the time about what we're doing. Other people, of course, enact these roles quite deliberately and consciously. When they do, it's not Shadow possession but rather a chosen role, or an embodied subpersonality (perhaps a Wounded Child, Loyal Soldier, Rescuer, Tyrant, or Puer/Puella), or what may be called a conscious archetypal possession (enacting a potential that exists in all human psyches but that is rarely embodied in one's culture or community), or any combination of the three.

"The Long Bag We Drag behind Us"

As I've been suggesting, people naturally strong in one facet of the Self are often weak in the facet on the opposite side of the circle. A strong West facet suggests a weak East facet. In addition, someone naturally strong in the West facet, the Muse-Beloved, is often prone to heavy reliance upon their West subpersonalities, their Shadow and Shadow Selves, in part because their East Self, the Innocent/Sage, is underdeveloped and unavailable to provide its wisdom, light, humor, and nonattachment to balance out the West subs' heaviness, overreaction, darkness, and denial. As we'll see, the East Self provides an essential key to the healing or liberation of the West's Shadow elements.

The Shadow contains the elements of our psyches that our Egos have rejected and labeled "not me," "evil," "bad," or perhaps "divine." Through Shadow work, we have the opportunity to reclaim some of these banished shades. Just as Lucifer is said to be God's fallen angel, our Shadows hold essential but exiled components of our wholeness, lost elements of the Self.

We each have a personal Shadow, but each culture, nation, and ethnic group has a collective Shadow, too. Perhaps it makes sense to say that even the human species as a whole has a Shadow — what almost everyone doesn't know about our species and would be horrified to discover (if we could).

Most elements of your personal Shadow — your wildness, say, or your carnality, daredevil proclivities, or telepathic capacities — are invaluable personal resources that were unconsciously disowned and repressed during childhood and early adolescence in your psyche's attempts (successful or not) to win acceptance from your family and peers. Far from being a mistake, this involuntary self-rejection and downsizing were necessary in order to form a socially adaptive Ego and personality, your first identity. Later, to grow whole, you must descend into those dark dominions to retrieve the vital, lost pieces of yourself.

Your Shadow contains values, perspectives, and capacities needed to round out and complete your adult personality. It contains personal powers you'll need when you befriend or wrestle with the inner and outer demons and angels encountered in the process of growing whole, and it holds the powers you'll need in order to embody the singular Soul gift you carry for the world.

How might Richard's life be enriched, for example, if he were able to access and cultivate his Wild Indigenous One (instead of unconsciously acting it out in juvenile, tequila-fueled ways)? What creative projects and fulfilling relationships might Harriet be capable of if she were to liberate and cultivate the bold assertiveness currently hidden (and dreadfully distorted) as the ax murderer of her nightmares? How might President Donald be humbled and softened by finding the "evil" in himself and in his own country rather than belligerently projecting it onto other, less militarily mighty nations he preemptively invades? How might the world be blessed by a change in his policies from military threat and conquest to true peacemaking and international cooperation?

Poet Robert Bly maintains we spend the first twenty years of our life stuffing 90 percent of our wholeness into "the long bag we drag behind us" and the rest of our life attempting to retrieve these items.[3] The bag is quite full. We drag it behind us, like our literal shadow, because we tend to walk toward the light. Because it's behind us, we can't see or understand its contents. It's always there with us because it is, after all, a part of us, despite our inability to acknowledge it.

How did all those rejected elements of our wholeness get into that long bag in the first place? Our Loyal Soldiers, early in life, were usually the ones wielding the shovels, the ones in charge of this Ego-downsizing operation.[4]

Or, to evoke another metaphor, think of Loyal Soldiers as part-time psychic bouncers who toss out of consciousness any elements of our psyches not deemed respectable by the management. The boss, in this case, is every child's family and cultural setting (and sometimes the Self). When the boss spots an undesirable, a Loyal Soldier tosses it out onto the street, and the Shadow police swoop in, haul it off, lock it up in Shadow jail, and throw away the key.[5]

But it's possible, later in life, to free these prisoners of our selves, to reclaim them. And even before we reclaim them, we might at least be able to remember that there is in fact an inner prison and that we have relatives in there, both Sinister and Golden.

Before being reclaimed, the elements of our Sinister Shadow tend to show up in guises our Egos regard as disagreeable and frightening. Often they appear as scary or unpleasant dreamworld characters, like Harriet's ax murderer. We also see them as dayworld people onto whom we project our own socially unacceptable traits, such as greed, cowardice, rage, weakness, arrogance, or cruelty. Sometimes we project our Sinister Shadow elements onto people of different-colored skin or from other nations or with different religious beliefs. We project these elements onto other-than-human nature, too: perhaps dark forests, swamps, tornadoes, wolves, bats, or snakes. And they turn up, of course, in the mythologies of all cultures in such guises as hairy beasts, werewolves, harpies, minotaurs, gorgons, and fire-breathing dragons.

The reason why elements of our Sinister Shadow seem so frightening upon first approach is this: When we banish a part of our self and lock it away in a prison or a closet for many years, it becomes angry, funky, bizarre, wild. (Wouldn't you?) Should we ever unlock the door, it rages at first. Demons become demons through their long imprisonment. But when we find the courage to really look at our disowned parts, they begin to shift shape. They often need only to be honored, heard, allowed to speak.

The initial goals of working with our Sinister Shadow are to uncover our unacknowledged negative traits, take responsibility for them, learn to soften or eliminate them, and cease to project them onto others. In this way, we're less likely to unconsciously undermine our relationships and opportunities. The objective of this foundational Shadow work is a neutralized Sinister Shadow and a healthier personality that functions better socially.

The more advanced goal of Sinister Shadow work, which we'll explore at the end of this chapter, is to get to know our Shadow elements intimately — so thoroughly and courageously that we uncover at their hearts psychospiritual resources we need in order to live our true life, to embody our Soul.

We often discover that our Sinister Shadow holds something sacred: our deepest passion. Perhaps it's a longing to dance, to create magic, to sing, or to love with abandon. When we're young, we name our passion something else — so we can more easily repress it. We name it foolish, selfish, odd, crazy, or evil. This mislabeling and repression protect us from social injury — from being rejected or marginalized by our family, peers, or community.

TRACKING DOWN ELEMENTS OF YOUR SHADOW

Given that Shadow is what you don't know about yourself and what you would, if confronted, steadfastly and honestly deny, how on Earth can you ever learn anything about it? How do you track down something you can't see and have every (unconscious) reason not to notice? All you can go on are shadowy clues. Where do you look for such clues? Your task is somewhat like searching for a never-before-seen, merely rumored, nocturnal animal. Actually, your mission is even more implausible than that — not only do you not know exactly what you're looking for, and not only is it the case that what you're looking for does not want to be found, but also, worse yet, you don't really want to find it.

Still, if you insist on seeking your Shadow, there's only one thing you can do: you must root around wherever you can for telltale signs. Where do you look? As Rumi notes, "Everybody's scandalous flaw is mine."[6] If you see scandalous flaws (or prodigious virtuosity) in others, those are great places to investigate. Harriet, if she's clever, is going to get awfully curious about the ax murderer of her dreams. Jack, the antiabortionist, will, at last, hunt for the killer in himself instead of the one he believes to be working at the clinic. President Donald, in a rare flash of insight, will decide to spend some truly intimate time with Iranians (or Iraqis, al-Qaeda jihadists, or the Taliban) and perhaps in this way find the humanity in the others and the "evil" in himself.

Before generalizing and elaborating, first a definition: projection is the unconscious transfer of your own emotions, desires, or traits onto another person (your "screen") or sometimes onto a whole class of persons. For example, people of one nation or ethnicity might project evil onto those of another, a man with repressed eroticism might experience certain others as lecherous but himself as hardly even amorous, or a woman CFO with three advanced degrees might criticize a female candidate for U.S. president as ruthlessly power hungry. The pot calls the kettle black. The invaluable thing about projection and screens is that they provide the opportunity to discover something about yourself through what you see in others. The process of projection is like looking in a psyche-revealing mirror — except at first we don't know it's a mirror; we think we're simply seeing someone else.

How do you know, then, when you're projecting? How do you know when what you see in another is true about *you* (whether or not you also happen to be right about the other)? Your primary clue is the intensity of the emotional reaction you have to that other person, especially when he or she is someone you don't know well, or at all, and especially when you have reason to believe relatively few people have quite the same emotional reaction — or such an intense one — to that person.

But projections are only one of the realms in which you might turn up elements of your Shadow. Here's a more complete list of some of the classic places to look, places that include dreams, strong emotions, myths and stories, archetypes, and denial, as well as projections:

- Dream characters (especially from nightmares) who spark a strong emotional charge in you, positive or negative or both, characters you'd swear you're not *anything* like (as did Harriet)
- People in your dayworld life to whom you have a strong emotional reaction (not just people you detest but also those you admire or fall in love with)
- The qualities of your over-the-top ideal romantic partner
- Personal qualities most of your best friends have in common but you believe you don't posses at all
- Other-than-human creatures or aspects of nature to which you strongly react[7]
- Villains or other characters from literature, film, or myth you feel are thoroughly despicable
- Heroes or other characters you feel are exceptionally admirable
- Strongly negative and/or positive feelings about people of different genders, professions, cultures, races, religions, nations, or political parties
- Deeply disturbing characters from your deep-imagery journeys
- Your most despised or revered archetypes, icons, or celebrities
- The antithesis of your personal characteristics that disturb you the most (For example, disturbed by your own shyness? What is the antithesis of your shyness? Perhaps aggressive self-assertion?)

- Your episodes of acting so unlike yourself, so bizarrely, that you swear afterward it could not have been you who did it (as happened to Richard)
- Your episodes of extreme emotional overreactions to events
- The three words used to describe you, in an article you imagine appearing in one of the world's most prestigious magazines — words that would destroy you, shame you, send you into a rage, render you suicidal
- Anything you've been accused of (by a friend or family member, including your own child) that you steadfastly believe could not possibly be less true about you
- The way you would complete this sentence: "The one thing absolutely not true about me is…!"
- The antithesis of the one thing that you feel is absolutely true about you

None of the items in this list are guaranteed indicators of Shadow. They're simply fruitful places to look.

But how, then, do you know if one of these shadowy hideouts has yielded the real thing? Simple: You treat it as if it is in fact an element of your Shadow and see what happens. If it's truly Shadow and you get psychologically close to it, dangerously intimate, you're likely to experience some intense emotions and memories and have a number of extraordinary insights. Lots of trapped vitality will eventually be released, which is to say you'll notice some substantial new degrees of freedom in your life.

This leaves the question "How, exactly, do you treat something as if it is an element of your Shadow for the purpose of discovering if it really is?" I'll offer several suggestions shortly.

It's important to keep in mind, when you first uncover an element of your Sinister Shadow, this does *not* reveal that you are socially unacceptable, immature, sinful, loathsome, villainous, black hearted, or demonic, and that you must immediately repent, reform, or change yourself in order to eliminate or suppress your negative qualities. (Well, at least it doesn't *necessarily* mean this, and, even if it does, this is not the primary meaning.) It does mean that here is an element of your psyche you have the opportunity to explore in order to, eventually, find and retrieve the resource it holds for you. As we'll see in this chapter, you've been given the chance to become more whole.

Likewise, when you encounter a piece of your Golden Shadow, you don't simply and immediately get to embody it. It will always take a lot of work (not necessarily a lot of time) and will, inconveniently, require a type of dying, because your ego-identity has been constructed in opposition to all that's in your Shadow, Golden as well as Sinister.

PROJECTION AND TRANSFERENCE

I defined *projection* earlier, but there's a special case essential to mention now: when what we project onto another is not our disowned characteristics but rather an "unfinished" relationship from our past. Unconsciously projecting an old relationship onto a current one is called transference. Perhaps we experience and treat a current lover, professor, or therapist, for example, in a way similar to how we experienced and treated our mother or father or someone else from childhood — a teacher or another child with whom we were infatuated — but we don't realize that's what we're doing or that's why we feel the way we do. The old relationship is unfinished in the sense that there was something we didn't have the capacity to be or do in that relationship, and this inability contributed to what made the relationship challenging, inconclusive, unfulfilling, and perhaps traumatic or tragic. There's some capacity or resource we didn't have then that, had we had it, we would not have been so limited or harmed by that relationship or felt so incomplete. If we have yet to sufficiently cultivate that resource, and if it's a vital one for our growing whole, something in our psyche will search our current life for someone with whom we can enter into a new relationship that has dynamics similar to the old one's. Doing so grants us the opportunity to "get it right" — to complete the old relationship in the present one. Until we're able to do this, we'll forever find ourselves in relationships that have the same tired dynamics — despite our ardent vow to never end up there again.

When we fall in love, launch a new friendship, or choose to become someone's student or therapy client, we're often entering a transference relationship but don't know it at the time (if ever). Our first clue will be the suspiciously strong emotional reaction (positive, negative, or both) we have to the other.

In our healing work with both "regular" projections and the transference variety, the goal is to "own back" our projections. We do this by experiencing precisely how the characteristic that we've projected onto another is true about us and/or how our current relationship dynamic is a repeat of an old one. We do the work of making conscious what was previously unconscious: With a projection, we own up to having acted in the same way we believe our screen acted, or to having secretly wanted to act that way. We make whatever apology, amends, or restitution might be relevant and appropriate. With an acknowledged transference, we cease to blame our current other for the challenges in our relationship and instead begin to cultivate the ability or resource that we lacked and needed in the old relationship (and now need in the current one).

Owning back our projection and/or transference results in our greatly enhanced empathy and appreciation for the other, opening up the possibilities of (1) a transformed relationship, (2) greater self-compassion, and (3) the opportunity to shift our behavior in other relationships, too. These three possibilities become actualities only through the hard work of cultivating a new relationship with self and other. The real benefits result from this hard work, not simply from any (relatively easy) insight.

When we project something of our Sinister Shadow onto another person, we typically dislike or even detest that person, as you might imagine. But it's also possible to admire our Sinister screens or find them surprisingly attractive. For example, if you see yourself as compassionate and self-sacrificing but have a repressed subpersonality that is egotistical and aggressively self-promoting, and you project this sub onto another person, you could end up marveling at or falling in love with that person.

Likewise, it's entirely possible to project your Golden Shadow — say, your repressed beauty, brilliance, or gregariousness — onto someone and find yourself despising that person as a result of envy that is unconscious... or at least very difficult to understand.

THE WEST SUBPERSONALITIES AS FRAGMENTED VERSIONS OF THE MUSE-BELOVED

Owing to the fact that it's where the Sun sets every day everywhere in the world, the west is cross-culturally linked with a shift into darkness and descent and, by association, a plunging into the unknown, the unconscious, dreams, the deep imagination, and even decay or death. This reveals what is held in common by the West subpersonalities and the West facet of the Self. The West subs are every bit as immersed in the unknown and the depths as is the West Self.

The difference is that the West Self, the Muse-Beloved, enables us to be in conscious relationship with these hidden realms, whereas the Shadow is designed to thwart and prevent exactly that, whether or not we're really ready for that conscious relationship. The Muse-Beloved enables us to reclaim and manifest (for ourselves, our people, and our world) what we find in the dark — the symbols, insights, meanings, dreams, myths, visions, and revelations. The West facet of the Self affords us the capacity to understand ourselves more deeply and to more fully appreciate our place in the world and our potential contributions to it. The Muse-Beloved empowers us to recognize, explore, and celebrate all that is mysterious, magical, and sacred, all that we find alluring and profoundly fascinating, including other humans.

But the depths into which the West Self ushers us can be overwhelming and dangerous to us (our Ego) and to our mainstream cultural world, so dangerous that there is a part of our psyche — the Shadow — that exists to protect us from this very realm. The Shadow not only protects us (our Ego) from the depths but also holds its dark treasures in safekeeping for us until we're ready and able to reclaim them. The resources warehoused in our Shadow are potent. They can be used for good or for ill. Our Shadow not only safeguards us from these powers but also defends our communities from the damage we're capable of inflicting before we possess the maturity and experience to employ these powers wisely. Without the repression-rendering resources of the Shadow, human life might simply be impossible. What does this suggest to you about our miraculous human psyches and consciousness?

HEALING OUR RELATIONSHIPS WITH OUR WEST SUBPERSONALITIES: SHADOW WORK

The Shadow keeps the lid on elements of our psyche that are dangerous to our Ego, yes, but it can keep that lid on too tight or too long. Many of the psychological resources we need in order to cocreate more fulfilling relationships or to perform our most creative work in the world are impounded in the dungeon of our psyche. The Shadow helps ensure our survival, but it also impedes our blossoming, often rendering our life into a series of so many dull days for want of the imaginative possibilities and visionary resources trapped and held in the long bag we drag behind us.

And it's actually worse than that. As we've seen, one way the Shadow keeps the lid on all those aspects of the psyche that would overwhelm the Ego is by projecting these characteristics onto other people and groups (so that we're less likely to see these characteristics in ourselves). But these projections often have a way of backfiring: For example, when we treat our screens as if our Sinister Shadow projections are true about them, our screens tend to experience this as irritating or offensive, for some reason (go figure). Our screens often retaliate, triggering a Wounded Child within us. In this fashion, a part of our psyche (the wounded South) that our Shadow had been protecting is now actually harmed, perhaps setting off the alarms (and survival strategies) of our Loyal Soldiers (North) or our Addicts and Escapists (East), and so on, the whole ramshackle castle potentially crumbling.

Then there are our Shadow Selves. When we unintentionally act out elements of our Shadow — as a last-ditch, unconscious means of venting inner pressure that could destroy us otherwise — we often cause further wounding to ourselves (and others). When, for example, the "family values" preacher gets drunk and caught in the midst of an extramarital dalliance, this enactment may have saved his life in one way, but in another way it ruins it (and perhaps those of his wife and kids, too) — even if "the devil made him do it." Even if we, as soulcentric observers, believe that getting caught is the best thing that could have happened to the preacher (now he might finally get real), you can bet that his Ego has been devastated by this event, and it's the Ego's safety, after all, that the Shadow (and the other subs) have been trying to protect all along.

The worst scenario by far would be to live in a community with no human Shadows at all — where everyone, no matter how immature, has totally empty bags, the contents strewn everywhere. This would be a community in the process of self-destruction. Second worst would be to have everyone's Shadow tightly sealed within impregnable long bags. (Think stereotypical 1950s America.) The downside to this conjectural scenario is mind-numbing dullness, and, besides, those long bags always turn out to have holes in them. Best is to have healthy human communities in which those who have truly matured (rare in the Western world today) are in the process of uncovering and assimilating elements of their Shadows.

Given the great psychological and social price we pay for the services of our Shadow and Shadow Selves, how might we uncover Shadow elements and integrate them in a way that enhances our wholeness and relationships or at least minimizes the damage they would otherwise wreak?

First my standard caution, but this time amplified: It's best not to attempt Shadow work unless you have excellent access to the fourfold resources of your Self. Short of this, you'll want to at least be working with someone who has established expertise in guiding others into and out of these dark precincts. Ideally, before commencing Shadow work, you'll be confident your War of Childhood Survival is over, and you'll have available both your inner resources and some outer guidance. (The war's end does not mean you no longer catch yourself using childhood survival strategies; it only means you have the inner and outer resources needed to nurture yourself and to be nurtured in the face of harsh criticism or abandonment by someone who matters to you. See "Self-Assessment: Is the War Over?" in chapter 6, pages 141–42, for a more complete reminder of what it means for the war to be over.)

In subpersonality healing work, the West seems to afford the most challenging and hazardous opportunities. When approaching the Shadow, you can truly be blindsided by what you fail to notice, which is what the Shadow is by definition. Even with a decent degree of Self-cultivation, your Ego can get profoundly overwhelmed by what your Shadow brings forth. It's best to have adequate support before entering these dungeons.[8]

Shadow work requires dependable access to all four facets of your Self, but especially important are the perspectives and capacities of your East Self, the Innocent/Sage. You need your East's wisdom, light, humor, and nonattachment in order to successfully address the heaviness and darkness in your Shadow and the Ego's denial and overreaction to it. When you approach your Sinister Shadow, your first glimpse can be horrifying and repulsive. You need your Sage to remind you that the truth beneath what you're seeing is not nearly so bad as it first looks, and that there is in fact an invaluable resource waiting within. Your East's sense of humor about this terribly serious business of exhuming crypts could come in handy. And when you're dusting off a piece of your Golden Shadow and beginning, perhaps, to puff up with it, there's nothing like your Sacred Fool or Trickster to help you get over yourself.

In addition, you'll need your Nurturing Generative Adult to care for your Wounded Children, who will be emotionally activated by what emerges from the Shadow. You'll hope your Wild Indigenous One is available to help you viscerally experience all the evoked emotions and to rejoice over the way every formerly repressed element is actually a vital and honored piece of your humanity and animality. And your Muse-Beloved (a.k.a. Guide to Soul) is, after all, your in-house connoisseur of dungeon diving.

Your first step in Shadow work is to identify the location of a possible element of your Shadow, perhaps by following the clues noted in the earlier section "Tracking Down Elements of Your Shadow." In other words, to begin, you need some evidence that you may indeed have found an element of your Shadow in a dream, relationship, emotion, or waking experience. Next, select one or more methods for treating this phenomenon as if it is in fact an element of your Shadow, with the intention of discovering if it really is. What follows is an introduction to an array of possible methods:

ADDITIONAL PRACTICES FOR SHADOW WORK (HEALING OUR WEST SUBPERSONALITIES)

The goal in the Shadow work practices offered here is to simply *be* with a potential element of your Shadow, to experience it and interact with it. If you approach this primarily as a treasure hunt, you'll be trying to figure out how you might benefit from the encounter and, as a result, relying too much on your strategic mind; consequently, you'll be unlikely to benefit at all. The primary goal of Shadow work is to be directly changed by the encounter, not to acquire information about your Shadow or yourself.

Voice Dialogue, Four-Directions Circles, Dreamwork, and Deep Imagery with the Shadow

Consult the appendix for these four ways of shining light on your Shadow.

A Shadow Exercise

This is a journal-based exercise that begins with guidelines for locating possible Shadow elements.

- Go to a place, indoors or out, that feels sufficiently private to you.
- Identify a person from your life (dead or alive, but not a member of your family of origin) — someone you very much dislike or who disturbs you. And identify another person you feel great admiration and/or affection for. Choose people to whom you overreact emotionally, positively or negatively or both (individuals that most other people don't respond to in the same way, as far as you know). Your selections can come from people you've known anytime in the present or past, as long as you still have an emotional charge in response to them.
- Writing in your journal, identify four traits or characteristics that disturb you in the former and four that you admire in the latter.
- From the perspective of the Self, describe the origin of your like/dislike:

  - If this is a transference, trace it back to your family of origin, early years, or key individuals in your life.
  - If this is a projection (it can be both a transference and a projection), identify your own disowned parts that might be revealed: As you contemplate and feel the characteristics you see in the other, look for versions of these characteristics in yourself, perhaps expressed in subtle or unexpected ways or only occasionally but with a vengeance or a flare. Can you name the parts of you that act this way (or want to)? They might be one or more subpersonalities or aspects of one or more facets of your Self.

- Describe the emotions (mad, sad, glad, scared, hurt, guilty, ashamed, envious, jealous, and so on) that your screens' traits or characteristics evoke in you. Are these emotions familiar? What's familiar about them? How do you feel about having these emotions? (It's important to answer all these questions.)
- In the case of projections, what qualities or personal resources does this person have that you don't, but that you could use or benefit from? (These qualities and resources are not necessarily the same

as the traits you listed earlier.) Do these qualities or resources seem to resonate mostly with one of the four facets of the Self? If so, which one? Which facet of the Self is your strongest? Weakest?

- In the case of transferences, who did you have the old relationship with? What was the nature of that relationship? (What were the dynamics? The roles?) In what way did you get stuck or caught in your role in that relationship? What weren't you able to do (probably because you were too young or immature) that would have improved the relationship or enabled you to better protect yourself? What underdeveloped personal resource do you now need to cultivate in order to improve your current relationship? What opportunity to "get it right" does your current relationship provide you?

- From the perspective of the Self, consider how you would change if you embraced your screen as an ally in your life (so that you and the other were now on the same level, the other no longer being beneath you or above you). How might you change if you absorbed and assimilated some of your screen's qualities? What existing aspects of yourself (both positive and negative) might in this way be integrated into your embodied personality? How might your patterns of behavior shift?

In addition to doing this exercise using, as your subjects, people from your dayworld life, try it with characters from your dreams or from literature, film, or myth; or with a nonhuman being or feature of nature; or with people from any of the other "classic places to look" listed earlier in this chapter, in the "Tracking Down Elements of Your Shadow" section.

Next, supplement this exercise, enriching and amplifying it, in any of the following ways. Your goal in each case is to become better acquainted with the other (your screen) and to allow this relationship development to have its emotional effect on you. Your goal is *not* to figure anything out about him or her — or even about yourself.

- Beginning with a relaxation exercise, enter your deep imagery and invite your screen to appear in your imagination in order to meet with you. With the resources of your fourfold Self, initiate a dialogue with this person. Unless you are experienced in deep-imagery

work, this is likely to go best if you have a skilled deep-imagery facilitator guiding you.

- Do some empty-chair dialogues: Set up two chairs facing each other
  a couple feet apart (or, if outside, choose two such places to sit on
  the ground). Sit in one chair and imagine your screen in the other.
  From the perspective of your Self, speak as authentically as you can
  to the other about how you see him or her, the emotions stirred in
  you by him or her, the nature of your relationship, and so on. Then
  take the other seat and speak back to yourself from the perspective
  of your screen. Keep the dialogue going, switching back and forth
  between the two chairs. Do this exercise several times, on different
  days, with the same screen. Let the relationship develop.[9]
- Using drawing materials or clay, create a likeness of your screen.
  This has great value in its own right, but you can also use this likeness when dialoguing with your screen.
- Draw a picture of you and your screen together.
- With or without music, use movement or dance to embody your
  reaction to your screen.
- In your imagination, merge with your screen and invite it to express
  itself through drawing, painting, writing, movement, music, or
  dance.
- Go for a long walk as your Self, accompanied (in your imagination)
  by your screen. Or go for a walk *as* your screen.
- If you have a small group to work with, enact psychodrama interactions between you and your screen. You can take the role of yourself one time and the role of your screen another. You choose who
  in the group would best enact your screen (or you) and carefully
  coach that person in how best to do this (for example, which characteristic movements, attitudes, language, speech patterns, or posture to use). There's an example later in this chapter.
- Share the results (emotions, insights, shifts in body awareness)
  from any of the above exercises with someone you trust.

Here's another method for tracking down and experiencing a potential
element of your Shadow: Try on, own, and express the opposite of your
emotional overreactions to other people's criticisms of you. For example,
instead of "How dare you call me selfish!" try on: "I *am* selfish!"

After completing the above exercises with an element of your Shadow, you may want to ask yourself some of the following questions and answer them in your journal:

- Preintegration awareness of Shadow elements: Before you became conscious of your Shadow element as Shadow per se, what did you think it was? What qualities or traits did you think you were embodying or enacting at those times? Were you aware in any way that this Shadow element was part of you? Or were you completely unaware that you were embodying it (if you did)? If you had some early awareness of what you later recognized as Shadow, what did you call it? What did your Loyal Soldiers say about it? Your Wounded Children? Your Escapists or Addicts?

- Preintegration projection: Before you uncovered this element of your Shadow, did you project it onto others (humans or nonhumans)? (Correct answer: Yes, or probably.) Onto who or what? Did you project both your Sinister Shadow and your Golden Shadow, both negatively (you didn't like your screen) and positively (you did)? For example, with the Sinister Shadow, did you secretly admire or long for or be turned on by others with qualities you felt were abhorrent?

- Emergence of Shadow: How did you first begin to become conscious of this Shadow element as Shadow? What conscious experience(s) provided your first clue? What does this suggest?

- Social or cultural context: What aspect of your early family or cultural environment (or your constitution) led to your repression of this Shadow element? How does this Shadow element (if it is now embodied consciously) lead to a wholing of you or your family, community, or humanity?

Dream Thugs

Many years ago, I had a series of dreams about thugs, Shadow figures to be sure. These were generally inner-city street people of color who ripped me off, mugged me, or stole my car. They treated me like a wealthy, unhip, Middle American — not worth offering the time of day and certainly not someone to sit down and be real with. I (the dream ego) felt victimized and saw them, in turn, as mean-spirited trash.

My initial work with these Shadow figures included dreamwork, journal exercises, and walks with my dream thugs (as my imagined companions), all of which enabled me to sense their presence within me and to feel the psychological atmosphere within which they operated. In this way, I found the previously unconscious thug of me. Looking and feeling through the windows of these dreams, I could remember times in my everyday life I had been a sort of thug with friends or colleagues. I had been unkind, unintentionally offensive, cross, or rude. This conflicted in a big way with how I experienced myself. This was not easy or pleasant to look at — but necessary. What I had thought I was doing at such times was courageously standing up for what was right, or being assertive, honest, appropriately insistent, perhaps even admirably decisive. In my mind, acting like a thug was how *others* acted — politicians, for example, or corporate officers, pundits, gang members, cops, or badass characters from films and novels. I had been projecting my inner thug onto these others (with no implication that I was necessarily wrong about them). I also had to admit there were times I had fantasies of mugging these dayworld thugs in revenge for, or to exact justice for, their misdeeds — another indicator of the unacknowledged thug of me.

This phase of the Shadow work enabled me to be more conscious of my own behavior and psyche, to make amends to those I may have hurt, and to modify my attitudes, perspectives, and interpersonal patterns to decrease the chance of behaving like a thug.

It was not until a few months later that I did the next, deeper layer of work with my dream thugs. I describe this at the end of the chapter, as an example of advanced Shadow work.

Advanced West Subpersonality Work: Shadow Work as a Path to Soul

Our Shadow and Shadow Selves have been protecting us by blocking our access to resources of our own psyches, powers that our subpersonalities — and often the Self, too — feel we're not ready for, not yet mature enough to understand, to appreciate, or to deploy wisely or safely. These subs and the Self are afraid we'd blow ourselves up or that we'd wind up in such hellish hot water in our relationships that we'd be boiled alive. It's as if their mission is to keep the little devils of ourselves locked away in our private dungeons — despite all the havoc they create down there — rather than to risk provoking the ire of the bigger devils of the world who might wipe us out in one fell swoop.

Our Shadow accomplishes this internment through outright repression — a triple-locked steel door to the cellar, with no security passes issued to anyone from the daylight floors — and our Shadow Selves help out on rare occasions in a kind of catch-and-release operation in which a Shadow actor from Hell's Central Casting is allowed to abduct the Ego for a brief spell, with the proviso that the Ego, after its wild ride, must be tossed back, more or less intact, into the River of Everyday Life.

In these ways, our Shadow has admirably assisted in defending our un-ripe Egos from grave danger, but by the same token it has been sealing us off from our greatest personal powers and, in this way, from our destinies, our mythopoetic identities, our full humanity. It's a clever and prudent arrange-ment. The immature, adolescent personality — as embodied by 80 percent or so of all contemporary, Western Egos over age twelve — is not prepared to reclaim the powers held in trust by the Shadow. But don't get me wrong: such Egos, as we've seen, can certainly benefit from the more basic form of Shadow work, the therapeutic or healing-oriented version discussed in this chapter so far. In the basic form of Shadow work, we become more con-scious of how we behave toward others, withdrawing and owning back our projections and transferences (both the Sinister and the Golden forms), be-ginning to see our own "stuff" more clearly, taking greater responsibility, and in this way improving our relationships, making them more real. But our Shadows contain dark treasures a good deal more potent and dangerous than this.

The advanced, bound-for-Soul form of Shadow work has the under-world goal of reclaiming not what we project onto others but the hidden resources and gifts that await us in the depths of, the very heart of, the Shadow element. Here's one way to think about this vital difference: Early in our lives, as we've seen, we stuffed much of our wholeness into the long bag we drag behind us. To keep ourselves safe from these risky elements of our wholeness, we mislabeled them without knowing we were distorting their true nature. We called them bad, divine, and so on. When we project onto others, it's actually only these labels that we consciously experience in (or as) the other. We don't see or understand what it is we've mislabeled — namely, the elements of our original wholeness. And that's what we're seeking in the advanced form of Shadow work: not the wrappers but the essence, not the signs but the significance. The original lost elements of our wholeness are what we're after, what we seek to locate and reclaim in order to more fully understand and brilliantly perform our soulwork in this lifetime.

The resources hidden in the deeper and darker layers of Shadow are not the personal characteristics you've been unconsciously projecting onto others. The hidden, Soul-level resources are more mysterious and concealed. You can't discover what they are by thinking about them or trying to figure out what they might be. The Shadow must be experientially engaged in a profound way. This can be harrowing and risky, as well as rapturous and enormously beneficial. But you wouldn't want to attempt it unless you were feeling very solid and stable, ready and willing to take some psychospiritual risks for the not-at-all-guaranteed possibility of retrieving elements of your mythopoetic identity. And because this advanced form of Shadow work profoundly challenges the adolescent personality, you wouldn't want to attempt it before you've reached the stage of human development I've referred to in previous chapters as the Cocoon.[10]

So, this time I must emphasize more than ever that advanced West subpersonality work can be hazardous — psychologically, spiritually, and interpersonally. It's essential for you to cultivate dependable access to your fourfold Self before attempting this. Please see the overview and cautions I've offered in the introductory section on advanced subpersonality work, on pages 148–50.

Advanced Shadow work requires you to deeply get to know your screens, whether human or otherwise, whether from your dayworld or nightworld. In so doing, you eventually discover something about your screens that you truly admire, something that takes your breath away, something that usually has no obvious relationship with the quality you projected on your screens, but something that you yourself possess as a latent resource. This discovery sparks the transformation and reveals the beauty and treasure behind the projection.

For example, say you harbor a negative stereotype of people of a particular race, nationality, religion, or personality type. By way of the basic, therapeutic level of Shadow work, you learned to own back this projection, to see that the negative quality you projected is an element of your own personality and behavior, actual or latent. You became more conscious of yourself and made the indicated changes in the ways you act and relate.

Now the advanced work can begin. There are two phases. The first is to get to know as intimately as you can someone of that race, nationality, religion, or personality type, the kind of person to whom you used to react very negatively, and may even now, to some degree. Making certain you're anchored in your fourfold Self, especially your East facet (Innocent/Sage), hang out with someone of this sort on his (or her) turf, learn his customs, or help him with his family and community projects. In other words, if your screen is an accessible, living human being in your world, have sustained real-time interactions with him or her. With screens who are unavailable or from your nightworld, you can employ the practices discussed earlier in this chapter, including deep-imagery work, empty-chair dialogues, journaling, expressive arts, movement, voice dialogue, four-directions circles, dreamwork, and psychodrama.

In deeply getting to know your screen, the odds are you'll discover (not figure out) that people of this description possess a certain positive quality — say, just as examples, sensuality, assertiveness, or joy — that is considerably underdeveloped in you, and without which you're not able to mature beyond your current plateau. And maturing in this way is exactly what many of your subpersonalities fear, because doing so will expose you to social risks and potential psychological losses. This is why, for example, your Loyal Soldier arranged for you to unconsciously judge these other people as wholly negative, keeping you safe from discovering the repressed resource in yourself.

The way this advanced form of Shadow work differs from the basic form is that here you're giving the work considerably more time, taking it much deeper, and keeping your focus on the actual person (or dream character or...) rather than on your previous beliefs about or reactions to this person.

In other words, Shadow work provides two kinds of opportunities: first, to discover aspects of your personality and relationship patterns that have been unconscious and that you've projected onto others (this is the basic level of Shadow work) and, second, to practice what Jungian analyst James Hollis calls "radical conversation" with someone fundamentally different from you.[11] To take advantage of this second opportunity, you must treat the other as a fully autonomous and mysterious other and not as a screen (mirror) for you. Doing so can be a mind-blowing experience; it can provide an opportunity for the dismantling and reconfiguration of your current ego-identity. Keep in mind that this opportunity exists only when you know you're projecting or transferring onto someone and choose to get to know him or her independently of your projection or transference. This isn't easy. You won't be looking in the mirror; you'll be looking *behind* the mirror — behind the projection or transference — to see the actual other person and enter a potentially life-shifting interaction. This is the "half-silvered mirror" feature of working with projections and transference. Radical conversation is one version of advanced work with Shadow. You can do this work not only with people in your waking life but also with dream characters and with animals and other nonhumans from both your nightworld and dayworld.

The goal of radical conversation is to discover the deeper layers of your Shadow — not the personality layer, but the layers closer to Soul.

Loving Thugs

My thug dreams did not end after my initial Shadow work, described earlier. As a matter of fact, a few months after completing that work I had a thug dream every night for a week. By the end of the week, I was, in my waking life, with a group of a dozen men and women on an eight-day spring backpacking journey in a redrock canyon of southern Utah. One warm evening in camp, I recounted my thug dreams in great detail and then asked my companions to help me more fully experience my dream thugs through psychodrama. Two of my companions, a man and a woman, stood up straight away with mischievous "Sure, I'm happy to help" gleams in their eyes. I knew instantly they'd be perfect to enact my thugs. Swallowing hard, I summarized for them the attitudes and actions of my dream thugs, asking my companions to improvise but to be sure to stay within the framework of my dreams. I would take the role of my victimized and frightened dream ego, who was rather less assertive and confident than I am in the dayworld.

My two companions did a shockingly good job at enacting my dream thugs. They pushed me around with their loud questions and taunts and, sometimes, with their hands. They got in my face, questioned my authenticity, my values, my realness. They didn't give a damn about my precious car or possessions. The other group members, sitting in a circle around us, called out additional invectives and angles for the thugs to use. The thugs invited them to join in. Before long, there were eleven thugs and me and no one left sitting. Things were getting quite uncomfortable, and uncomfortably real. What they were saying about me had truth in it and remained true to the feel of the dreams. They were expressing a reality I hadn't seen before. Tears of grief and shame spilled from my eyes — and, astonishingly, tears of admiration for these thugs. I could see they possessed a fierce, no-holds-barred genuineness, the ability to look the other guy in the eye and speak the plain truth regardless of how much pain it might inflict. Their words came from the heart. These thugs possessed an authenticity, courage, chutzpah, and tough love my Ego lacked. This came as a humbling shock: where I had earlier felt self-righteously victimized, I now felt chagrin for my blindness to the rich world of these "poor" people of my nightworld. I could see that in my dayworld I exhibited a constraint, a timidity, a social distance that restricted the range and power in my work as a soul guide and in my intimate relationships.

Following this psychodrama, I adopted the practice of embodying the loving thug of me, of looking people in the eye and speaking the plain truth to the best of my ability and with full love and compassion. My job was to *become* that loving thug, to assimilate him. This required emulation of the heart warrior archetype about whom I had spoken for years but had not embodied as much as I might have. I found that when I did it skillfully, it worked; people felt seen, honored, deeply met. With few exceptions, they went away feeling not mugged but loved. Imagine.

This advanced work with my thugs contrasted with, but complemented, the foundational Shadow work I had done earlier. The first layer enabled me to explore how I had unconsciously engaged in harmful behaviors that were symbolically the same as those of my dream thugs. The second, deeper layer of Shadow work, however, allowed me to discover and reclaim an invaluable resource hidden in the thugs of me. Within the first layer, I found a *negative* characteristic that I could choose to stop acting out and replace with a relationship-enhancing pattern. Within the second layer, I unearthed a *positive* resource at the depths of the Sinister Shadow that I could choose to cultivate and, in so doing, more fully live my way into my Soul's destiny.

———

Once you experientially encounter the resource in the deeper layer of Shadow projection, you can move on to the second phase of advanced Shadow work, which is the very challenging project of cultivating the positive resources uncovered in both your Sinister and your Golden Shadow projections, practicing the embodiment of these resources in your decisions, actions, and interactions. Doing so will further undermine your previous, less mature way of belonging to the world. Each element of the Shadow holds particular strengths, unique perspectives, and sensitivities you could not have imagined when you made that first half-turn toward what you had previously failed to notice.

Coda

Beyond Here Be Dragons

The most remarkable feature of this historical moment on Earth is not that we are on the way to destroying the world — we've actually been on the way for quite a while. It is that we are beginning to wake up, as from a millennia-long sleep, to a whole new relationship to our world, to ourselves and each other.

— Joanna Macy

The major problems in the world are the result of the difference between how nature works and the way people think.

— Gregory Bateson

The human psyche — our wild, multifaceted mind in its natural habitat of the more-than-human world — is complex and dynamic. In its mature fullness, it grants us an astonishing array of personal resources: a rainbow spectrum of skills and sensibilities applicable to almost any circumstance. It affords us multiple ways to heal our psychological wounds — and to benefit from them. It gifts us with deeply imaginative capacities for engendering life-enhancing relationships and cultures and for meaningfully participating in the world we cocreate with the other members of the Earth community.

The Nature-Based Map of the Psyche identifies eleven elements, in a three-dimensional matrix, and suggests some of the diverse relationships these elements can have with each another. As we've seen, there are four facets of the Self, four groupings of subpersonalities, plus the Ego, Soul, and Spirit.

In the presentation of the map offered in this book, I've focused on the nature of the fourfold Self.[1] The deep structure of the Self can be summarized by saying that the West facet is fundamentally about romance, transformation, metaphor, and deep imagination; South, about wildness, indigenity, belonging, and full-bodied feeling; East, about innocence, wisdom, paradoxical humor, and full-presence sensing; and North, about nurturance, generativity, visionary action, and heart-centered thinking. Another, perhaps more poetic way to say this — as I did in this book's introduction — is that the Self is what enables us to dream the impossible and to romance the world, to feel and honor our kinship with all species and habitats, to embrace the troubling wisdom of paradox, and to shape ourselves into visionaries with the artistry to revitalize our enchanted and endangered world.

One of my intentions in constructing this Nature-Based Map of the Psyche has been to recognize and appreciate the full spectrum of our humanity. I especially wanted to portray the psyche in a way that allows its paired opposites to coexist. The map celebrates the paradoxes of our human nature and the tension existing within each paradox, tensions that perchance make possible the very structure of our human psyches. For example, some of the tensions identified in the map:

- wild/acculturated (S/N)
- sensuous/conceptual (S/N)
- Dionysian/Apollonian (S/N, or S-W/N-E)
- dark/light (W/E, or Underworld/Upperworld)
- Soul/Spirit (Underworld/Upperworld)
- unique/universal (Underworld/Upperworld)
- introversion/extroversion (W/E)
- personal/transpersonal (N-S/E-W)
- doing/being (N-W/S-E)
- arational/rational/(S-W/N-E)
- feminine/masculine (found within every dimension of our psyches, but in the Western world often embodied as S-W/N-E as a consequence of the gender imbalances endemic in our culture)

This book is a first presentation of the map, a work in progress.[2] There is undoubtedly much more to learn about these eleven elements of the human psyche and the relationships between them. And it may be the case that an adequate portrayal of the psyche cannot be accomplished with only eleven elements. Any map of the psyche can be responsive, at most, to our current needs for self-orientation and can represent only what we've discovered so far. As the old mapmakers used to say, "Beyond here be dragons."

Quite possibly in the future, it will better serve the ever-evolving project of human self-understanding to portray the human psyche differently or in greater detail. A map, we must always remember, is not the territory.

THREE DIMENSIONS OF HUMAN SELF-UNDERSTANDING

In the project of human self-understanding, the Nature-Based Map of the Psyche, whether or not it provides the optimal amount of detail, identifies only one set of ways in which one person can be similar to or different from another — namely, their degree of cultivation of the Self, their level of integration of subpersonalities, and the nature of their conscious relationship with Soul and Spirit. To fully understand any person, we must consider at least two additional dimensions beyond the structural elements of the psyche explored in this book. These additional dimensions are the person's stage of personal development and their personality type.[3] Since 1985, my colleagues and I have been fashioning an eight-stage, nature-based model of human development, which we call the Eco-Soulcentric Developmental Wheel, and which I introduced in *Nature and the Human Soul*. We've also sketched out a nature-based model of personality, also mapped onto the four-directions matrix but not yet published.

At Animas Valley Institute, we've found it essential to regard each person we work with, as well as ourselves, through the lenses of all three kinds of models: structural, developmental, and personality. For example, most people come to Animas experiential immersions because Mystery has ushered them into the multiyear process of Soul initiation (their descent into the mysteries of nature and psyche for the purpose of discovering their unique mythopoetic identity, their ultimate place in the world, their singular contribution to the Earth community), which is to say they are in the fourth of the eight life stages (the stage we call the Cocoon) or sometimes the fifth stage (the Wellspring). Cultivating their fourfold Self serves them primarily as preparation for the descent to Soul, or it enhances their capacity for benefiting from their underworld experiences. But cultivating the four facets is not the central focus of their work; *utilizing* these resources in their soulcraft practices and underworld experiences is. People in stage 5, in contrast, are most often assisted in developing a culturally relevant delivery system (a craft, project, profession, or way of being) for living what they discovered (in stage 4) about their mythopoetic identity. Which facets of the Self they most need to cultivate and which kind of delivery system makes most sense for them depends, in part, on their personality type. Meanwhile, people in stage 3 (the Oasis), because they are not developmentally ready for the descent to Soul, are more likely to be cultivating personal authenticity and balancing it with social acceptance. Their cultivation of the Self serves two purposes: it stimulates the multidimensional aliveness that wholing evokes and enables them to heal their relationships with their subpersonalities (two processes that continue through the later stages as well).

How the Self Serves Us

There are two ways the Self serves us. In one case — the ideal one — we consciously cultivate (via our 3-D Ego) the facets of the Self and learn to act from our horizontal wholeness. In this way, the resources of the Self are consciously available to us, through our Ego.

But the Self can also serve us independently of the Ego — without our intending it or even knowing how it happens: when our Ego is identified with one or more subpersonalities, the Self may nonetheless come to our aid through, for example, an intuition, an inner voice of wisdom "out of nowhere," a sudden inspiration or creative spark, or a profound feeling of presence, compassion, or interconnectedness. Almost everyone has had numerous experiences of this sort, moments of grace that we perhaps attributed to the intervention of a guardian angel, a still, small voice in the midst of a dark night of the soul, the voice of God, or a self-preservation instinct. To me, these experiences seem to be instances when the Self (and sometimes the Soul or Spirit) shows up to serve us or when the Ego, at least momentarily, accesses the realm of the Self.

Although such moments of grace are of great value, I believe we can do better than to passively wait or pray for them. The process of individuation is more effectively engaged when we consciously choose to cultivate our relationships with the fourfold Self.

THE SELF AS A TURNING WHEEL

The four facets of the Self work together, hand in hand. Sometimes they're all equally activated, fully participating together in the same moment. At other times, or in another sense, each facet offers the results of its perspective to the next — in a sunwise (clockwise) progression. Here's how this might look:

The East — the Innocent/Sage — possesses the genius to perceive the world simply as it is, in its constant changes and renewals, in its radiant and often paradoxical fullness, observing each thing with the East's uncompli-cated, composed manner, noticing how everything contributes to the whole.

The South takes up where the East leaves off. The Wild Indigenous One embraces and yet embellishes the East's clear and straightforward per-ceptions with its own Southerly sensuous, emotional, and enchanted com-munion with our animate world. The Wild Indigenous One fully *feels* the world, with its alluring, erotic enchantments as well as its grievous horrors. It puts South flesh on East bones — Tantric flesh, you might say, on Zen bones.

The West, then, receives the handoff from the South. The Muse-Beloved gathers up the fecund intricacies of the Wild Indigenous One and passion-ately imagines where we might go from there, envisioning what that South-erly communion might evolve into — what mystery blossoms might be coaxed from that fertile soil — dreaming up dangerous opportunities to fur-ther cooperate with and enhance life, and conceiving never-before-suspected and ecstatically troubling ways of participating in our astounding world.

And then, with a seductive wink, the West turns to the North: "Here, take *this*." The Nurturing Generative Adult beholds the Muse-Beloved's in-novative imaginings of being and participating and contrives skillful ways to embody these very possibilities in service to life, to a world in need. Through deliberate choice and action, the North transforms the West's inspired prospects into groundbreaking actualities, pioneering new cultural realities.

Then, coming full circle, the North offers its results to the East, and the East steps back (sometimes off a cliff, like the Tarot's Fool), enjoys a deep breath, and takes a gander not only at what the North has manifested but also at the whole cycle just completed, appreciating the big picture, including how the human realm participates in the greater Earth community — both the good fit, when there is one, and the cosmic comedy-tragedy wrought by what always seems to be overlooked, misunderstood, or misappropriated. And then, with a twinkle the Innocent/Sage offers its diamond-like clarity to the emotional dishevelment services of the South. And so on.

INDIVIDUAL DIFFERENCES: A GLIMPSE AT PERSONALITY TYPES

Among the people you know who have achieved some degree of human fullness or maturity, you probably know some who are extraordinary in their embodiment of two or more of the facets of the Self. Sometimes this also means they're lacking in their development of one or two of the other facets. Sometimes it doesn't. A person particularly adept in one facet, no matter how impressive, is not necessarily someone to emulate in one's own individuation process.

There seems to be a tendency among people who are strong in one particular facet of the Self to be weak in the complementary facet (the one on the opposite side of the circle). Take me, for example. I've been rather West my whole life: As a child and youth, I was utterly introverted, solitude loving, idealistic, dreamy, moody, and romantic (especially in the sense of being allured/obsessed by the possibilities of love affairs — not merely sex — with mysterious young women). Beginning in my twenties, I became prone to visionary experiences and developed a great fascination with dreams, the unconscious, the hidden and occult, spiritual practices, nonordinary consciousness, death, mythology, and symbols. Professionally, in my twenties I was a research psychologist studying dreams, hypnosis, meditation, and other nonordinary states, and then a soul-oriented psychotherapist, and my primary work for the past thirty years has been wilderness-based underworld guiding. My earliest dream was of an occult ritual occurring in a dim underground crypt in a mysterious, ancient cemetery. Some of my friends have conferred on me endearments such as "Dr. Death" or "Impossible Dreamer." My favorite color is black. (Really.) A person just doesn't get much more West.

Meanwhile, the East has been an enigma for me most of my life. It seems that only in recent years have I been able to say anything coherent about it. Twenty years ago, when speaking about the psychological qualities of the four directions, I would sometimes draw a complete blank when I got to the East, or I would simply omit it entirely as if there were really only three cardinal directions. Or I found myself describing the East in ways that implied disapproval. It would be fair to say I was not a particularly lighthearted person; nor did I have a single detectable extroverted bone in my psychosocial body. My sense of humor was, uh, a bit limited. I was not exactly the life of the party. Appearing as a Fool was not my idea of a good time. Nor was appearing as an Innocent. The idea of seeking the light seemed to me to be the flakiest of New Age spiritual escapisms.

And yet, something in me knew what I was missing. Something in me was in fact powerfully attracted to the Eastern light. I have been, since my early twenties, a student of Buddhism, Sufism, and Yoga. Most of my best friends have always been exceptionally East people, extraordinarily funny folks, extroverted, innocent, and lighthearted, as well as wise and perceptive. I achieved a provisional kind of East-West balance through spiritual pursuits and by hanging out with very East types.

But a more thorough intrapsychic redemption is also possible. About fifteen years ago, having at last conceded my off-the-graph bias toward the West, I resolved to cultivate my relationship with the Eastern precinct of my own psyche. I began an apprenticeship to unabashed Joy. I embarked upon an embodied rapprochement with the Sacred Fool of me. I invited my inner comedian to show up as outrageously as he wished, even (especially) while guiding intense and serious underworld-tending immersions. I like to think I've made a good deal of progress. I even experienced some joy while working on chapter 4 of this book! If *I* can do it, anyone can.

You may wonder: if every person's Self possesses the same fourfold resources, shouldn't we expect Self-realized people (those who have fully cultivated all four facets) to seem quite similar to one another? Not at all. Our embodiment of the Self always takes on the tenor of our personality; the color of our culture, ethnicity, and language; the climate, land shapes, waterways, flora, and fauna of our bioregion; our historical epoch; and our current stage of life, not to mention the desires of our Soul — our one-of-a-kind mythopoetic identity.

THE CULTURAL, ECOLOGICAL, AND EVOLUTIONARY IMPORTANCE OF INDIVIDUATION

Toward the end of chapter 1, I proposed that there are five dimensions of the lifelong process of individuation, the process by which each one of us can become fully human. But individuation is not solely or even primarily for ourselves as individuals.

A person with a well-developed Self seeks to restore and enhance the more-than-human world and to coconceive and cocreate a healthy, mature, life-enhancing culture (North); feels himself to be indigenous, kin to all other creatures and a native member of the Earth community (South); sees the big picture, being mindful of the human story as a component of an ever-evolving cosmic unfolding (East); imagines possible futures that resonate with our deepest potentials (West) — possibilities that we could never figure out with the everyday, strategic mind; and makes those futures real, in this way participating in the evolution of our species and planet, perhaps even of the cosmos (North again).

These fourfold resources of the Self enable us to develop our relationships with our subpersonalities, with Spirit, and with Soul and in this way to change our relationship with the world and to transform the world itself. With a well-developed Self, we can most effectively

- heal our individual wounds (our subpersonalities), enhancing our capacity to contribute to our world;
- cultivate a conscious relationship to Spirit and so enjoy an intimacy with all of life, experiencing our oneness with all things and with the Universe as a whole; and
- cultivate a conscious relationship with Soul and so discover our singular and ultimate place in the world, enabling us to serve the world most effectively as initiated adults and true elders.

With a well-developed Self, we experience and embody ourselves as agents of cultural transformation. After Soul initiation, we become visionary participants in and proponents of an evolving world.

CULTURAL TRANSFORMATION:
FROM PSYCHOTHERAPY TO SELF-HEALING
TO SOUL INITIATION

How do we achieve a well-developed Self? Although people navigate toward maturity by their own internal compasses, having a map can make all the difference in a culture that does not adequately support human flowering. The Nature-Based Map of the Psyche can be used as a basis for psychotherapy or life coaching, but it can also be used as a self-implemented alternative, a means by which people can, on their own, cultivate personal wholeness and, from that wholeness, learn to embrace their wounded subpersonalities.

A skilled psychotherapist develops a relationship between her wholeness and the fragmented parts of her client. Although of great value, this alone does not help the client develop *his* wholeness (Self), and the latter is the substance and sign of psychological health — much more so than merely healing his emotional wounds or reducing the frequency with which his subpersonalities act out his woundedness. In the best contemporary psychotherapies, the therapist supports the client's Self-development.

Every child and teenager can and should be coached in the cultivation of wholeness and, from that wholeness, the embrace of their subpersonalities. This ought to be a matter of course in the process of growing up. If it were, the need for psychotherapy (and other forms of other-assisted psychological healing) would be significantly reduced.

Widespread wholing and Self-healing would transform our patho-adolescent society into a healthy adolescent society — a major transformation! Then, the process of Soul initiation, if widely available, would eventually transform a healthy adolescent society into a truly mature one.

BEYOND HERE BE DRAGONS

As a culture and as a planet, we're now collectively toppling over the edge of the world as we've known and mapped it, into a future that, without doubt, will confront us with unprecedented danger, hardship, and suffering

— greater, even, than that of past centuries — as well as unparalleled opportunities. As of 2012, we've already been besieged for quite some time by the formidable human-spawned dragons of climate destabilization, environmental and genetic poisoning, species loss, nuclear accidents and weaponry, epidemics, resource scarcity (not only "peak oil," peak coal extraction, and peak grain harvests but actually "peak everything"),[4] overpopulation, and endless resource wars (masquerading as rescue missions). And there will be additional dragons of these kinds, possibly fiercer, materializing soon enough.

But at least we're beginning to consciously recognize that we have, in fact, wandered, irreversibly, beyond the edge of our previous world and outside the range of the prosaic stories we've been telling each other for millennia. We've crossed beyond all familiar borders into an unknown mysterious territory, a mythic realm in which we no longer recognize our world or ourselves. Here, if we are to survive, we must be radically reshaped. We must be transformed by our encounters with dragons of another sort — dragons that have been waiting for us in the depths of our individual and collective Shadows, the dragons of our own forsaken or never-known potentials, the dragons of our human destiny. Engaging *these* demons, angels, and shape-shifters constitutes the necessary dangerous opportunity of our time, the current initiatory journey of our species and planet.

The future — ours, and that of everything else on Earth — will be what we make it: we, the humans of the generations currently alive. We're going to need all the resources of our innate wholeness if we, as a species, are going to accomplish something our ancestors would be proud of and future generations will be grateful for.

In one sense, we're all emigrants now, on a great sea voyage, and a long way yet from the shores of the new world, a place no one has yet visited. We're not even sure such a place really exists or, if it does, whether we'll ever arrive there. We could all perish in the great storm while still in our lifeboats.

But in another sense, emigration is entirely the wrong metaphor. We're not actually going to reach a new world, the reason simply being that this time a new world does not exist somewhere "out there." A new world, a new story for us, is one we'll manifest ourselves — or there won't be one.

The great crises and predicaments of our time are not due to bad luck, evil people, or a fatal flaw in the human species. They are, rather, a result of unhealthy human cultures. (And unhealthy cultures are the result not of a defective species but of a species brilliantly designed by Mystery to bear a sacred wound as an essential ingredient of its journey and its promise and destiny. But that's another story.) The Great Work before us is to invent or re-invent healthy, mature cultures — not merely sustainable, just, cooperation-based cultures but life-enhancing, visionary cultures capable of cooperating with evolution itself, with the emerging future, with the cosmos.[5]

Where do healthy, mature cultures come from? There are several good answers, but I believe they all amount to different ways of saying the same thing. Healthy, mature cultures emerge from, and have always emerged from, nature, from the depths of our individual and collective psyches, from the Earth's imagination acting through us,[6] from the mythic realm of dreams or the Dreamtime, from Soul, from the Soul of the world, from Mystery.

Where healthy, mature cultures *don't* come from is the strategic mind — even from blue-ribbon panels of experts in ecocentric culture design. Never did. Never will. Yes, we can design ecocentric social and environmental policies and so on, but the strategic human mind is incapable of fig-uring out the organic, wildly imaginative, multifaceted, constantly shifting mythic structure of a truly mature culture. The strategic mind is not capable of even understanding or fully appreciating such a mythic structure. Impli-cation: it's not possible to simply think our way out of the mess we're in.

Mature cultures emerge and evolve naturally and organically through the coordinated activities of multitudes of mature humans, humans who have learned again what it means to dream the impossible and to romance the world. Mature cultures are self-organizing. They can only be *dreamed* into existence.

To end up with a truly mature culture, you need to start with the right ingredients — namely, mature humans, in addition to a thriving, diverse, re-silient environment. This is a case of what Buddhists call dependent coaris-ing: Mature cultures come from mature humans, and mature humans emerge from mature cultures, or at least mature communities or families. Mature hu-mans and mature cultures arise together. Consequently, the knowledge and skill to foster optimal human development means everything for the emer-gence and evolution of healthy cultures. If what we want is a thriving planet, the most essential project is to raise children who have the capacity to grow into true adults and authentic elders — mature humans.

How do you become a mature human? As described in these pages, my answer is that you must achieve two things, two dimensions of wholeness:

- Some degree of success in cultivating the four innate facets of your Self, which enables you to contribute magnificently to the more-than-human world and also to embrace and heal your own woundedness (this is your horizontal wholeness)

- An encounter with the mysteries of your Soul, enabling you to actively embody your unique mythopoetic identity, plus the cultivation of a personal relationship with Spirit, enabling you to maintain a vast, universal perspective (this is your vertical, transpersonal, or spiritual wholeness)

In order to cultivate these two dimensions of wholeness, you must have sufficient success with the developmental tasks of the first half of life (the stages of childhood and adolescence).[7] Success with these developmental tasks leads to true adulthood and, eventually, authentic elderhood.

Authentic elders in a mature culture don't advise the youths of their communities to simply pick a career or a mate, nor do they send them to vocational guidance counselors or matchmakers. Rather, when their youths are developmentally ready, the elders push them beyond the edge of their adolescent maps, to the realm where dragons prowl, the kinds of dragons youths need to encounter, the magical dragons of nature and psyche. In other words, the elders usher the members of the next generation into the process of Soul initiation so that they can discover for themselves what it is that Mystery or the Dreamtime or the Soul of the World intends for their lives. Upon their return, months or years later, young women and men are then capable of cultivating life-enhancing crafts or careers and, if they choose, becoming healthy, soulcentric parents.

How do youths become psychospiritually ready for the process of Soul initiation? The (true) adults of their society support them in addressing the developmental tasks of adolescence and in the foundational cultivation of their fourfold horizontal wholeness and their ability to Self-heal.

Given that authentic elders are essential to human development, where do *they* come from? From true (soul-initiated) adults who have completed their deeply fulfilling adult work of wildly creative cultural artistry. Where do true adults come from? From healthy adolescents who've been supported by elders and adult initiation guides through the process of Soul initiation. Where do healthy adolescents come from? From eco-soulcentric communities and families that include parents and others who are true adults and elders.

A healthy, mature culture is what we get when a majority of our people (over a certain age) have discovered their individual mythopoetic identities and are embodying those identities (via culturally relevant delivery systems) for the benefit of their more-than-human community. Mature cultures, in other words, emerge from the mystery-blossoming lives of Soul-initiated people. And because Soul is our most authentic and deepest human nature, we could just as well say that mature cultures come from nature — from nature's deep imagination.

How, you may wonder, can we create healthy, mature human cultures when we clearly don't live in one? We must generate family and community practices for eco-soulcentric human development that allow all children and teenagers to one day discover and embody their individual, Soul-infused contributions to a mature culture and, in this way, to take their places as visionary artisans of cultural evolution. The new dreams, stories, and practices of future healthy cultures are waiting within the depths of our own wild psyches. (In *Nature and the Human Soul*, I've offered a description of what optimal human development might look like, stage by stage, in contemporary societies.)

Where, then, do healthy, mature cultures come from? From each of us as we cultivate our wholeness and, when ready, undergo the journey to Soul, in this way tapping into Earth's imagination as it wants to live through us. Individual human fulfillment emerges in the same way, as does our greatest individual service to the world, as does cultural evolution.

———

Individuation is a lifelong adventure of many challenges and joys. I hope this book serves you as a helpful guide along the way. I didn't write it to be merely read but to be engaged and applied in the cultivation of your own wild mind, in your process of becoming fully human, on your journey of Soul initiation, in the midst of your life as a visionary artisan. I wrote it to spur you on to deeply imaginative acts of cultural revolution and renaissance. *What are you waiting for?*

Appendix

Four Practices for Wholing and Self-Healing

As a complement to the specialized practices included in each of the chapters on the facets of the Self and the subpersonalities, here are four of the best methods for cultivating our relationship to all facets and subs.

VOICE DIALOGUE

Voice dialogue, as developed by Hal and Sidra Stone, is a technique for cultivating awareness of, dialoguing with, and integrating the many parts or aspects of the human psyche.[1] You can use voice dialogue on your own, with a companion, or in a group. Below is a brief outline of one approach. (A more complete version can be found at www.wildmindbook.com.) Feel free to creatively modify it. If one or more others are joining you, designate a facilitator. If you're alone, your 3-D Ego is the facilitator. Here I assume you're working with a group and that you are the facilitator:

STEP 1. Invite the others to make themselves comfortable; most will prefer lying on the floor; some may prefer a chair. To aid relaxation and deepen the process, invite everyone to become aware of any muscle tension and to release it (you might guide them to sequentially place their awareness in each major part of the body). Next, invite them to be aware of their thoughts, simply observing them for a minute or so without getting caught in them, and then letting them come to a rest. Then do the same with emotions. (Substitute or blend in other relaxation strategies you prefer.)

STEP 2. Explain that this voice dialogue session is an opportunity to access and explore one or more facets of their wholeness and/or one or more dimensions of their woundedness. (When accessing all eight aspects, I usually begin with the subpersonalities, starting in the North and working around clockwise, and then the facets of the Self in the same order.) Let them know that in a moment you'll be inviting them to speak aloud, in brief phrases or short sentences, from the perspective and consciousness of one or more of these parts of themselves, and that it's perfectly okay for more than one person to be speaking at the same time.

STEP 3. Read to them (or speak your own version of) a description of the first part of the psyche you want to evoke. For example, with the Muse-Beloved (West facet), you might say something like: "I want to remind you that there's an aspect of your psyche, a facet of your wholeness, that is darkly mysterious, profoundly and startlingly creative, entirely at home with death and the undoing of things, and that loves to explore dreams and other worlds, remembers the future, regularly imagines the 'impossible,' is wildly romantic, and that you often find to be both disturbingly alluring and dangerous. This aspect of your psyche, which we might call the Muse or Inner Beloved or Lover of Fruitful Darkness or Guide to Soul, is something you can feel right now in your body. Perhaps you can hear its voice, too. It may, in fact, have something to say in this very moment, something like..." Here, pause, letting people spontaneously complete your sentence, but if no one leaps in, you can suggest an example yourself: "Something like: 'How interesting! The way that all of us are lying here on the floor with our eyes closed, awake and speaking randomly — this reminds me of a dream I once had' or 'I wonder what it means about the human species that we each have an inner Lover of Fruitful Darkness' or 'Death is my best friend and most trustworthy guide.'" Soon the imaginations of their Muse-Beloveds will be evoked, and they'll be volunteering a great variety of creative observations. If it seems helpful, encourage them, at times, with a "Yes!" "Good," "Mmm-hmmm," and so on.

STEP 4. If you're going to include more than one part of the psyche in this session, then, after several minutes (or when the West-facet verbalizations subside), invite everyone to shift his or her body position at least a bit, and then introduce the next aspect of the psyche with a brief description (step 3, again). And so on. See www.wildmindbook.com for examples of descriptions you can use for the North, South, and East facets of the Self.

STEP 5. When completed, offer gratitude to all parts for being present and perhaps voice the aspiration that all elements of our human psyches learn to support each other and work together for the highest and deepest good of both the individual and the more-than-human community.

Doing this exercise in a group provides the benefit of the collective consciousness that develops, helping each person find the unique perspective and voice of each part of their psyche. Hearing others' perspectives evokes, broadens, and diversifies our own experience of the possibilities.

Here's another kind of voice dialogue practice: Imagine four people at a dinner party — an Innocent/Sage, a Wild Indigenous One, a Muse-Beloved, and a

Nurturing Generative Adult. Suddenly, a precious vase falls to the ground and shatters. How does each person react? (Speak out loud from each perspective.)

The benefits of all exercises in this appendix, where a facet of the Self is evoked, are deepened and extended by practicing the embodiment of that facet in any and all interactions with the world in the immediately following hours and days. Adopt the perspectives, consciousness, bodily postures, and gestures of this facet while you're observing, planning, feeling, speaking, doing, or interacting. In the case of the North facet, for example, you might actively ask yourself: "In this moment, what would my Nurturing Generative Adult do, say, feel, perceive, imagine, or think?"

Voice Dialogue with Subpersonalities

You can also employ voice dialogue to heal your relationships with your subpersonalities: to get to know them better, to discover subs you had previously been unaware of, to explore the nature of their survival strategies, and to welcome them back into your circle of care.

With your South subpersonalities, for example, step 3 might go something like this: "I want to remind you that there's an aspect of your psyche that's like a wounded child or an orphan. This aspect of your psyche has been doing its best to get your basic needs met — through its immature emotional strategies — or it's been a casualty of your own attempts to self-protect, or perhaps a victim of other people's actions. This part of you feels harmed by the way it's been treated — and angry about that — and it's often afraid on account of the dire condition it believes it is in. It might also feel hurt, sad, guilty, or ashamed. Sometimes it plays the role of Conformist, Victim, Rebel, or Prince or Princess. Perhaps it feels like, and is, an Outcast within your own psyche. Right now, you might be able to feel the presence within your own body of this Wounded Child or Orphan. It may, in fact, have something to say right now, something like..." Here, pause, letting people spontaneously complete your sentence, but if no one leaps in right away, you can suggest examples of what one of these subpersonalities might be saying right then: "Something like: 'I'll wait until someone else volunteers so I can be sure to get it right and be acceptable here' or 'I always get it wrong and no one likes me anyway' or 'I'm angry and ain't gonna take it anymore!'" Their Wounded Children and Orphans will quickly get the idea and start volunteering examples. Encourage them, if necessary, with words or sounds like: "Yes!" "Ahh-hunh," "Yup," or other expressions of empathy.

See www.wildmindbook.com for examples of ways to evoke your North, East, and West subpersonalities.

Inviting the West subs through voice dialogue is, of course, particularly tricky given that, by definition, these are parts of ourselves we don't know. But our Shadows know they're being invited, and if we're sufficiently rooted in our fourfold Selves, we may be in a safe enough container for an element of Shadow to actually make an appearance. Most commonly, with the West subs, people volunteer statements that feel to them like Sinister or Golden projections they suspect or know they have.

When using voice dialogue with the subpersonalities, you may want to immediately follow up their spontaneous expressions with an added step. When working with yourself or another, read the following very slowly, pausing for ten to sixty seconds or so where indicated: "Now I want to invite you to empathically surround your subpersonality with all four facets of your Self. From the compassionate and holistic perspective of the Self, imagine this subpersonality, for whom you were just speaking, sitting before you. Observe him with care." (Pause.)

Then, to work with your Loyal Soldiers, for example, you might say: "Be aware of his (or her) long-standing intention to serve you by protecting you from psychological or physical harm. Be aware of his loyalty, faith, and skill and of the ways he has in fact been successful." (Pause.) "Take some time now to remember both the hazards he saved you from and the strategies he used." (Pause.) "Either silently or speaking out loud, tell him what you know about his good intentions, his creative strategies, and his successes. Speak from the Nurturing Generative Adult of you, but also from your Wild Indigenous One, your Innocent/Sage, and your Muse-Beloved." (Pause.) "Wholeheartedly thank your Loyal Soldier for his years of service." (Pause.) "Welcome him home. Let him know the War of Childhood Survival is over (if it is). Let him know you have more mature methods for keeping yourself safe enough. Give him some examples of strategies you might use in one or two specific scenarios in your current life in which he, the Loyal Soldier, might be tempted to use one of his old strategies." (Pause.) "Let him know that he can always choose to use one of his old strategies if you, the Self, don't show up soon enough to use one of yours." (Pause.) "Let him know that his skills are admired and needed and that there will always be opportunities for him to employ these skills." (Pause.) "And, finally, ask him if there's anything he'd like to say. Listen empathically and respond to him from this perspective. Keep the dialogue going as long as it feels right. Remember: If he disapproves of your approach, worries about your safety or your capacity to protect yourself, or otherwise refuses to budge from his perspective, your task is to neither agree nor disagree. Your opportunity is to love him, thank him, tell him the war is over, welcome him home, and remind him you'll be employing your own methods of self-protection."

For examples of how you might work with your South, East, and West sub-personalities, see www.wildmindbook.com.

If in your voice dialogue session you're including one or more subpersonalities, be sure to complete the exercise with step 5, as described earlier in this appendix. And remember that the benefits derived from this voice dialogue and other exercises are immensely deepened and extended by practicing the embodiment of the fourfold Self in relationship to your subpersonalities when they become active and in any and all interactions in the immediately following hours and days.

In the course of embracing your subpersonalities, you're likely to unearth old wounds or buried feelings of hurt or grief concerning events in your life that have felt like troubles or torments. When this happens, practice embracing these wounds and feelings from the fourfold perspective of the Self.

FOUR-DIRECTIONS CIRCLES

Venture out onto the land, preferably in a wild or semiwild place, or at least a spot some distance from buildings, cars, and human clamor. The less altered by humans and the more inhabited by undomesticated plants and trees and animals, the better. But even a backyard or city park will do.

Find a flattish spot at least six to ten feet in diameter in which your presence won't significantly disturb the soil, plants, or creatures that live there. Perhaps you'll find a spot that already has one or more of the four cardinal directions "anchored" by a rock, tree, creek, or other natural feature.

Place a small thing — a rock, pine cone, or stick — to mark each of the four cardinal directions not already "preanchored," so that you have a circle about eight feet or so in diameter. The precise compass directions are not important. Usually south, in the Northern Hemisphere (or north in the Southern Hemisphere) is obvious simply by where the Sun is at midday. Then you can extrapolate the other three directions from there. If you're going to move anything to anchor the directions, it's a good practice to first let those things (subjects, not objects) know, with audible speech, why you want to do so, ask for permission, and express gratitude if you feel you've received consent. This can feel odd or fanciful if you're not used to granting animate agency to the things of our world, but you'll probably feel good about doing it even if your worldview is not yet ready to shift. By treating your world as if it's more alive than you had previously imagined, you're likely to experience an enhancement in your *own* sense of aliveness.

You've now created a simple four-directions circle. You might feel a need to remind yourself that this is not a flaky or New Age exercise. Rather, it's an embodied acknowledgment of the panhuman intuition that wholeness, including your own, can be effectively embodied in a quadrisected circle aligned with the cardinal directions. It's also an acknowledgment of the fact that most cultures around the world, including a variety of Western traditions, have understood this, and that you, as a member of the human species, take the form you do as a result of millions of years of interdependent evolution with the other myriad forms and forces of the Earth community.

Here are some practices you can use in a four-directions circle.

Core Practice: Cultivating the Four Facets of the Self

STEP 1. Stand or sit in the center of the circle, the position of the 3-D Ego. Attentively look toward each of the four directions, one at a time. What do you see in that direction, both near and far? What sounds emanate from that direction? Scents? Winds? What do you feel when focused on this direction? What do you notice about the ground below you? About the sky above and the air in which you move?

STEP 2. Now face the direction of the facet of Self you want to cultivate. Let's say this time it's the North. Facing the north and the landforms, waterways, and vegetation in that direction, call out, audibly, to your Nurturing Generative Adult. Let it know why you want to cultivate your relationship to it. Tell it a relevant story or two from your life that illustrate why this is important to you now. Then give it an example or two of people in your life, past or present, who have embodied in an exemplary way the qualities of a Nurturing Generative Adult. If no one from your own life comes to mind, or even if someone does, evoke a biographical or archetypal figure. Imagine such a person or persons standing or sitting in this direction. Ask them to help you access and cultivate your own Nurturing Generative Adult. Take some time with this. Express your gratitude for the support you receive.

STEP 3. When you're ready, move to or next to the thing that is anchoring the north for you and stand there yourself. Breathe in and feel the essence of all the persons who have anchored for you the qualities of the Nurturing Generative Adult. Stand, sit, dance, move, sing, or speak there in the posture and manner of your own North facet of Self. Observe the world from this place. Imagine how your life would shift with the fully incorporated resources of the North. Address the world, out loud, from this consciousness. Breathe deeply and feel your body filling with this perspective and consciousness.

STEP 4. Now move back to the center of your circle and allow yourself to recall a significant and emotionally challenging issue in your current life: a question, conflict, dilemma, opportunity, dream, relationship, or feeling. Then speak aloud to the North facet about this issue, in exactly the way it has been feeling to you, in order to help yourself become more present to it. Take your time. Allow yourself to feel any emotions that arise without trying to modify them or make them go away.

STEP 5. Then once again move and stand in the north, merging again with this facet of the Self, and face the center of the circle. Speak to the issue from the perspective and consciousness of your Nurturing Generative Adult. Speak to it about how you experience it from this perspective or about what you feel ought to be done in relation to it. How do you understand this issue? What do you think about it? What are the best ways to care for yourself and any others involved? If you sense a response from the issue itself, good. Allow the interaction to become a dialogue. Keep it going. Take your time. Don't let the conversation fade until it feels complete to you or, better, to both you and it.

When you feel complete with this time in your four-directions circle, but before leaving, offer your gratitude to the place in which your circle sits. Present a gift, perhaps the mindful offering of your breath.

To amplify your work with the North facet of the Self, you might consider going, at least sometimes, to this place late at night and even in the winter, if you can do this safely, but any time of day or year is good. For the South facet, ideally go there in midday, and especially in summer. For the East facet, best is at first light, and especially in spring. For the West facet, ideal are the west-oriented times: toward sunset and in autumn.

When cultivating your relationship with your South facet, it's important, in step 3, to open your awareness to your feelings: your emotions and your sensations of being indigenous to Earth and thoroughly rooted in the land. In step 4, when you speak to your life issue, ask yourself what you *feel* about it. How does it feel in your body? With your indigenous sense of belonging to the more-than-human world, what's your perspective on this issue?

When you're cultivating your relationship with your East facet, be aware, in step 3, of your sensations of big-picture wisdom, innocence, clear-sightedness, and full presence in the now. In step 4, ask yourself what you sense about your life issue. What bits of wisdom are revealed? What does your Sage, Innocent, Trickster, or Sacred Fool have to say?

When you're cultivating your relationship with your West facet, imagine yourself, in step 3, to be as mysterious, mythic, imaginative, and mortal as anything in the cosmos. In step 4, ask yourself what you imagine about your life issue. What symbols, images, stories, or hidden meanings emerge from the depths? What magical aspects of the issue do you discover from this West perspective?

Other ways to work within a four-directions circle to cultivate the facets of the Self:

- While standing on the circumference of your circle in the place of one of your facets, speak to or converse with a plant, creature, or landform you observe in any direction. If this other being is in or near one of the other cardinal directions of your circle, speak to it as if it represents the facet of the Self associated with that direction.

- You can also converse directly with the other facets of the Self from the perspective of the facet you're standing with or as.

- While sitting or standing in the center as the 3-D Ego, converse with one of the facets. You can also move back and forth between the two positions.

- From the perspective of one of your facets, converse with your Soul (which you might imagine being deep below you) or with Spirit (above you or, better, surrounding you in all directions or, even better, permeating you and all things).

You can, of course, make a four-directions circle indoors and access the Self in this way, but there is a great, added advantage in doing this out on the land and in the most ecologically diversified place you can conveniently get yourself to. The more diverse, the more that place will evoke the varied potentialities of your own psyche.

Four-Directions Circles with Subpersonalities

When working with your North subpersonalities (any variety of your Loyal Soldiers, Rescuers, and Pseudo-Warriors), address them in a way similar to that described in the Loyal Soldier exercise described in chapter 6 (see pages 146–48). Imagine them on the north side of your circle, just inside the place of your Nurturing Generative Adult, representing them with found items or ones you brought with you. Then stand or sit in the place of each of your four facets of Self, one at a time, and address your North sub(s). Begin by fully embodying that facet of the Self in its emotions, thoughts, imagination, senses, and physical presence. It's especially important to address your North subs from your Wild Indigenous One, but all four facets will embrace them from their own unique perspectives.

When working with your South subpersonalities (any of your Wounded Children, Outcasts, or Orphans), address them in a way similar to that described in the chapter 7 practices (see pages 170–75). Place them on the south side of your circle, representing them with found items or ones you brought with you. It's especially important to address them from your Nurturing Generative Adult (whose place is on the opposite side of your circle).

When working with your East subpersonalities (your Escapists, Addicts, Bliss-heads, or Puers/Puellas), address them in a way similar to that described in the

Addicts and Escapists exercise in chapter 8 (see pages 193–99). Be sure to address them from the perspective of your Muse-Beloved.

When working with your West subpersonalities (suspected Shadow elements), address them in a way similar to that described in the Shadow exercise in chapter 9 (see pages 224–26). Be sure to address them from the perspective of your Innocent/Sage.

DREAMWORK WITH THE FACETS OF THE SELF

If you work with your dreams in a soulcentric manner,[2] you can use the following variation when your dream includes a figure or feature that feels very much like one of the facets of the Self (or like the Self as a whole).

A _North_-like figure might be someone like Saint Francis. Or someone like Mother Teresa, Gandhi, or Martin Luther King. Or sometimes it's a tree, mountain, or bison with a strong aura of competence, compassion, and caregiving. Or a house or community that embodies these same qualities.

A compelling _South_-like presence might be a wild man or woman, like Artemis, the Green Man, or Pan; a fertility figure, like the Native American Kokopeli or the Greek harvest goddess Demeter; an instinctive, muscular man, like Tarzan; a love-and-beauty figure, like Venus or Aphrodite; an earthy or indigenous person or an inhabitant of the forest, mountains, or desert. Perhaps it's a lustful or sensual creature, like a monkey, goat, horse, dog, or wildcat. Or possibly a Southerly thing or place, such as a lush meadow, garden, rain forest, or waterfall.

A strong _East_-like presence could be a wise woman or man, a saint, a fool, a comic, an infant, a faerie, or an innocent. Or maybe it's a creature that exemplifies innocence, like almost any newborn mammal; or one that embodies wisdom, like an owl; one that embraces a big picture, like an eagle; or a mischievous one, like a raven or coyote.

A potent _West_-like presence could take the form of a wizardly figure, like Merlin or Morgaine; an alluring and dangerous woman or man; a handsome and charming thief, bandit, or pirate; a femme fatale, like Mata Hari; a shaman; a medium; a Sphinx; Hades or Persephone; or Death. Often it's an underworld-ish creature, like a snake, mole, badger, bear, frog, fish, chameleon, caterpillar-chrysalis-butterfly, or worms. Or perhaps it's a Westerly place or thing, such as a cave, compost, falling and decaying leaves, a swamp, shadow, crypt, or sewer.

Begin this phase of your dreamwork by dropping back deeply into the dream so that you're reexperiencing the dream just as it unfolded while you were asleep. It's essential that you're able to experience yourself fully back in the dream's reality. This often takes some practice and might not work with every dream. Don't proceed with the next step unless you're able to do this.

Once you find yourself reimmersed in the dreamscape, observe the dream character or element carefully, using your eyes and ears within the dream. Let yourself fully feel its presence, allowing a full empathic resonance with this other. Then begin a dialogue with this dream figure, in which you tell it about its qualities in the way you experience them. Or ask it questions, which might include: "Is there anything you want to tell me, show me, or teach me?" Within the dreamscape, move in closer. Hope to be surprised as you get to know this dream figure. Don't interpret or draw conclusions. You may want to offer a gift — a physical thing or symbol.

Then you might ask if it would be willing to allow you to merge with it. If so, feel yourself become one with it until you can experience the dream scene from its perspective. How does this feel physically? What emotions are stirred? What thoughts or insights? If the dream ego (the you in your dreams) is present in this dream scene, take the opportunity to focus on the dream ego from the perspective of the being — the facet of the Self — with which you're now merged. What do you notice about the dream ego? What do you sense to be true of him or her? What seems to be missing in the dream ego's awareness or actions? What do you want to say to the dream ego? What object or symbol, if any, do you want to offer?

When you feel complete, gently bring yourself back to your dayworld by shifting your position a little, stretching a bit, and then slowly opening your eyes and taking a few deep breaths. Take journal notes, if you'd like, or draw some of the images from the dreamwork.

———

You can also use this method when working with dream characters that feel to you like subpersonalities in any of their intrapersonal or interpersonal guises. As in the dreamwork with the Self, reimmerse yourself in the dreamscape and observe the subpersonality character very carefully. One possibility, of course, is that the dream ego — the "you" in your dream — is the subpersonality. This is not unusual. But the subpersonality is often a non-Ego figure. In either case, you have the opportunity to empathically discover more of what it's like to be this subpersonality. Also, the next time you go out to your four-directions circle, you'll have a new dream-anchored image for one of your subpersonalities.

Following your dreamwork with your subpersonality characters, you may want to imagine them sitting in the corresponding quadrant of a four-directions circle, as discussed above, in which you address them from the perspective of your Self — in order to discover what they really want, how they've been trying to serve you, and what you can learn from them.

When using this form of dreamwork with a suspected element of your

Shadow — Sinister or Golden — you have the opportunity to empathically discover what it's like to be a character who is profoundly different from the way
you think of yourself. Let yourself be surprised by what happens. After completing
your dreamwork with your Shadow character, you may want to imagine this character sitting on the west side of your four-directions circle and then address it from
the perspective of your Self.

DEEP IMAGERY:
ANIMALS OF THE FOUR FACETS OF THE SELF

Deep imagery refers to inner journeys in which you interact, while awake, with the
other-than-Ego inhabitants of your psyche. Also known as *active imagination* by
Jungians, deep imagery is distinct from guided imagery, in which another person
(the guide) invites you to imagine specific scenes suggested by the guide. With deep
imagery, in contrast, the images come from the hidden depths of your own psyche,
and the guide (when there is one) doesn't know any more than you what will take
place on the journey. (See *Soulcraft* or www.wildmindbook.com for more background on deep-imagery work.)

There are many methods for cultivating deep imagery, but among the most
effective are those that involve imaginal animals, inner guides to healing, wholing,
and soul encounter. Psychologist Eligio Stephen Gallegos has developed a potent
method for working with imaginal animals.[3]

Gallegos implores us not to interpret imaginal animals. The goal is to interact
with them, develop a respectful relationship, and see how things unfold. Your 3-D
Ego accompanies the animal on journeys through the nonordinary realms of the
psyche and the body, receives information, advice, or other gifts, and assists the
animal with its needs. You might also merge with the animal to perceive its world
through its eyes, ears, and nose, move with its wings, paws, or fins, and be embodied within its feathers, fur, or scales.

Through deep-imagery work, you can cultivate your relationship with the
four facets of the Self. Most people find that their deep-imagery work is most effective when they are guided by another person highly experienced in this kind of
work.

Here is an example of how you can meet the animal of your North, whether
self-guided or guided by another:

Get into a comfortable position, either lying down on the floor or a couch or
sitting in a comfortable chair. (Use any relaxation or centering technique you prefer. See suggestions above for voice dialogue.) Then imagine you're facing the direction of north, and call out in this direction, asking for your animal of the North
facet of the Self to appear to you. Continue calling slowly and with some faith, and

soon enough you'll sense an animal (through visual, auditory, and/or kinesthetic imagery). Often it's an animal you're familiar with, one you know to exist in the real world, but sometimes it's a species of animal you never knew existed (and perhaps doesn't). Take some time to simply observe this animal. How does it move? What color is it? Does it make any sounds? Can you catch its scent? What does it seem to be doing? Tell it why you have come to meet it, and ask it if it has anything to tell you, show you, or teach you — perhaps something about cultivating your nurturing and generative capacities. Whatever it says or does, offer your careful and grateful attention. Maybe it will communicate with you in words or in gestures, sounds, emotions, images, or symbols or by taking you on a journey to experience something of importance. If you have any questions about what it says or does or how its response applies to you, ask it. Keep the dialogue or interaction going until it feels complete. Then ask if there is anything you can do for it, anything to help it in *its* world (as distinct from *your* everyday world). If it does make a request, do your best to assist it right then and there in your imagination. Whether or not it asks for your help, it's good to offer a gift. Then ask both yourself and the animal if there is anything else that needs to happen between the two of you at this time. If there is, continue the interaction. When the encounter feels complete, be sure to thank the animal for being there and let it know you hope to meet with it again before too long. Make some notes in your journal.

In the same way, meet your animals of the South, East, and West.

You can meet with these imaginal animals any time you need assistance from the Self or when you simply want to cultivate your access to or embodiment of any facet of Self. When working with challenging or traumatic experiences, it can be enormously helpful to begin by checking in with one or more of the animals of the four facets of your Self or to explore the experience from the perspective of these animals.

You can also use this deep-imagery process to meet animals of any of your subpersonalities.

If you've previously met and developed relationships with the imaginal animals of the four facets of your Self, then, after meeting your subpersonality animal, you might ask if it would be willing to meet with your Self animals. If it is, then call out, in your imagination, to these four animals, greet them as they appear, and let them know you've been meeting with your subpersonality animal. Allow them all to interact. It's best if you participate with them, and that you do so from the perspective of the 3-D Ego. If it feels right to all, you might invite your subpersonality animal to stand or sit in the center of a circle formed by you and the animals of your Self. The five of you might spontaneously interact with your subpersonality animal in a manner similar to what I described in discussing the four-directions circles.

Acknowledgments

The Nature-Based Map of the Human Psyche emerged gradually over the past twenty-five years from several interdependent sources. First to be acknowledged are the thousands of people who have participated in Animas Valley Institute's multiday, ceremonial immersions into the mysteries of nature and psyche. I'm grateful beyond measure for the privilege to serve as a guide for these bold women and men on their descent to Soul as well as on their journey of wholing and Self-healing. Every element of the map has roots in what I and my Animas colleagues have learned from tending the individuation of the people we've guided — and from navigating the labyrinths of our own personal development.

Each of these discoveries about human nature was clarified and amplified by locating it within the universal design pattern of the more-than-human world, which has provided innumerable cultures with the essential template of the four cardinal directions (and the four seasons and the four times of day), along with skyward (the above), downward (the below), and the center. Over the past hundred thousand years or so, this seven-directions template of wholeness has been enriched and further fleshed out by the symbols and images of the human archetypes, which together constellate what Carl Jung called the collective unconscious, or what might also be named Human Nature, or Mystery Expressing Itself through the Human. These archetypes are found abundantly in the myths (sacred stories), arts, and rituals of all peoples of the world.

Many other elements of the map derive from the insights, concepts, theories, and models contributed by Western psychologists, beginning in the early twentieth century, and from the work of countless Western poets, artists, and philosophers of the past several hundred years. I am grateful to all these individuals and traditions and for the crucial support of the Muse, who faithfully and generously directed my gaze toward the images and insights that have found their way onto the map.

My heartfelt gratitude goes to my border-eclipsing teachers Steven Foster and Meredith Little, who, beginning in the 1970s, pioneered the reintroduction to Western culture of the panhuman vision fast, and who developed their own model of human nature called the Four Shields, which they introduced in 1999 in their book of that title. I had the great fortune to study with Steven and Meredith in the 1980s — in person and through correspondence and by way of their books and essays — and was immeasurably enriched and informed by an early version of their model of human nature. Many seeds of the Nature-Based Map of the Human Psyche were sown by what I learned from Steven and Meredith.

Additional seeds for the map were sown by other great teachers with whom I've been privileged to study in person. These include Dorothy Wergin and her inspired map of the phases of the moon, "a guide to evolving human nature"; Peter G. Ossorio and his brilliantly articulated concepts of *person, behavior, language,* and *world,* as presented through descriptive psychology (to my knowledge, the first and only comprehensive conceptual framework for the science of psychology); Gregory Bateson and his visionary ecology of mind; Roger Strachan and his provocateur arts of wilderness encounter, gestalt therapy, and personal mandalas; Dolores LaChapelle and her wild guidance in experiential deep ecology and powder skiing; Elizabeth Cogburn and her elegantly embodied lessons on the four directions offered through the long dance and the talking staff council; Molly Young Brown and Morgan Farley and their innovative rendering of the psychosynthesis path to growing whole; Eligio Stephen Gallegos and his deeply imaginative elucidation of the "four windows of knowing"; Thomas Berry and his inspiring celebration of the dream of the Earth and, with Brian Swimme, the story of the Universe; Joanna Macy and her activist-empowering and culture-transforming Work That Reconnects; and David Abram and his eloquent articulation and embodiment of the art of "becoming animal." Aspects of the map have also been enriched by what I've learned from the published works of many seminal authors, including C. G. Jung, Roberto Assagioli, Rainer Maria Rilke, Joseph Campbell, Paul Shepard, Gary Snyder, James Hillman, Robert A. Johnson, Jean Houston, James Hollis, Chellis Glendinning, Carol Pearson, and David Whyte.

While the central ideas in this book ultimately derive from all the sources noted above — and more — there are many gifted and generous colleagues who have been indispensable in fleshing out and refining this map of the psyche.

My greatest debt is to consummate imagineer Geneen Marie Haugen, my beloved partner and underworld coguide, who, over the past ten years, has brought perception-expanding clarity and extension to the ideas and images embedded in the map. Indeed, many of the insights and practices found in these pages were originally suggested or coshaped by her. An immensely talented writer, Geneen also brought her literary and editorial eye to the crafting of this book, a great gift, especially while she was in the midst of her own major writing project, her doctoral dissertation on planetary imagination.

My greathearted Swiss friend and Animas colleague, Sabina Wyss, likewise edited every chapter of this book, often two or more times, graciously illuminating and questioning ideas and passages that were poorly formed and suggesting innumerable improvements in content and structure. Many of the practices offered here were suggested, developed, and modified by Sabina, an exceptionally gifted soul guide.

Two other dear friends, colleagues, and brilliant teachers, Peter Scanlan and Donna Medeiros, also reviewed every chapter with discerning eyes and wild creativity and deserve credit for much of the clarity and value I hope this book offers.

Other friends and treasured colleagues who helped shape the ideas and practices in these pages include Rebecca Wildbear, Gene Dilworth, Sheila Belanger, Anne Hayden, Mary Marsden, and Tony Putman.

As noted earlier, the Nature-Based Map of the Human Psyche was developed over many years in the midst of guiding a variety of Animas programs. My darkly radiant fellow guides during these years, in addition to those named above, include Jade Sherer, Jeffrey Allen, Jim Marsden, Annie Bloom, Jamie Reaser, Lauren Chambliss, Nate Bacon, Len Fleischer, Dianne Timberlake, Dorothy Mason, Doug Van Houten, Ann Roberts, Cristin DeVine, Louden Kiracofe, Bill Ball, Ron Pevny, Rob Meltzer, Kerry Brady, Trebbe Johnson, Wes Burwell, Patti Rieser, and Rachel Posner. I have immense gratitude for you all.

New World Library editorial director Georgia Hughes profoundly influenced the shape and content of this book. She saw its essence even before I did and worked with me for two years to bring forward its most worthy offerings. Georgia, too, reviewed and edited each chapter at least twice, helping me structure each and identify the many opportunities to trim and condense.

Great gratitude goes to my literary agent, Anne Depue, for representing and shepherding my work, for edits and suggestions on every chapter, for wrestling with and improving many of my ideas, and for coaching me in overall approach and form.

I'm grateful for Bonita Hurd's and Kristen Cashman's meticulous editorial expertise and for the investigative editorial assistance of Jonathan Wichmann.

Special thanks are due to Barbara Ford, Lane Lasater, Kenji Akahoshi, Michael Thunder, Deborah Demme, Steve and Jessie Zeller, Roger Strachan, Mado Reid, Wendy Sarno, Aryeh Margolis, Maria Cristina Grabiel, Christina Stout, Suzannah Bacon, and, as always, my beloved parents, Betty and Bernie Plotkin.

And the writing of this book would not have been possible without the loving and visionary support of the extraordinary individuals who have served on the Animas Valley Institute Board of Directors over the past few years, especially

Julian Norris, Barbara Ford, Sheila Belanger, Martin Goldberg, Tony Putman, David Ellisor, Cathy Edgerly, and Beverly Winterscheid, as well as our amazing Animas staff and team volunteers, who, in recent years, have included, among those not named earlier, Mary Karis, Elizabeth Shephard, Tracey Belt, Angela Atkinson, Nancy Petrik, Pete Fonken, Joe Mazza, Hilary Leighton, Tootie Jones, Ro Babcock, Chelle Nagle, and Sara Papathakis.

As noted a few times in these pages, a map is not to be confused with the territory. Notwithstanding all the human and archetypal help I've been blessed with, the Nature-Based Map of the Human Psyche is limited in its accuracy and usefulness by my conscious and unconscious assumptions, misunderstandings, cultural biases, and blind spots, and by the impatience that kept me from sensibly waiting another twenty-five years before first introducing the map in book form, as well as by the impossibility of fashioning any map that can reflect the endless nuances of the actual thing.

Finally, how does one thank the Earth and Universe that make possible each life and every creative project? How does one pay proper tribute to the thundering mountains, the enigmatic canyons, and the rivers that run through them? How does one meaningfully acknowledge the whirling galaxies of star worlds or the equally diverse flora and fauna of our home planet? Perhaps by daily celebrations of the miracle of each and our kinship with all, bows to how we've been formed and informed by them, conscious participation in the story we're spinning with them, and dedication of our lives to the flourishing of theirs. In this way, our human story might continue to unfold and, if we are amply graced, unfold in a way that serves and enhances all life on Earth and beyond.

Notes

Book Epigraphs

C. G. Jung, letter written in 1940, in *The Earth Has a Soul: C. G. Jung on Nature, Technology, and Modern Life*, ed. Meredith Sabina (Berkeley, CA: North Atlantic Books, 2008), p. 219.

David Whyte, from "The Sun," in *The House of Belonging* (Langley, WA: Many Rivers Press, 1997), p. 90.

Introduction: Re-Visioning Our Selves

Epigraph: Derek Walcott, "Earth," in *Sea Grapes* (London: Jonathan Cape, 1976), p. 87.

1. Psychology needs a fresh start in at least four ways. The two ways to which I hope to contribute with this book are substantive and applied: a structural map of the human psyche and, based on this map, new practices for growing whole. But Western psychology is also in need of a fresh start conceptually and methodologically: we must begin anew with a thoughtful and thorough articulation of the basic concepts of psychology — in particular, *behavior, person, language,* and *world* — and we must develop new methods for finding out what is and is not true about people and behavior (in addition to conventional forms of empirical science). These conceptual and methodological features of a fresh start, which are more fundamental and ambitious than what I attempt in this book, have been brilliantly and comprehensively addressed over the past fifty years in the work of Peter G. Ossorio and his colleagues through the discipline of descriptive psychology. See, for example, Ossorio's *Behavior of Persons* (Ann Arbor, MI: Descriptive Psychology Press, 2012), *Place* (Ann Arbor, MI: Descriptive Psychology Press, 2013), and www.sdp.org. Ossorio has launched what many consider to be the most foundational and essential project in the history of psychology, Western or otherwise.

2. Twentieth-century depth psychologists, beginning with Carl Jung, have expanded the scope of psychology beyond the mitigation of psychopathology, advocating goals such as Jung's individuation (the self-formation of the personality into a coherent whole,

enabling the embodiment of one's "true self") and James Hillman's soul-making (discovering and living the images at the depths of our psyches). The most prominent contemporary neo-Jungian depth psychologists, in addition to Hillman, include Marion Woodman, Thomas Moore, James Hollis, Jean Shinoda Bolen, Arnold Mindell, and Clarissa Pinkola Estés. Although depth psychology fully embraces the goal of wholeness, it has not, to my knowledge, offered a systematic and comprehensive means of identifying, assessing, and cultivating the dimensions or facets of our wholeness.

3. Launched in the late 1990s, positive psychology advocates a shift of emphasis from human dysfunction to positive functioning or thriving. The goal of positive psychology is to help people become "happier" and more "fulfilled." In this book, I suggest that psychological wholeness, soul embodiment, Spirit-realization, and gratifying participation in and contribution to the more-than-human world, rather than happiness, are more mature and enlivening goals of personal development. Happiness is more likely to find us if we're not chasing it but, instead, cultivating our capacity to fully belong to and love the world. True fulfillment allows for grief and longing, sometimes fear, and certainly uncertainty. Happiness might be too small a goal, inhibiting the deep joy and complex spectrum of experience and participation afforded by our psyches and our world.

    Positive psychology focuses on the emotional and social resources needed to function well in a human community, the types of skills and values developed in a healthy adolescence (rare in the Western world today). Beyond adolescent development, however, are the spiritual, ecological, and mythopoetic potentials of the psyche — the skills, values, and human resources we need in order to uncover our deeper identities and to participate fully as evolutionary partners in the more-than-human community.

4. David Abram, *The Spell of the Sensuous: Perception and Language in a More-Than-Human World* (New York: Pantheon, 1996).

5. One reason Western psychology has been pathology oriented rather than wholeness enhancing is that pathology howls — it gets our attention and calls for intervention — while health is relatively inconspicuous. When things go wrong, we take notice and seek solutions. When all is well, we tend to take our good fortune for granted — no intercession needed.

    A second reason is that the constituents of wholeness are much more difficult to inventory than are the symptoms of pathology. First, what tells us something is going right, other than the absence of something going wrong? It's tempting to crumple intellectually and simply conclude that wholeness, or health, is merely the absence of illness, in which case we have nothing to say about wholeness itself. Second, when enumerating the components of wholeness, how do we know we've identified them all, or even half? We need a nonarbitrary and comprehensive way of inventorying psychological wholeness, and it hasn't been obvious how to do this.

6. There are, of course, in the Western world outside the mainstream, instances of extraordinary educational and religious endeavors that are holistic and nature based. See, for example, Richard Lewis, *Living by Wonder: The Imaginative Life of Childhood* (New

York: Touchstone Center, 1998); Michael K. Stone and Zenobia Barlow, eds., *Ecological Literacy: Educating Our Children for a Sustainable World* (San Francisco: Sierra Club Books, 2005); Gregory Cajete, *Look to the Mountain: An Ecology of Indigenous Education* (Durango, CO: Kivaki Press, 1994); Richard Rohr, *Falling Upward: A Spirituality for the Two Halves of Life* (New York: Jossey-Bass, 2011); and Matthew Fox, *Original Blessing* (New York: Tarcher/Putnam, 2000).

7. Western science is in the midst of another outbreak of diehard reductionism, as seen for example in the neurosciences, in which brains are conceptually misconstrued as minds, as if certain neurological events are the same thing as empathy, love, or psychopathology. It should be simple enough to understand that neurology is one aspect of the way that human beings experience and do things, not the same thing as experience or behavior. Neurology is to behavior as wings are to bird flight (not the same thing as flight), or as fingers, brains, musical instruments, and musicians are to the orchestral performance of a symphony. The fact that certain things happen in certain parts of the brain when we feel empathy, or that our capacity for empathy might be impaired when that part of the brain is injured, tells us only that that part of the brain is part of how we do empathy (a valuable thing to know). The fact that you can't have an acoustic piano concerto without a piano does not make vibrations of piano strings the same thing as a concerto.

There are many well-established problems with reductionism, but the one I want to highlight is the way that reductionism shrinks and perhaps trivializes our way of conceiving and responding to the opportunities of human and cultural development and to the challenges in human life, including cultural and environmental degradation. If we reduce human difficulties to brain dysfunction, then, while we're preoccupied with neurology, we'll be oblivious to all the generally more significant opportunities to enhance life through endeavors in our psychological, social, cultural, and ecological realms. Intrapsychic reductionism — treating our human difficulties as solely the result of troubles within individual psyches — is only one step less limiting than neurological reductionism.

8. Foundational texts of ecopsychology include Gregory Bateson, *Mind and Nature: A Necessary Unity* (New York: Dutton, 1979); Paul Shepard, *Nature and Madness* (San Francisco: Sierra Club Books, 1982); Theodore Roszak, *The Voice of the Earth: An Exploration of Ecopsychology* (New York: Touchstone, 1993); Theodore Roszak, Mary Gomes, and Allen Kanner, eds., *Ecopsychology: Restoring the Earth, Healing the Mind* (San Francisco: Sierra Club Books, 1995); Ralph Metzner, *Green Psychology: Transforming Our Relationship to the Earth* (Rochester, VT: Park Street Press, 1999); and Andy Fisher, *Radical Ecopsychology: Psychology in the Service of Life* (Albany, NY: State University of New York Press, 2002).

9. Thomas Berry, *The Dream of the Earth* (San Francisco: Sierra Club Books, 1988).

10. Thomas Berry, *The Great Work: Our Way into the Future* (New York: Bell Tower, 1999), p. 3.

11. Joanna Macy and Chris Johnstone, *Active Hope: How to Face the Mess We're in without Going Crazy* (Novato, CA: New World Library, 2012), p. 26.

CHAPTER 1. THE NATURE-BASED MAP
OF THE HUMAN PSYCHE: AN OVERVIEW

Epigraph: Gary Snyder, *The Practice of the Wild* (Berkeley, CA: North Point Press, 1990), p. 12.

1. If our goal is to portray the human psyche in its integral wholeness, how can we be confident we've included all its features or components — that we haven't overlooked something essential? We need what architect Christopher Alexander calls "a design pattern," a formal way of generating a solution to a design problem. In this case, we need a design pattern that provides guidance in creating a map of the psyche — and in particular, a map that is complete. See my book *Nature and the Human Soul* (Novato, CA: New World Library, 2008), chapter 3, for a review of four-direction and seven-direction templates as found in traditions throughout the world, especially Native American, but also Tibetan, Egyptian, Buddhist, Hindu, Jewish, and Christian. Given the near ubiquity of such templates, it's tempting to conclude that the Nature-Based Map of the Psyche has its origins in nature itself or, if you prefer, in the collective human unconscious.

2. With the phrase *ecological niche*, I mean that Soul can be defined by a person's unique place not in human culture but in the more-than-human world. A person's *cultural* place is expressed in the social roles he enacts, including the ways he socially or vocationally embodies or manifests his ecological place (these embodiments being his delivery systems for Soul). The concept of Soul utilized in this and my previous books is equally and simultaneously ecological and psychological (and neither cultural nor religious). Our Souls belong to the natural world as much as they do to our psyches. This is analogous to light having properties of both a wave and a particle. Or you could say that each human Soul is an element in the Soul of the world, the *anima mundi*.

3. The first three definitions of Soul in this sentence are from poet David Whyte and are drawn from, respectively, *Crossing the Unknown Sea: Work as a Pilgrimage of Identity* (New York: Riverhead, 2002), and "All the True Vows" and "What to Remember When Waking," in *The House of Belonging* (Langley, WA: Many Rivers Press, 1997), pp. 24 and 28. The fourth quote is from Geneen Marie Haugen, personal communication, 2008.

4. The Yeats quote is from "The Song of Wandering Aengus," in *The Collected Poems of W. B. Yeats*, ed. Richard J. Finneran (New York: Scribner, 1996), p. 59.

5. Joanna Macy, *Widening Circles: A Memoir* (Gabriola Island, BC: New Society Publishers, 2001), p. 106. Also see my *Nature and the Human Soul*, pp. 269–71, for a discussion of this and a second of Joanna's encounters with Soul.

6. Thomas Berry, *The Great Work: Our Way into the Future* (New York: Bell Tower, 1999), p. 13, and *The Dream of the Earth* (San Francisco: Sierra Club Books, 2006). See my books *Soulcraft* and *Nature and the Human Soul* for many more examples, all with much greater elaboration, of ways that people have understood and articulated their mythopoetic identities.

7. My use of *Self* is similar to that of Carl Jung, who defined it as the "archetype of wholeness and the regulating center of the psyche." Jung understood the Self to be a coherent

whole, encompassing and unifying both the conscious and unconscious realms of the psyche and often symbolized by a quadrisected circle. I, too, conceive of the Self as a coherent whole, one that encompasses both conscious and unconscious elements and is in fact both symbolized *and represented* as a quadrisected circle. One major difference is that I have specifically characterized the four facets of the Self, something that to my knowledge Jung did not do. Another difference is that Jung thought of the Self as the totality of the entire psyche, including the ego, while I prefer to think of it as a whole within the psyche, where the psyche also includes the Ego, subpersonalities, Soul, and our connection with Spirit.

8. This idea of different versions of ourselves comes from Anthony O. Putman, "Being, Becoming, and Belonging," in *Advances in Descriptive Psychology*, vol. 7, ed. H. Joel Jeffrey and Raymond M. Bergner (Ann Arbor, MI: Descriptive Psychology Press, 1998), pp. 127–60.

9. It's also possible to act by way of our subs or Self when we are unconscious or asleep — that is, without the Ego's participation (for example, when sleepwalking, dreaming, or in deep trance or coma).

10. Although our subpersonalities and the facets of our Selves act *in the world* only when we, as persons, do, it makes sense to say that the subpersonalities and the facets of the Self often act *within our psyches* independent of our Egos.

11. The concept of the Self presented here, in addition to being similar to Jung's, is fully resonant with what deep ecologists call, following Norwegian philosopher Arne Naess, the *ecological self*. See "Self Realization: An Ecological Approach to Being in the World," in *Thinking Like a Mountain: Toward a Council of All Beings*, by John Seed, Joanna Macy, Pat Fleming, and Arne Naess (Gabriola Island, BC: New Society Publishers, 1988).

12. As I wrote earlier, in *Nature and the Human Soul*, "We live in a largely adolescent world. And it is, in great measure, a pathological adolescence. There is absolutely nothing wrong with (healthy) adolescence, but our cultural resources have been so degraded over the centuries that the majority of humans in 'developed' societies now never reach true adulthood. An adolescent world, being unnatural and unbalanced, inevitably spawns a variety of cultural pathologies, resulting in contemporary societies that are materialistic, greed-based, hostilely competitive, violent, racist, sexist, ageist, and ultimately self-destructive. These societal symptoms of patho-adolescence, which we see everywhere in the industrialized world today, are not at the root of our human nature, but rather are an effect of egocentrism on our humanity" (p. 7).

13. It's challenging to identify names for parts of the psyche, names that might enjoy widespread resonance and acceptance. Although in these pages I've selected words that work for me, my colleagues, and most participants in our programs, there will be some readers for whom some of these words won't resonate. But the names are not essential; the meanings are. I've tried to offer clear descriptions and definitions so you can understand what I'm pointing to, even if you might prefer other pointers. The important thing is to have a common language to refer to shared concepts and images.

In your own use of the Nature-Based Map of the Psyche, feel free to substitute other names when those work better for you.

14. In earlier times, "the environment" meant the local ecosystem; but now, in the twenty-first century, with global industrialization it means the entire planetary biosphere.

15. See David Abram, *The Spell of the Sensuous: Perception and Language in a More-Than-Human World* (New York: Pantheon, 1996).

16. Mary Oliver, from "The Summer Day," in *New and Selected Poems* (Boston: Beacon Press, 1992), p. 94.

17. By protecting us in the ways they do, our subs also increase our chances of surviving long enough, psychologically and physically, to enable us someday to cultivate a relationship to Self and to the transpersonal (both Spirit and Soul).

    Our subpersonalities also benefit us by providing a type of spiritual support: the wounds associated with our subpersonalities suggest something about the Soul's desires and the resources or qualities we must cultivate in order to manifest those desires. The process of uncovering these desires and resources is what I call "advanced subpersonality work." It's advanced because this work is possible and psychologically safe enough only after a person has realized some success at cultivating the facets of the Self and has reached the developmental stage in which the psyche is prepared for the journey of descent to Soul. We'll explore the nature of this advanced work in each of the subpersonality chapters.

18. The English language seems to lack a simple, single word that means "to make whole." This absence, in itself, might reflect Western proclivities to analyze and fragment more than to synthesize and unite. Although wholing at first seems an awkward word, I think you'll soon enough grow accustomed to it and perhaps appreciate it as indispensable, as I have. I borrowed it from psychologist Jean Houston.

    To make whole is not the same as to perfect. As Jung emphasized, the goal of individuation (meaning, roughly, to become fully human and uniquely oneself) is decidedly not perfection but wholeness. To become fully human is to cultivate our relationships with all aspects of our psyche and all things of the world.

19. Sad to say, Western psychotherapy often involves an immature therapist attempting to heal while operating from his own woundedness — from subpersonalities such as Rescuer or Conformist.

20. This is not to say that we can grow whole on our own, only that it is possible to *heal* on our own (via the Self). The larger process of becoming fully human requires a community: we need to be mirrored by others to be able to clearly see ourselves; we need positive role models to help us understand what it is to be whole or fully human; and we all need teachers, true adults, initiators, and elders to guide us along the way.

21. See James Hillman and Michael Ventura, *We've Had a Hundred Years of Psychotherapy — and the World's Getting Worse* (San Francisco: Harper, 1993).

22. In my view, these are the two foremost criteria for an adequate psychological assessment model:

    • It must help us understand the specific restrictions and strengths in a person's psychological repertoire — in his capacity to embody wholeness and to be in healthy relationships with other persons, society, and the natural environment.

- It must help us understand what to do to expand that capacity, to cultivate wholeness.

The most commonly employed assessment system in Western psychology and psychiatry, the *Diagnostic and Statistical Manual of Mental Disorders* (DSM), does not even meaningfully attempt to meet either of these criteria, but instead simply categorizes psychological deficits and symptoms, often in a way that is pejorative and demeaning. The Nature-Based Map of the Psyche (NMP), in contrast, has been shaped with both criteria as primary design influences and with respect for all persons and their potential.

A large percentage of psychologists, psychiatrists, and counselors have for many years found the DSM to be a thoroughly unsatisfactory framework for understanding or helping people (although pharmaceutical companies seem to like it quite well). The NMP is a contribution to the development of an affirmative, holistic, nature-based, twenty-first-century approach to psychological assessment and personal development.

23. Consider, for example, Freud's map of the psyche, his famous tripartite "structural model" of id, ego, and superego. For Freud, the id is the unconscious, impulsive, childlike part of the psyche that "wants what it wants when it wants it" and is the source of basic impulses and drives; it avoids pain and seeks immediate pleasure and gratification. On the Nature-Based Map of the Psyche, we find the id's impulses and drives in three places: in some features of our Wounded Children (the South subpersonalities), in some features of the Wild Indigenous One (South facet of the Self), and in some elements of both of the first two that have been hidden away (repressed) in the Shadow (the collection of West subpersonalities). In other words, we find aspects of the id in both the wounded and the healthy South and in the repressed South, but with no distinctions made between these three very different realms of the South.

The superego, for Freud, is the self-righteous, moral component of the psyche that strives for perfection and social appropriateness and acceptance; it criticizes us, prohibits immoral actions, and is, in essence, our conscience. The subject matter of the superego corresponds to what the NMP calls the Inner Critic or Critical Parent (two among the North subpersonalities) and, in some ways, to the mature protective qualities of the Nurturing Generative Adult (the North facet of the Self) — in short, some aspects of the North, but again without distinguishing mature and immature versions. And Freud's "ego" corresponds to what I, too, call Ego, but more specifically, an *immature* Ego. Freud, like many Western psychologists, overlooked most aspects of our human horizontal wholeness (collectively, what I call the Self), but especially its East and West facets, as well as our vertical wholeness — our relationship with both Soul and Spirit (underworld and upperworld).

Carl Jung, Roberto Assagioli, and others came closer to offering a map of the whole psyche, yet without identifying all aspects that become evident when using the design pattern of nature's seven directions.

24. The Nature-Based Map of the Psyche can aid us in self-discovery somewhat in the way

that physical scientists once used the periodic table of the elements to know "where" to look for never-before-encountered atomic elements.

Chapter 2. North: The Nurturing Generative Adult

Epigraph: Wendell Berry, from "A Vision," in *The Selected Poems of Wendell Berry* (Washington, DC: Counterpoint, 1999), p. 102.

1. Thomas Berry, *The Great Work: Our Way into the Future* (New York: Bell Tower, 1999), pp. 12–13.

2. By "initiated adults" I mean people who experience themselves, first and foremost, as members of the Earth community (in contrast to members of a family, tribe, culture, or nation), have had a revelatory experience of their unique, mythopoetic place in that community, and are embodying that unique place as a gift to their people and the Earth community. Even briefer: initiated adults are those who know who they really are. See my book *Nature and the Human Soul* for a more complete definition and description of the initiated adult.

3. Lewis Hyde, *The Gift: Imagination and the Erotic Life of Property* (New York: Vintage, 1983).

4. Aldo Leopold, *A Sand County Almanac* (New York: Ballantine, 1970), p. 240. The actual quotation is: "In short, a land ethic changes the role of *Homo sapiens* from conqueror of the land-community to plain member and citizen of it. It implies respect for his fellow-members, and also respect for the community as such."

5. Eligio Stephen Gallegos, *Animals of the Four Windows: Integrating Thinking, Sensing, Feeling, and Imagery* (Santa Fe, NM: Moon Bear Press, 1991).

6. Gallegos understands thinking, feeling, and sensing much the way that Carl Jung did, but where Jung wrote of intuition as the fourth "function of consciousness," Gallegos offers the insight that the fourth function is actually imagination. Gallegos explains that intuition is our ability to know things "beyond the present moment and circumstance and for which there is no immediate evidence" (ibid., p. 6). Intuition, he notes, can operate by means of any of the four windows, although for any given person it tends to operate primarily through one in particular. In other words, for some people intuitions arrive in the form of an image — say, of a loved one's face just before that person walks in the door. Other people intuit by way of a thought "out of nowhere" that enables them to understand more deeply something happening at the moment. Some people intuit by way of a feeling or emotion. A fourth group experiences intuition primarily through sensory perception — say, the appearance of a certain bird, breeze, or blossom, which suggests to them that some specific event (such as a birth or a death) has just happened or is about to happen. Jung's own intuition, as it turns out, operated primarily through his imagination, which led him to identify the fourth function as intuition.

7. In contemporary America, our schools tend to overvalue thinking and ignore the development of emotional, imaginal, and sensory intelligence. In fact, even genuine thinking is discouraged in our schools, which tend to teach only memorization and mimicry. By overemphasizing shallow thinking and inconsequential strategizing, we shortchange indigenous human desires and developmental needs, such as for

exploration and celebration of the wondrous and beautiful, as well as for creativity and artistic expression, emotional growth and healing, healthy relationships, and personal fulfillment and meaning.

Our schools place a secondary emphasis, after shallow thinking, on sensing, but here the focus is mostly on seeing and hearing, with little attention to tasting, smelling, or touching. Even with visual and auditory perception, there is little effort invested in helping children to see or hear clearly, to employ their full appreciation for nuance and depth in the play of light and sound.

Creative thinking and emotional, imaginal, and sensory experience should receive full attention in our classrooms, at home, at work, and in our social and recreational lives, so that we can all grow into mature humans with full mastery of all four of our fundamental human faculties of knowing.

8. What I write here about the north is true, of course, only in the Northern Hemisphere; in the Southern Hemisphere, the qualities discussed in this chapter are those of the South.

9. Rainer Maria Rilke, *Rilke's Book of Hours: Love Poems to God*, trans. Anita Barrows and Joanna Macy (New York: Riverhead Books, 1996), p. 67.

CHAPTER 3. SOUTH: THE WILD INDIGENOUS ONE

Epigraph: David Abram, *Becoming Animal: An Earthly Cosmology* (New York: Pantheon, 2010), p. 3.

1. Robert MacLean, from "Nass River," in *Heartwood* (Silverton, CO: Way of the Mountain Center, 1985), p. 10.

2. Hermann Hesse, "Sometimes," trans. Robert Bly, in *News of the Universe*, ed. Robert Bly (Berkeley, CA: University of California Press, 1995), p. 86.

3. Mary Oliver, from "Wild Geese," in *New and Selected Poems* (Boston: Beacon Press, 1992), p. 110.

4. Read *Song of the World*, Jean Giono's extraordinary novel, for the rare adventure of a reading experience that viscerally evokes the consciousness of the Wild One.

5. David Whyte, from "Revelation Must Be Terrible," in *Fire in the Earth* (Langley, WA: Many Rivers Press, 1992), p. 33.

6. The Self experiences our emotions very differently than do our subpersonalities. From the perspective of the Self, the experience of shame, for example, tells us that we have acted in a way that has violated our own authentic values. Shame, in this way, is an invaluable, although painful, experience that serves notice that we must make amends in order to do what's right, to repair any relationship damage, and to reinstate our sense of personal integrity. As we'll see in chapter 7, the Wounded Children elements of our psyches experience shame in a very different way — as devastating evidence that we are unworthy and ineligible. For our Wounded Children, shame is often a toxic experience.

7. Wendell Berry, from "1988: II," in *A Timbered Choir* (Washington, DC: Counterpoint, 1998), p. 98.

8. Joanna Macy and Chris Johnstone, *Active Hope: How to Face the Mess We're in without Going Crazy* (Novato, CA: New World Library, 2012).

9. Quoted in Meredith Sabini, *The Earth Has a Soul: C. G. Jung on Nature, Technology and Modern Life* (Berkeley, CA: North Atlantic Books, 2008), p. 98.

10. Paul Shepard, *Coming Home to the Pleistocene*, ed. Florence R. Shepard (Washington, DC: Island Press, 1998).

11. We could conclude, then, that elements of the instinctual nature of contemporary Western people can be found in both the South facet of wholeness and the West component of woundedness, the Shadow. In other words, what Jung and others called our unconscious "instincts" might largely be repressed aspects of our South wholeness now mostly hidden in the Shadow. These are resources of inestimable value that can be reclaimed when we are developmentally prepared to do so. Accessing them before we are psychospiritually ready could be dangerous to both the individual and his society. For example, the 1930s eruption of the collective German Shadow (in the form of the archaic figure of Wotan), Jung believed, is what made the Nazi movement possible. A god of ancient Germanic paganism, Wotan is associated with states of ecstasy, fury, prophecy, and poetic inspiration, a mix of South and West aspects of the psyche. Hitler managed to awaken and harness these positive cultural capacities for his own pathological ends.

12. Sigmund Freud, *New Introductory Lectures on Psycho-Analysis* (New York: Norton, 1969), p. 100.

13. In an egocentric society, it may be necessary for some of this wildness to be kept hidden from the mainstream, shared openly only with family members and other intimates. For an *ecocentric* perspective on childhood development, see my book *Nature and the Human Soul* (Novato, CA: New World Library, 2008), chaps. 4 and 5.

14. Theodore Roszak, *The Voice of the Earth: An Exploration of Ecopsychology* (New York: Touchstone, 1992), p. 290.

15. Rainer Maria Rilke, *Rilke's Book of Hours: Love Poems to God*, trans. Anita Barrows and Joanna Macy (New York: Riverhead Books, 1996), p. 116.

16. D. H. Lawrence, *Lady Chatterley's Lover and A Propos of "Lady Chatterley's Lover,"* ed. Michael Squires (Cambridge: Cambridge University Press, 2002), p. 323.

17. When a person's innate wildness and indigenity is culturally suppressed in childhood, as is common in Western societies, the Wild One gradually disappears into the dark, hidden recesses of the psyche, either to awkwardly reappear in the sexual hunger and emotional storms of the teen years or to smolder indefinitely beneath the civilized veneer of socioeconomic propriety. Sometimes the repressed Wild One will briefly burst out of the smoldering shadows in shocking and often ruinous displays of antisocial exploits — not because the Wild One is antisocial, but because its repression corrupts and warps our natural, wholesome wildness. (We'll explore the Shadow in some depth in chapter 9.)

18. See Stephen Harrod Buhner, *Ensouling Language: On the Art of Nonfiction and the Writer's Life* (Rochester, VT: Inner Traditions, 2010), especially chapter 5.

19. It's probably not a coincidence that people from southern countries, like Italy and Greece, or Mexico and Brazil, are said to be highly attuned to their feelings. The northern

countries, in contrast, are better known for North-like people, as seen, for example, in the Germanic attitude of *ʒackʒack* (getting things done quickly) and in the North American fondness for bigger, better, faster, more, and progress-as-our-most-important-product). The South might respond with "mañana" or all-night salsa dancing.

20. See Richard Louv's *Last Child in the Woods: Saving Our Children from Nature-Deficit Disorder* (Chapel Hill, NC: Algonquin Books, 2005).
21. Gary Snyder, *The Practice of the Wild* (Berkeley, CA: North Point, 1990), p. 192.
22. Many Jews, Christians, and Muslims have an additional reason to speak of ascension to Spirit: from their monotheistic, transcendental perspective, the divine and heaven are above and beyond this world entirely.

CHAPTER 4. EAST: THE INNOCENT/SAGE

Epigraph: Mary Oliver, *Why I Wake Early* (Boston: Beacon Press, 2004), pp. 58–59.

1. Hafiz, from "Tired of Speaking Sweetly," in *The Gift: Poems by Hafiz*, trans. Daniel Ladinsky (New York: Penguin, 1999), p. 187.
2. Healthy competition is a special case of cooperation; it enables the contestants or adversaries to cultivate skills and conjure creative innovations, all for the benefit of the community. Aggressive and vicious competition, in contrast (routinely found in, for example, Western politics, business, and sports), springs from personal woundedness and from the psychopathologies commonly engendered by egocentric society.
3. Robinson Jeffers, from "The Tower beyond Tragedy," in *The Selected Poetry of Robinson Jeffers*, ed. Tim Hunt (Palo Alto, CA: Stanford University Press, 2002), p. 113.
4. The eighty-one sayings are published as the *Tao Te Ching*, translated as *The Way of Life*.
5. Jelaluddin Rumi, from "A Spider Playing in the House," in *Feeling the Shoulder of the Lion: Poetry and Teaching Stories of Rumi*, trans. Coleman Barks (Boston: Shambhala, 2000), pp. 56–57.
6. Jay Leeming, "Ego," in *Dynamite on a China Plate* (Omaha: Backwaters Press, 2006), p. 65.
7. Here I am blending the acute sensing of the East with the embodied sensuousness of the South. The East and South naturally work together in this way: the South's sensuousness adds and blends emotion, feeling, and eroticism into what the East purely perceives through the five senses.
8. The death of the Ego is not the same as its elimination. If we understand the Ego to be the conscious self and its current way of self-understanding, then "death of the Ego" means the death of our current self-concept. The Ego is "reborn" in another form as soon as it dies in its previous one — at least until the end of our life. But this is no comfort to the Ego as it embarks on either the ascent or the descent.

CHAPTER 5. WEST: THE MUSE-BELOVED

Epigraph: William Stafford, "When I Met My Muse," in *The Way It Is: New and Selected Poems* (Saint Paul, MN: Graywolf Press, 1998), p. 222.

1. Ken Kesey, "The Art of Fiction No. 136," interview by Robert Faggen, *Paris Review*, no. 130 (Spring 1994), www.theparisreview.org/interviews/1830/the-art-of-fiction-no-136-ken-kesey (accessed October 2, 2012).

2. John Fowles, *The Magus: A Revised Version* (Boston: Back Bay Books, 2001), p. 235.

3. Apparently the early Greeks fully honored the imagination in a way that Western culture has mostly lost; many contemporary Westerners believe that all knowledge derives exclusively from observation and thinking, and that imagination is mere fantasy and fiction (and that emotions are irrational and unreliable).

4. From a letter to the Reverend Dr. Trusler, August 23, 1799, in *The Complete Poetry and Prose of William Blake*, ed. David V. Erdman (Berkeley: University of California Press, 1982), p. 702.

5. Geneen Marie Haugen, "Awakening Planetary Imagination: A Theory and Practice" (PhD diss., California Institute of Integral Studies, San Francisco, forthcoming).

6. A biocracy is a society in which all species, not just individual humans, are granted (by humans) their habitat and freedom.

7. Jelaluddin Rumi, *Open Secret: Versions of Rumi*, trans. John Moyne and Coleman Barks (Boston: Shambhala, 1999), quatrain 388, p. 8.

8. As we cultivate the gender qualities in which we are innately weaker, we don't become gender ambiguous or nondescript, and we don't find ourselves less attracted or attractive to others. To the contrary, our masculine or feminine core becomes more attractive because it can now be more fully expressed and embodied in the world: A masculine person's action orientation and intellectual-spiritual insights are now manifested more sensitively, flexibly, and imaginatively and, consequently, more effectively and masterfully. A feminine person's intuition and sensitivity are now expressed more eloquently and embodied more dynamically and, consequently, more visibly and seductively.

9. Another way the Inner Beloved shows up is when a masculine person notices himself being attracted to feminine endeavors, as when a masculine man desires to study ballet or massage. Or the Inner Beloved may manifest for a feminine woman in her attraction to the role of preacher or mountaineer.

10. The art of romance is obviously a vast topic that can only be touched on here. For a soulcentric perspective, see my book *Soulcraft: Crossing into the Mysteries of Nature and Psyche* (Novato, CA: New World Library, 2003), chap. 12.

11. The East and West facets of the Self lie on the horizontal plane, while Spirit and Soul constitute the vertical axis. Self is our horizontal wholeness. Soul is our depths. Spirit is the immanent and transcendent unity that contains all. (See the definitions at the beginning of chapter 1.)

12. We form crushes in childhood, too, in the first grade or even earlier. These are likely early projections of the Inner Beloved onto another, years before mature romance or sexual allurement occurs.

13. People with highly developed North and East facets, too, are a threat to consumer society, in part because no facet of the Self can be fully embodied without some degree of cultivation of the other three. But the North facet, considered in isolation, is not as great a threat, because this facet is able to care for others and get things done without

having to rock the boat of empire. And the East facet is not as subversive as the South and West, because the East is able to rise above the everyday fray, be present to the daily miracles, and chuckle ironically about itself without necessarily challenging business as usual.

14. Contemporary Western life is commonly lauded as an across-the-board advancement. We're told that things used to be a lot worse, that back in premodern times life was simply "poor, nasty, brutish, and short," as the seventeenth-century English philosopher Thomas Hobbes famously put it, whereas now we have modern hygiene and health care, uncountable channels of television, fast food, and "better living through chemistry." This perspective reveals a misunderstanding of life in healthy, nature-based societies; cultural prejudice; unwarranted Western self-congratulations; and utter denial of the brutish, life-destroying aspects of contemporary Western culture — as well as an accurate appraisal of how science and technology have in many ways enhanced the quality of Western life.

15. Diane di Prima, from "Rant," in *From the Margin: Writings in Italian Americana*, ed. Anthony Julian Tamburri, Paolo A. Giordano, and Fred L. Gardaphé, rev. ed. (West Lafayette, IN: Purdue University Press, 2000), p. 143.

16. David Whyte, from "Sometimes," in *Everything Is Waiting for You* (Langley, WA: Many Rivers Press, 2003), p. 5.

17. Robert Bly, trans., from "The Man Watching," in *Selected Poems of Rainer Maria Rilke* (New York: Harper and Row, 1981), p. 107.

18. David Whyte, from "All the True Vows," in *The House of Belonging* (Langley, WA: Many Rivers Press, 1997), p. 25.

19. People are psychospiritually prepared for the descent when they reach what I call the Cocoon, the fourth of eight life stages in the Eco-Soulcentric Developmental Wheel; see my book *Nature and the Human Soul*.

20. For more on the descent to Soul, see *Soulcraft* or chapter 7 of *Nature and the Human Soul*.

21. David Whyte, from "What to Remember When Waking," in *The House of Belonging* (Langley, WA: Many Rivers Press, 1997), p. 27.

22. Rainer Maria Rilke, *Rilke's Book of Hours: Love Poems to God*, trans. Anita Barrows and Joanna Macy (New York: Riverhead, 1996), p. 49.

23. Ibid., p. 61.

CHAPTER 6. NORTH: LOYAL SOLDIERS

Epigraph: Robert Bly, "One Source of Bad Information," in *Morning Poems* (New York: Harper, 1998), p. 85.

1. I'm indebted to master psychosynthesists Morgan Farley and Molly Young Brown, who introduced me to the image of the Loyal Soldier in 1981. See Molly Young Brown, *Unfolding Self: The Practice of Psychosynthesis* (New York: Allworth Press, 2004).

2. David Whyte, from "The Fire in the Song," in *Fire in the Earth* (Langley, WA: Many Rivers Press, 1997), p. 35.

3. For an example of how you might assist others with their Loyal Soldier work, see www .wildmindbook.com.

4. My estimate is that 80 percent of Westerners never reach the Cocoon stage — on account of widespread developmental deficits from childhood and early adolescence. A full explanation can be found in my book *Nature and the Human Soul*.

5. See my book *Soulcraft* or *Nature and the Human Soul*, chapter 7, for an exploration of a great variety of core methods for Soul encounter.

6. Anita Barrows, from "Questo Muro," in *Kindred Flame* (Berkeley, CA: Quelquefois Press, 2010).

CHAPTER 7. SOUTH: WOUNDED CHILDREN

Epigraph: Lisel Mueller, "Sometimes, When the Light," in *Alive Together: New and Selected Poems* (Baton Rouge: Louisiana State University Press, 1996), p. 115.

1. Our Outcasts are the parts of ourselves we've banished but remain conscious of. If, however, we so completely banish an Outcast that we're no longer conscious of its existence, then it becomes an element of our Shadow — the realm of our West subpersonalities, which we'll explore in chapter 9. For an excellent discussion of Outcasts, see Francis Weller's *Entering the Healing Ground: Grief, Ritual, and the Soul of the World* (Santa Rosa, CA: WisdomBridge Press, 2011).

2. Psychologists refer to this tactic as "identification with the aggressor."

3. For examples of communal grieving practices, see Weller's *Entering the Healing Ground* and Malidoma Somé, *The Healing Wisdom of Africa: Finding Life Purpose through Nature, Ritual, and Community* (New York: Tarcher/Putnam, 1998).

4. This is not to deny there are times when antidepressants are useful. Sometimes a person is so depressed (has so many strong emotions stuck inside for so long) that there's value or even necessity in buying some time to get beyond an acute suicidal phase, after which the person can be helped to fully feel.

    Some believe there are valid uses of antidepressants for forms of depression caused by deficits in brain chemistry as opposed to unassimilated emotions. Although this may be the case, we may also wonder what percentage of people said to be in the former category are really in the latter. Antidepressants and other tools of psychopharmacology are often used as regrettable substitutes because there's a lack of expertise among many psychotherapists and most physicians to facilitate emotional access, embodiment, expression, and assimilation. It is likely that, more often than not, antidepressants, as currently used, are causing greater depression (increased suppression of emotions) and should be called what they really are: depressants. They "assist" people to feel "better" by feeling less — when the true cure is to feel more.

5. There are actually four kinds of depression, four varieties of obstructed human nature:

    - South: blocked emotions
    - West: blocked access to meaning, imagination, inspiration, or life purpose
    - North: blocked ability to creatively manifest life purpose (for example, writer's block)
    - East: blocked capacity for present-centeredness, humor, or a big-picture perspective, or a blocked relationship to Spirit

    The kind of depression discussed in this chapter is the South variety.

6. This is not to blame the poor for being poor. When a poor or oppressed person is as retarded in his personal development as most egocentric middle-class and upper-class people, a likely factor is societal or class oppression and the resulting lack of opportunities.

7. Egocentric society functions largely as a system of Victims and Rescuers (and Perpetrators). Consider America's dysfunctional tort system and its disempowering approach to welfare, to name just two examples.

8. We can also *choose* to act as a Prince or Princess. When we do, we know we're doing it and feel fully justified because we are, after all, better than others — smarter, more talented, more important, and perhaps from an upper-crust family — and people *should*, come to think of it, defer to us.

9. The same is true, of course, of ecocentric nations and corporations, which are very rare in the world today. Among nations, Ecuador and Bolivia are leading the way by legislatively affirming the rights of other-than-human nature.

   The extent to which individuals or nations care for their environment reveals something much more important than their political alliance or philosophical perspective; it is nothing less than a measure of their psychological and spiritual maturity and wholeness and of their capacity for compassion — for self, others, their fellow species, and their own future generations.

10. Edward O. Wilson, *The Diversity of Life* (Cambridge, MA: Harvard University Press, 1992), p. 280.

11. I'm referring to conformity not necessarily in the way things are done but in the shared values and identities that underlie the consumer way of life — the implicit belief, for example, that it's acceptable to have jobs that are poverty exporting, life degrading, habitat destroying, and deadly to one's own soul and to have them not just to survive but in order to purchase mountains of stuff of dubious worth.

12. You might, for example, employ the principles of nonviolent communication.

13. I am grateful to my teachers Steven Foster and Meredith Little for introducing me, in 1985, to their version of this walk.

14. Although the existence of the core wound is necessary for the eventual emergence of adulthood, it's not at all sufficient. A developmentally prepared adolescent must recognize, accept, and respond to the call from the depths — the summons to spiritual adventure — and most youth don't know how to do this or aren't able without the support of genuine elders or adult initiators. A society with few true adults and elders will eventually self-destruct...unless the paths to initiation are unearthed, reclaimed, and restored. See my books *Soulcraft* and *Nature and the Human Soul*.

15. Arno Kohlhoff of Germany has told me that the Enneagram can be understood as a description of nine categories of core vulnerabilities.

16. This perspective is brilliantly articulated by psychologist Jean Houston in *The Search for the Beloved: Journeys in Mythology and Sacred Psychology* (Los Angeles: Tarcher, 1987).

CHAPTER 8. EAST: ADDICTS AND ESCAPISTS

Epigraph: Dawna Markova, *I Will Not Die an Unlived Life: Reclaiming Purpose and Passion* (Berkeley, CA: Conari, 2000), p. 1.

1. In childhood, it's possible to develop Escapist tactics so effective and reliable that there's little need for Loyal Soldier or Wounded Child strategies. When a person stays stuck in their woundedness even after doing first-rate healing work with their Loyal Soldiers and Wounded Children, it's often because there's a potent Escapist strategy still at work. This can be, for example, a dissociative pattern such as "leaving" one's body, used for so many years it has become reflexive. It's also possible there's an element of Shadow that needs to be discovered and integrated (see next chapter).

2. If these social gambits are inspired by self-criticism (such as a feeling of being socially unworthy), they can actually be Loyal Soldier strategies or a combination of Loyal Soldier and Escapist. But if they simply enable evasion without psychological downsizing, they are probably pure Escapist activity.

3. See the discussion of depression in chapter 7, pp. 159–60.

4. Not all addictions are negative. *Addiction* can refer to positive, life-enhancing activities to which a person is devoted, such as skiing, yoga, or dance. In this book, an addiction is considered negative simply and only if it is a survival strategy used by an East subpersonality. The topic of this chapter, in other words, is not addictions but East subs. Not all addictions are East sub strategies, and not all East subs use addictions as their strategies.

5. In the Western world, alcohol and marijuana have been among the most commonly abused substances. When used addictively, they create a barrier between our Egos and our Selves in somewhat opposite but equally consequential ways. Alcohol, a central nervous system depressant, disinhibits us when used in small to moderate doses. If used to excess, it simply numbs us, and we become zombies unable to access the Self to any depth. Marijuana, on the other hand, provides something like experiential binoculars — wherever we turn our attention, we experience what's there in greater detail and intensity. We're drawn in. When used compulsively, however, these binoculars can become blinders, concealing the painful emotional areas so much in need of our attention.

6. Chellis Glendinning, *My Name Is Chellis and I'm in Recovery from Western Civilization* (Boston: Shambhala, 1994).

7. Many current suggestions for cultural change are too little, too late, because they take Western civilization (for example, "the American way of life") as a nonnegotiable given. Suggesting that fixes such as solar power and hybrid cars will, by themselves, solve our problems without any substantial changes in the adolescent-consumer lifestyle is something like a heroin addict saying he'll address his addiction by using cleaner needles or 20 percent less heroin.

8. This is the message of, for example, the 2006 self-help book and film by Rhonda Byrne, *The Secret*, which Bill Moyers referred to as "the spiritualization of greed." See Barbara Ehrenreich's critique, *Bright-Sided: How the Relentless Promotion of Positive Thinking Has Undermined America* (New York: Metropolitan Books, 2009).

9. See Chogyam Trungpa, *Cutting Through Spiritual Materialism* (Berkeley, CA: Shambhala, 1973).

10. Jelaluddin Rumi, *The Essential Rumi*, trans. Coleman Barks (San Francisco: Harper, 1995), p. 103.

11. Kabir, "The Time before Death," in *The Soul is Here for Its Own Joy: Sacred Poems from Many Cultures*, ed. Robert Bly (New York: Ecco, 1999), p. 81.

CHAPTER 9. WEST: THE SHADOW AND SHADOW SELVES

Epigraph: Daniel Goleman, *Vital Lies, Simple Truths: The Psychology of Self Deception* (New York: Simon and Schuster, 1996), p. 24.

1. R. D. Laing, *Knots* (New York: Vintage, 1972).
2. Helpful books on Shadow and Shadow work include: Robert Bly, *A Little Book on the Human Shadow* (San Francisco: Harper and Row, 1988); Robert A. Johnson, *Owning Your Own Shadow: Understanding the Dark Side of the Psyche* (San Francisco: Harper, 1993); David Richo, *Shadow Dance: Liberating the Power and Creativity of Your Dark Side* (Boston: Shambhala, 1999); Connie Zweig and Jeremiah Abrams, eds., *Meeting the Shadow: The Hidden Power of the Dark Side of Human Nature* (New York: Tarcher/ Putnam, 1991).
3. Bly, *A Little Book on the Human Shadow*, p. 17.
4. Sometimes it's the Self that wields the shovel. The Self recognizes aspects of the psyche that could overwhelm the Ego were it to become aware of those aspects before reaching a later stage of development. The Self wants to protect the Ego from such premature meltdowns. Our Loyal Soldiers, on the other hand, simply want to shape the Ego in a way acceptable to family and culture.
5. We may wonder what sorts of things are imprisoned in our Shadow, what elements of self have been relegated to the dungeon of our psyche. Here are some of the possibilities:

    • Any of the following when deemed by a Loyal Soldier and/or the Self as undesirable or dangerous to the Ego: subpersonalities from the other three directions; aspects of any of the facets of the Self; or our masculine or feminine qualities

    • Aspects of the Self that were never actively discarded and concealed by a Loyal Soldier or the Self, but that, because of the nature of family or culture or our species' stage of evolution, were preempted from being embodied (the "quarantined" unconscious, which includes the cultural unconscious and species unconscious), such as aspects of our human origins or destiny we're not yet ready as a species to assimilate

    • Aspects of Soul or Spirit deemed by a Loyal Soldier and/or the Self as undesirable or dangerous to the Ego in its current stage

6. Jelaluddin Rumi, *Rumi: The Big Red Book: The Great Masterpiece Celebrating Mystical Love and Friendship*, ed. Coleman Barks (New York: HarperOne, 2010), p. 471.
7. An animal species you love, especially if it is one many people don't like, can be a clue to elements of both your Sinister and your Golden Shadows (for example, maybe you admire crows — as I do — because they're imaginatively naughty, even though many people dislike them and consider them simply rude and pesky). Which animal scares you the most? Which do you find most repulsive? Most admirable? What things in nature most appeal to you or most repel you?

8. Of the four groupings of subpersonalities, our Loyal Soldiers seem to be the safest and easiest to work with because of the stay-in-control quality of the North. Our Loyal Soldiers are dedicated to keeping our Egos safe, and they do so by limiting our options, keeping things controllable. They also have plenty of ways to ignore us if our psyches aren't yet ready to live without their services (when the war is not yet over). They're good at recruiting reinforcements as needed. Generally, the worse thing that can happen when working with our North subs is nothing — no change. Working with our Wounded Children, on the other hand, can be more dangerous, because these South subs are sitting on volatile emotions that could overwhelm our Egos if we're not sufficiently rooted in the Self. Riskier yet is working with our Addicts and Escapists, because, under their thrall, we often go unconscious, especially when substance addictions are involved, and if we're unaware of our escapes in progress, we're powerless to alter them. Shadow work, as I say, is generally the most risky, simply because we have no idea what we're dealing with until it's in our face.

9. A variation: Use three chairs, the third forming a triangle with the other two. The first chair is for you in the consciousness of one of your subpersonalities, the one most triggered by your screen. The second is for your screen. The third is for your fourfold Self. After you speak from either of the first two chairs, always go to the third; sit there and access the perspective of your Self regarding what is happening between the other two; you can speak from this chair, too, if you want.

10. See my book *Nature and the Human Soul*.

11. James Hollis, *The Middle Passage: From Misery to Meaning in Midlife* (Toronto: Inner City Books, 1993).

CODA: BEYOND HERE BE DRAGONS

Epigraphs: Joanna Macy, from the website Joanna Macy and Her Work, www.joannamacy .net, accessed November 29, 2012; Gregory Bateson, quoted at the website for the film *An Ecology of Mind: A Daughter's Portrait of Gregory Bateson*, by Nora Bateson, www .anecologyofmind.com/thefilm, accessed October 3, 2012.

1. In contrast, in *Soulcraft* I focused on the nature of the descent to Soul, while my book *Nature and the Human Soul* describes the stages of human development, discussing the facets of the Self only in passing.

2. This introduction to the map is written primarily for the general reader. A presentation for psychotherapists or scholars would include additional distinctions, concepts, theory, therapeutic methods, case studies, references, and comparisons with other models. The general reader can thank my publisher and its wise editorial director for what this book doesn't include. Professional readers may want to visit www.wildmindbook.com and consider enrolling in an experiential training program (see www.animas.org).

3. Fully understanding a person also requires us to know about their context, their relationship with the world — their historical epoch, cultural setting, ethnicity, language, family and social relationships, gender and gender roles, vocational and community roles, ecological place, and the nature and extent of their ecological awareness and participation.

4. Richard Heinberg, *Peak Everything: Waking Up to the Century of Declines* (Gabriola Island, BC: New Society Publishers, 2010).

5. See Thomas Berry, *The Great Work: Our Way into the Future* (New York: Bell Tower, 1999).

6. Geneen Marie Haugen, "Awakening Planetary Imagination: A Theory and Practice" (PhD diss., California Institute of Integral Studies, San Francisco, forthcoming).

7. In the Eco-Soulcentric Developmental Wheel, there are two developmental tasks unique to each stage of life, one being a nature-oriented task and the other a culture-oriented task. See *Nature and the Human Soul*.

APPENDIX: FOUR PRACTICES FOR WHOLING AND SELF-HEALING

1. H. Stone and S. Stone, *Embracing Our Selves: The Voice Dialogue Manual* (Novato, CA: Nataraj Publishing, 1993). The specific voice dialogue approach outlined in this chapter was developed by Geneen Marie Haugen.

2. See my book *Soulcraft: Crossing into the Mysteries of Nature and Psyche* (Novato, CA: New World Library, 2003), pp. 129–45; also Robert Bosnak, *A Little Course in Dreams* (Boston: Shambhala, 1998), and *Tracks in the Wilderness of Dreaming* (New York: Delta, 1997); and James Hillman, *The Dream and the Underworld* (New York: Harper and Row, 1979).

3. Eligio Stephen Gallegos, *The Personal Totem Pole: Animal Imagery, the Chakras, and Psychotherapy* (Santa Fe: Moon Bear Press, 1990), and *Animals of the Four Windows: Integrating Thinking, Sensing, Feeling, and Imagery* (Santa Fe: Moon Bear Press, 1991).

Permission Acknowledgments

Chapter 4. East: The Innocent/Sage

"Mindful" from *Why I Wake Early: New Poems* by Mary Oliver, published by Beacon Press Boston, copyright © 2004 by Mary Oliver. Reprinted by permission of the Charlotte Sheedy Literary Agency Inc.

From "Tired of Speaking Sweetly" from the Penguin publication *The Gift: Poems by Hafiz*, translated by Daniel Ladinsky. Copyright © 1999 by Daniel Ladinsky and used with his permission.

Excerpt from "The Tower beyond Tragedy" from *The Collected Poetry of Robinson Jeffers*, Volume 1, edited by Tim Hunt. Poem copyright © 1938, renewed 1966, by Donnan and Garth Jeffers. All rights reserved. Used with permission of Stanford University Press, www.sup.org.

Excerpt from "A Spider Playing in the House" from *Feeling the Shoulder of the Lion: Poetry and Teaching Stories of Rumi*, translated by Coleman Barks. Copyright © 2000 by Coleman Barks.

"Ego" from *Dynamite on a China Plate* by Jay Leeming. Copyright © 2006 by Jay Leeming.

Chapter 5. West: The Muse-Beloved

"When I Met My Muse" from *The Way It Is: New and Selected Poems by William Stafford*, copyright © 1986, 1998 by William Stafford and the Estate of William Stafford. Reprinted with the permission of the Permissions Company, Inc., on behalf of Graywolf Press, Minneapolis, MN, www.graywolfpress.org.

Quatrain 388 from *Open Secret: Versions of Rumi*, translated by John Moyne and Coleman Barks. Copyright © 1999 by John Moyne and Coleman Barks. Used by permission of Coleman Barks.

From *Rilke's Book of Hours: Love Poems to God* by Rainer Maria Rilke, translated by Anita Barrows and Joanna Macy, translation copyright © 1996 by Anita Barrows and Joanna Macy. Used by permission of Riverhead Books, an imprint of Penguin Group (USA) Inc.

Chapter 6. North: Loyal Soldiers

"One Source of Bad Information" from *Morning Poems* by Robert Bly, copyright © 1998 by Robert Bly. Reprinted by permission of Robert Bly.

Excerpt from "The Fire in the Song" from *Fire in the Earth* by David Whyte, copyright © 1997 by Many Rivers Press, Langley, WA. Printed with permission from Many Rivers Press, www.davidwhyte.com.

Excerpt from "Questo Muro" from *Kindred Flame* by Anita Barrows. Copyright © 2010 by Anita Barrows. Printed with permission from Anita Barrows.

Chapter 7. South: Wounded Children

"Sometimes, When the Light" in *Alive Together: New and Selected Poems* by Lisel Mueller, copyright © 1996 by Lisel Mueller. Reprinted by permission of Louisiana State University Press.

CHAPTER 8. EAST: ADDICTS AND ESCAPISTS

Index

Abram, David, 3, 51, 53
action, mature, 197
Addict/Escapist Exercise, 198–99
addiction, 185–86, 189–91, 193–94, 202–5,
    280nn4–5
Addicts, 158, 181, 183, 185–86
    See also Escapists and Addicts
adolescents. *See* children/adolescents
agape, 80
alcohol, 200, 202–5, 280n5
Alexander, Christopher, 268n1
anger, 58, 172
Anima/Animus, 100, 103–4, 107, 117
animals. *See* animals, imaginal; other-than-
    human world
animals, imaginal, 259–60
anima mundi, 98, 268n2
Animas Valley Institute, 237–38
"Anthem" (song; Cohen), 177
antidepressants, 278n4
Apollo (Greek deity), 76
apprenticeships, 91
"archaic man," 61–62
archetypes
    of collective unconscious, 72–73
    of East Self, 17, 78, 80, 82, 83
    of North Self, 16, 43
    Shadow elements in, 216

of South Self, 16, 64–65
of West Self, 17, 208
Artemis (Greek deity), 64
asceticism, 74–75
Assagioli, Roberto, 271n23
awe, feelings of, 55–56

Barrows, Anita, 150–51
Bateson, Gregory, 235
"beginner's mind," 81
behavior, 265n1
Beloved. *See* Inner Beloved; West Self
    (Muse-Beloved)
Berry, Thomas, 13, 35, 42, 56, 105
Berry, Wendell, 33, 34, 41–42, 60
bhakti (Hindu devotional worship), 120
biocracies, 105, 276n6
biosphere, 270n14
Blake, William, 105
Blissheads, 181–82, 183, 187–88, 193
Bly, Robert, 127, 130–31, 213
body
    feeling and, 66
    South Self at home in, 51, 52, 57
Bolen, Jean Shinoda, 266n2
Book of Hours (Rilke), 48
Buddha Dharma, 41
Buddhism, 38, 81, 84, 90, 245

About the Author

*B*ill Plotkin, PhD, is a depth psychologist, wilderness guide, and agent of cultural evolution. As founder of southwest Colorado's Animas Valley Institute, he has, since 1980, guided thousands of women and men through nature-based initiatory passages, including a contemporary Western adaptation of the pancultural vision fast. He's also been a research psychologist (studying nonordinary states of consciousness), professor of psychology, rock musician, and whitewater river guide. Bill is the author of *Soulcraft: Crossing into the Mysteries of Nature and Psyche* (an experiential guidebook) and *Nature and the Human Soul: Cultivating Wholeness and Community in a Fragmented World* (a nature-based stage model of human development). He has a doctorate in psychology from the University of Colorado at Boulder.

Animas Valley Institute

Animas Valley Institute — founded in 1980 by Bill Plotkin — offers a rich assortment of journeys into the mysteries of nature and psyche, including Soulcraft™ intensives, contemporary vision fasts, and training programs for nature-based Soul guides.

> Individually and collectively, we launch into an uncertain future — at once, both perilous and saturated with possibility. Our accustomed, culturally determined roles and identities are inadequate for navigating the sea change of our time. Our collective journey requires a radical shift in the human relationship with the community of all life — a cultural transformation so profound that future humans might regard it as an evolution of consciousness. Safe passage requires each of us to offer our full magnificence to the world. Popular culture cannot help us uncover our singular gifts; contemporary institutions do not invite their expression. Our particular genius can be discovered only in an initiatory journey — an accidental or intentional descent into the mysteries of Soul. Guiding the *intentional* descent to Soul has been the unfolding work of Animas Valley Institute for over thirty years.
>
> — Geneen Marie Haugen, Animas guide, author,
> and wilderness wanderer

Soulcraft skills and practices evoke the world-shifting experience of Soul encounter — the revelation of our unique mythopoetic identity, an identity expressed through symbol and metaphor, image and dream, archetype and myth, an identity embodied in a mysterious story that whispers to us in moments of expanded awareness and exquisite aliveness. The shape and rhythm of this story reveals the hidden treasure that each of us carries for the world — a world longing for the transformative contributions of visionary leaders and artisans of cultural renaissance. Soulcraft practices spring from wilderness rites, depth psychology, ecopsychology, the poetic tradition, nature-based peoples, and the wild Earth itself — and constitute a contemporary, Western, and nature-rooted path to the *terra mysterium* of Soul initiation.

Animas Valley Institute offers multiday experiential explorations into wild landscapes and into the wilds of Soul with the goal of discovering the meaning and destiny at the heart of each life. We are guides to the initiatory journey — the descent into the mysteries of nature and psyche, where the husk of outgrown ego-identity is shed; where tricksters, demons, and perhaps angels are encountered; and from which a new self emerges as a vessel for one's distinctive genius and world-transforming gifts. Although our work evokes nonordinary perception and ways of knowing, it is not shamanism, nor is it primarily rites of passage, wilderness-based psychotherapy, or emotional healing. Our immersions are not designed to transcend the Ego, solve everyday personal problems, or help people better adjust to — or be happier in — the flatland of contemporary Western culture. Rather, our intent is a deep-structure shift that *matures* the Ego and elicits each person's most creative, soul-rooted response to our critical, liminal moment in the unfolding of the world's story — on the threshold of a future shaped by those who can see beyond our own time.

To learn more about the Nature-Based Map of the Human Psyche and experiential programs and trainings based on the map, please visit:

www.wildmindbook.com

Each year, Animas Valley Institute and its twenty guides offer approximately forty programs for adults — in various locations and ecosystems in North America and Europe — including a comprehensive, multiyear training program in the arts of nature-based underworld guiding.

To learn more about Animas programs and trainings,
visit our website: www.animas.org,
email us: soulcraft@animas.org,
call: 800-451-6327 (U.S.A. only)
or 970-259-0585,
or fax: 970-259-1225

or write:
Animas Valley Institute
P. O. Box 1020
Durango, CO 81302
U.S.A.

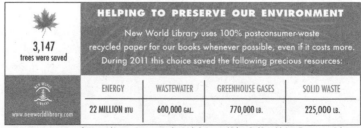